SUCCESS

is a

STATE

of

MIND

To Diane —
You have a big heart —
give the love away.

Insight Publishing
Sevierville, TN

To Your Success
Dr. Judy

TABLE OF CONTENTS

—

A MESSAGE FROM THE PUBLISHER

Success is an attitude and when we consider achieving success in life, attitude is everything. Having a positive outlook can help us overcome obstacles and discouragement. We must discipline the mind to be positive and this discipline can mean the difference between hitting the wall or pushing through.

The ideas communicated by the writers in this book, *Success is a State of Mind*, will help you in your success journey. As I talked with these authors I found that they have valid and proven strategies that will inspire you to do the mental preparation it takes to make the best of each and every opportunity that comes your way.

To have a successful attitude means believing that you can do what needs to be done. These authors have demonstrated in their own lives how they achieved the inner satisfaction and confidence they needed. They realized that true success is not the end of the road but the journey itself. Take advantage of this unique opportunity to learn from these successful people. I think you just may find some answers here. You will certainly find a wealth of information. And remember, no rules for success will work if you don't.

Interviews Conducted by:
David E. Wright, President
Insight Publishing & International Speakers Network

An interview with…

Ivy Meadors

David Wright (Wright)

It is my sincere pleasure to be talking with Ivy Meadors, founder and CEO of High Tech High Touch Solutions in Woodinville, Washington, a conference and events producer and a consulting firm specializing in help desks and call centers. Ivy has over thirty years of experience in the customer service and support industry. She is a seasoned consultant and a world-renowned professional speaker. She has traveled the globe to deliver her content rich in-demand presentations. Ivy is the owner and producer of the Signature Customer Service and Support Professionals Conference and Expo and the Government Customer Support Conference and Expo. She is the sole woman owner of conferences and events in this industry.

Ivy is considered one of this industry's most respected leaders. She received the honor of being one of the Top 10 Legends in the Help Desk Industry and was awarded for being one of the "Top 25

Most Influential Professionals in the Service and Support Industry" by Service News. She publishes the online newsletter, *eSharings,* read by thousands around the world, and has also been published in the top industry magazines and newsletters. You can sign up for her content-rich newsletter at www.hthts.com.

Ivy has included steps and encouragement at the end of this chapter to help you get started to begin your personal journey to success. If you need help along your journey, email Ivy at solutions4u@hthts.com.

Ivy, welcome to *Success is a State of Mind.*

Let's start with how you define success.

Ivy Meadors (Meadors)

For me, success means engaging with others, transforming lives, and seeing those same people then influence the lives of others. Though often overused, "pay it forward" understandably represents my definition for success. My definition of success is using multi-faceted communication levels to connect with people at a deeper level, understand their dreams and goals, and connect them with other people who will contribute to their journey for success.

Wright

Wow, so for you, success doesn't involve "arriving" somewhere, but is a way of being?

Meadors

Exactly. Success is when I can contribute to the favorable transformation of lives. By being fully engaged and communicating with others at a deeper and more complete level, I help them expand their beliefs and views of life in general, as well as their own. This includes providing an avenue for people to network for personal and professional growth, to influence personal transformation, and to learn from others who will inspire them to be ambitious and achieve their goals. A friend of mine, Seanna Sams, said, "You help people believe in themselves. You move them to inspire themselves and I think that that growth is what overflows and makes us want to "pay it forward" because we have so much more now to share."

Wright

It sounds like this definition and your own measure of success has been very deliberately crafted and honed.

Meadors

Yes, I have been very aware of my own development in terms of the many experiences I have had, both in business and with personal relationships. The common theme is leadership and connections at different levels of communication. It is based on what it means to be a strong leader others want to emulate.

You know, I just turned fifty, which is a wonderful milestone on its own merit. But I see this point in my life as a time when I have just reached base camp and now I'm headed up to the summit. Those who show up at base camp are already accomplished climbers—they have come fully equipped with the skills, resources, and mindset to tackle the next ascent.

Having the right attitude and being in the right state of mind, sets the stage for victory. I have it written on a mirror to remind myself daily that *"I am 100 percent responsible for my own success."* I encourage others to follow my lead and use this sort of attitude to reach their own base camp and then head onward and upward to reach their summit.

Wright

If you could narrow it down to the most important, what skills or attitudes do you think are most critical in order to achieve this level of success not only in people's own lives, but to influence others as well?

Meadors

Being successful requires having a positive attitude, working extremely hard, and wanting it bad enough to reach the goal that represents success. You have to be confident, strong willed, and tough minded to ensure the journey is victorious. I love the saying, "Do what you gotta do to get what you wanna get." Success doesn't come to those who wait or those who hope to win the lottery. You have to make concessions and work very hard at it. I am a very driven person, like many other successful people. You really have to have a "get tough, focused, pull out all the stops attitude" to arrive. Having the right attitude and fortitude isn't enough though, you have to take the first step and get started. This is the reason a lot of people never reach their goals—they never start.

Wright

What were your early influences that helped in developing those attributes?

Meadors

All my life I have challenged the norm, from how I grew up to the accomplishments I have realized in my life. My parents were very non-traditional. I wasn't raised like most little girls. I drove a truck when I was eight and a motorcycle at ten. I could change a tire and do basic work on a car or motorcycle engine as a young girl—enough at least to get me back on the road to safety. I could even protect myself with a gun before I was eleven. You needed these skills to survive in the deep country. I'm proud to say I never had to shoot any animals but I sure hit a lot of cans. Having these sorts of skills at such a young age affords a level of confidence not typically realized in a child. It makes you very tough and strong-willed.

My parents were also very giving people. They helped total strangers and friends alike. They would give the shirt off their backs—literally. When people were in need, they would do whatever they could to help them. I remember times when young girls who came from abuse or had children when they were too young would be invited into our home to stay until they got their feet on the ground. There are innumerable stories like this throughout my childhood. My parents never expected anything in return from anyone they helped. Their example had an incredible influence on me and the attitudes and insights that formed my own trust and belief in me and my ability to help others.

I have since lived my life and built my business on the notion of giving to others and not expecting anything in return. In fact, it is one of our corporate mission statements: "Maintain and foster a philosophy of giving without the expectation of receiving anything in return." Success means transforming lives. I use my influence and expertise in our industry and the gift of having multi-faceted communication skills to make a difference. Consulting, speaking, and conferences generate the revenue that affords me the means to reach, teach, mentor, and influence others using connections at many different levels.

Wright

Clearly your own communication skills are highly advanced. How did that particular strength develop?

Meadors

Animals were a significant part of my life living in the country where I grew up. From raising a baby bear for one year after its mother was killed and then releasing it, to raising a fawn from a bottle to adulthood and regularly being around horses, cats, and dogs, I learned communication skills that often didn't use words. I realized early on I had a gift for connecting at a different level. These skills have been fine-tuned over the years. They have given me the ability to influence and help others using these deeper non-traditional communication skills.

The primary non-traditional factors include: hearing the unspoken word, reading the unwritten message, having a deep intuition and feel from a behavioral and energy standpoint, and being fully present in the now. You can become adept at these things but it takes a concentrated awareness of energy levels and active practice. Mostly it takes a strong sense of caring about connecting with others.

Wright

Do you have an example of using non-traditional communication? Explain how it can contribute to someone's success.

Meadors

Success in life is found by having a clear direction, a goal, and an understanding of what must be done. Good leaders and mentors can guide you in identifying the steps to achieve your goals. These individuals have exceptional communication and people skills. When helping others or attempting to reach your own goals, the following exemplifies the importance of listening carefully and communicating clearly.

Let's use horses to make the point effectively. Many of the problems that horses have are the direct result of being confused by riders who are confused themselves. The horse cannot know what is expected of him unless, and until, the rider understands how the horse needs to have information presented to him, at which time he understands what he is expected to do to succeed.

By working with my horses, using horse-whispering techniques, I have learned how to gain trust and respect through feel and by being fully present. Using the forces of energy of pressure and release, horses cooperate and are more likely to do what they are asked willingly and with enthusiasm and when they are provided clear directions. The key to success includes offering them the assurance to have them succeed.

Horses, like people, lose trust if they are asked to do something that may harm them, cause them to feel fear, or be subjected to danger. Their instinctive senses through intuition, touch, and energy, along with limited verbal communication give them the understanding they need to respond to a request. If there is pressure they will resist and move away from it. If there is a release from the pressure, they will return and connect back up with you. This can be mastered through feel and by being fully present.

When horses have been given a clear definition of what to do, pressure from a rope or whip is not required. Horses will give to you willingly and do their very best if they know you appreciate their effort and will reward them for their accomplishments. They should not be punished for failure; but instead, are to be rewarded when they succeed at accomplishing the desired request.

This is true for people too. People will willingly follow or be influenced by someone if they have a clear understanding of what needs to be accomplished and are offered the opportunity to perform without pressure. They need to feel confident they will be afforded the chance to make manageable mistakes without serious reprimand. Once they realize their success, receive appreciation for their effort, and receive encouragement, they will perform at this level again. If they feel they can succeed, they can, they will, and they do.

Successful people benefit from others who reassure and offer them the confidence to understand what needs to be done and provide the necessary support, direction, and guidance. Control is an attempt to lead using a rope, and people will shy away from this sort of domination. When the fear of failure is reduced, though not always removed, the willingness to pursue the goal is less of a risk.

Proper pressure is necessary to move people toward their goal but too much negative pressure with no release will get undesirable results. Think about a time you pushed a child or someone at work to do something. Did the person resist? How hard was it to get the child or person to succeed? When people feel the release of the pressure, combined with clear instructions, they respond more favorably.

When you sense discomfort from people after asking them to do a task, offering them reassurances will make them feel more encouraged. It is important to be able to "feel" their fear and offer them support. You must "hear" their unspoken words just as you need to clearly communicate.

I created a keynote speech titled, "Lead Without a Rope" to teach these techniques of motivating people successfully. If people want to benefit from this presentation, they can contact me to deliver the speech at their company or other venue. It's a great session at corporate retreats or conferences for personal reflection.

Wright

How is it that you have been able to not only connect, but to influence so many people?

Meadors

In retrospect I see that coming from a non-traditional childhood with variations of good and bad behaviors have made it easier to connect with people and understand their emotional and intellectual needs. As a manager in business, I applied this same approach intuitively; it was how I connected best with others at a very real and meaningful level. I am a professional speaker, consultant, mentor/coach, and own conference venues. These avenues for communicating with others afford a means to help people develop professionally, advance personally, and grow intellectually. I can use these venues to encourage them to aggressively reach for the summit and help others move forward to achieve their goals. Having the right state of mind, a strong confident attitude, being a hard worker, and having great mentors to push, guide, and open doors made my success a reality. I want to share that knowledge with others.

Wright

How do you use the venues you mention to help others realize their success?

Meadors

I am the only female in the United States—perhaps worldwide— who owns conference venues in the customer service and technology support industry. As one of few females in the top of the technology support industry and one of the more recognized names in the Help Desk industry, I now have a place where I can help people connect with others and a place where I can deliver speeches to transform and influence lives. Again, anyone can succeed if they want it bad enough, get tough, have the right attitude, and are willing to work hard for it.

Incidentally, you can read more about our events on our Web site at www.hthts.com. The Web site is loaded with free resources from leadership and mentoring to professional development—even things on being a conservationist and animal activist, which is also one of my passions. There is much information on the website for those in the service and support industry.

My friend, Mary Kay Wegner, is an example of someone who permitted me to push her to reach her goals and leverage the use of our conferences. She wanted to be a better speaker and move from the ranks of frontline manager to the executive level. By being open to the feedback and trusting my leadership experience, she used the conference venues to practice her speaking and networking skills. In less than five years she has become a polished speaker and has reached an executive management level after years as a frontline manager. She's a driven person who was willing and open to feedback and gentle pushing to help her reach these goals. Networking at conferences and speaking gave her the resources and opportunity to excel in both of these arenas. From competence comes confidence, and she wasted no time applying that to reach the executive ranks.

Wright

How do people fail when defining success?

Meadors

Sometimes people encourage others to live the dream they had for themselves. If you are defining success by someone else's definition, this is not your true success. Parents, managers, and other influencers will encourage or direct people to do something specific. Often this influence is because the person didn't realize his or her own dreams and want to see someone else experience it.

An example is the story of the little boy whose father pushes him to play baseball yet the boy has no desire to play. He does it only because his father wants it. The boy isn't happy living his father's dream, he has his own, but he wants to please his dad. He plays baseball miserably, doesn't enjoy the game, and becomes discouraged. Years are lost from not doing what he could have been doing to realize his own dreams. He could have been developing skills, building up a network of friends on the desired journey, and gaining confidence in himself from doing something he is passionate about and does really well. It transforms your life when you do what you are the most passionate about.

People need to become confident in themselves and trust their instincts. They need to enthusiastically go after their idea of success— after their own dream—and not the one someone else wants for them.

The questions I want our readers to contemplate are: "Are you pushing someone to achieve your dream and not theirs? Is someone pushing you to do something that isn't your definition of success?" If the answer is yes to either question, it is time to make a radical change.

Wright

If someone wants to apply your expertise in communication to everyday improvements, what is one of the simplest techniques anyone can use to positively influence others?

Meadors

The easiest thing, and it doesn't cost a dime, is to intentionally share a smile or fully listen to someone. It touches lives in many positive ways when you smile and/or listen fully to someone. A smile can be "heard" and "seen" even over the phone. It would be wonderful if this chapter influences the readers to share a smile with others they meet or speak to on the phone and listen fully with those they engage in a conversation.

I try to share a smile with most people I pass, especially in airports and grocery stores where people seem tense. It's a nice feeling when they smile back because you know you made them feel special even if for a moment. Again, it is about being in the moment with people and making them feel important and letting them know that they matter.

Have you ever gone to your boss's desk and needed some time only to have him or her answer the phone or keep doing e-mail? How did it make you feel? Have you ever walked up to a cashier in a store who was engaged in a conversation either on the phone (personal cell phone is even worse) or with another employee and the person doesn't acknowledge your presence? The sales clerk can ring out the sale and never greet you or say thank you. Personally, I don't always let sales clerks get away with this behavior by pointing it out to them. The more we tolerate this behavior, the more likely it will continue.

Wright

How do we then move from simple steps to deeper connections?

Meadors

When people are engaged in a conversation it would be wonderful if they could apply the technique my friend, Max Dixon (also a professional speaker) taught me. He said you should "show up ready to be no place else." For me this translates to "being fully present" as I mentioned in the example about communicating with horses. If you can maintain a sense of undivided attention with any interaction you have, you are then better prepared to "hear the unspoken word" and "read the unwritten message." These are the fully developed skills that will allow you, either in work or personal exchanges, to reach a deeper level of communication.

Being fully present has two values in the goal to succeed. If you are the influencer—the listener—making people feel important and discussing their ideas with them helps them become more confident and successful. If you are working on your own dream or goal, being fully present and completely engaged at the moment keeps outside distractions from impacting you. It's easy to lose site of the goal when e-mails are popping up, the cell phone is ringing and people are constantly sending text messages.

Wright

You emphasized, "hearing the unspoken word." Will you share an example of where you heard the unspoken word and what was the end result?

Meadors

It is necessary to be mentally focused and cognizant of the energy being transmitted through feel or by hearing the unspoken word. It is more then just listening, but actually "hearing" what someone is saying or not saying.

Being fully present is very simple as a concept, but difficult to practice for most people. In this information-loaded era of technology, with everyone expecting things now, it becomes difficult to practice. It means stopping whatever you are doing and being fully engaged with the other person. Being fully present means quieting the mind and stopping the endless chatter, even for a moment while engaging with someone.

An eighteen-year-old high school senior, Kevin Osborne, asked for help with a speech to be delivered at school. His father knew my unique skills and suggested we meet. I immediately saw incredible potential in Kevin but also "heard" something else being said—the part that didn't contain any words. He was scared and insecure at a deeper level for reasons that were not outwardly shared until later. The approach I used with him needed to be different from the way I coached other aspiring speakers. We needed to go someplace he had never gone to help him learn something about himself to get beyond the internal dilemmas. We also needed to establish a trust that was unlike any he had in the past, outside of his family.

Making the deeper connection and understanding Kevin and his personal concerns at an unspoken level helped me to help him overcome his perceived insurmountable issues. One year later, at our Ninth Annual Customer Service and Support Professionals Conference (www.helpdeskconference.com), Kevin co-presented a keynote session with me in front of hundreds of people. He received a standing ovation—the only one in the entire event. He was nineteen and had arrived at his first base camp. He had learned how to deal with the deep insecurities and put them behind him. He was on to his next new challenge.

Summary statement:

Realizing success takes being in the right state of mind. I hope this chapter has demonstrated that being fully engaged and present, listening deeply to hear the unspoken word, reading carefully to read the unwritten message, and having the attitude to succeed will offer a great start to reaching whatever summit you are climbing toward.

Anyone can achieve their goal by resolving to succeed. You must take the first step, stop making excuses for not getting started, and go for the top. There will always be a reason you can come up with for not taking the first step, but there are no reasons good enough to prevent you from starting the climb. The summit is always achievable—you just have to start the climb.

The overall theme is communication at a much deeper level and keying in on the success of the others in our lives. Any time we communicate with people, more will be achieved if we are in it for their agenda, not just our own. This is so important because it frees our state of mind to succeed in the next step—pressure and release. We can help others achieve their goals by not attempting to control them, by pushing them toward their dreams without pushing too hard, and by releasing pressure in such a way that they are encouraged and not afraid of failure.

In making our success and others' successes possible, we must ourselves focus more deeply on communication beyond the spoken word. It is important to pay attention to the otherwise minor details— the telling signs that can show us what is really going on for the other person. Giving deeply of our attention transcends walls and breaks down barriers, and makes us much more human; a new level of relationship is formed as a result. Undivided attention to others' true needs makes achieving dreams possible.

The following information should help you take the first step to begin the ascent to the summit of success.

My favorite quote is "what would you attempt to do if you knew you could not fail?"—Dr. Robert Schuller. Ask yourself this question and be honest with the answer. It is difficult to operate from a position of fear to realize success.

The first step to success is to take a step. The reasons not to take the first step are mostly just excuses. These excuses might include; after the kids graduate, when the house is paid off, when the next promotion comes, and when we retire. If you never take the first step, there will always be another excuse to postpone taking it. It's about choice—do you choose to fail, stay where you are or succeed? I'm going for success, how about you?

1. Write down one thing you would like to accomplish that defines success for you.
2. List five to seven major milestones to reach the point of success and when you will reach the top—the summit.
3. Working backward from the final date, set dates for when you will reach the major milestones. Resources, funds, training, life balance, vacations, and other key factors should be considered when you define the dates. When people fail to meet their

commitments, negative thinking begins and will discourage the state of mind, dates are pushed out and before you know it, the potential to realize success is prolonged or never realized.

4. Identify a date when you will start the climb. You must start on the date you set.

5. Give the date to a reliable person who can push you to start on this day. It's fine if they gently intimidate you or offer moderate encouragement, as long as they don't accept your excuse not to meet your commitment.

6. Identify how you will reward yourself as you reach each milestone.

7. Each time you reach a milestone, celebrate your success. Be sure to reward yourself. The positive affirmation encourages movement to the next milestone.

Summary:

- Write a mission statement
- Establish the goals and objectives
- Agree on the "contract" and expectations
- Discuss what means of feedback and inspiration works best
- Review what makes for the best relationship with the person who is going to help keep you on target
- Identify milestones to celebrate major accomplishments along the journey
- Understand that the journey should be as equally rewarding as realizing the success at the end.

12 Key Factors to Contribute to Having a Successful State of Mind

1. **Work hard no matter how bad the job is and do it better then anyone else.** I worked as a maid at a coastal resort when I was

sixteen. Toilets are not everyone's favorite thing to clean. Customers are unhappy when they arrive at a dirty hotel room. The toilet is usually the first or second thing they notice. I learned to take pride in having the cleanest toilets in the facility. It represented success because the customers were happy and so was my boss. That was a good thing. Adhere to nothing but the highest standards in your work.

2. **Stop working so much.** Make constructive use of your time and ensure a balanced home and work life. It isn't the quantity of the work you do but the quality. People will work eighty to ninety hours a week and tell everyone how busy they are. They may not realize the success that someone else might achieve by working only forty to fifty hours per week. It is easy to get caught up in the work and forget about the balance. A tired mind no longer focuses on the pleasure of reaching the goal and instead becomes discouraged.

3. **Change your clothes and your walk.** How you dress, your behavior, how you walk and carry yourself all contribute to a different mindset. People who work at home and never change out of their sweats are able to do their jobs but the real driving force that changes one's mindset is to feel successful. A young lady, Lauren Stewart, who works for me went to a business dinner with her father. She had on a professional looking white sweater, black slacks, but no jacket, and tennis shoes. She said that when the executives came in the room she felt intimidated and uncomfortable. On other occasions, she had gone to meetings with people of the same executive stature and did not feel uncomfortable. The difference was simply wearing a suit jacket and black pumps with the same white sweater and pants.

How you feel about yourself will change your state of mind. Shine from the inside out.

4. **Get reading.** Learn constantly and be an avid reader. It is likely that you have heard the quote "Leaders are readers, but not all readers are leaders." It is true that leaders read regularly. Learning is a motivator in itself but the education and inspiration you can gain is invaluable. I read at least one book per week. Most are non-fiction, but occasionally I will read a fiction book for pleasure. The principle is to develop knowledge and have constant exposure to learning opportunities. Knowledge is one of the greatest assets to have for people to realize their dreams.

Listening to educational tapes and watching DVDs are very valuable too. If you don't have the time to read as much as you would like, adding tapes and DVDs can compliment your reading efforts.

5. **Surround yourself with great people and avoid toxic relationships.** Avoid relationships that discourage success and bring you down. To maintain a state of mind of success, the people you associate with should be those you aspire to be like or respect. Toxic relationships drain your strength and positive thoughts away from the goal. You have heard the stories where people are told, "you will fail," "don't do it because it won't work," or even "what a stupid idea." These are toxic thoughts and people who discourage you should be avoided as much as possible or taken with a grain of salt. Other people's words or deeds can influence our view of ourselves and directly affect our ability to succeed. Learn how to become immune to negative criticism and develop a thick skin.

6. **Change your mindset from "why should I?" to "why shouldn't I?"** I went through challenges in my life that resulted in a period of time of anorexia and bulimia. It was suggested I take up a body-building program to help regain confidence in myself and learn a better eating program to alleviate my issues. It turned out that by becoming a body-builder I studied nutrition in depth, got myself back on the road to better health, and became a titled competitor in a regional competition.

   Everyone said I couldn't do it—I was too small. Since childhood, a severe case of hypoglycemia (in the five percent worst levels of the population) hindered my ability to put on a lot of muscle mass. My personal coach said I would need steroids to succeed. When I walked off that platform with a two-foot gold trophy in my hand as a drug-fee competitor, competing against others who were not drug-free, it didn't matter that I didn't get first place (though that was what I was aiming for), I had succeeded and won. Why shouldn't I have gone drug free, giving it my all?

7. **Don't fear failure and take risks.** Ask yourself, "What's the worse thing that can happen?" Failure can be tolerable as long as you learn from it. Don't make the same mistake twice—discover a better way.

   I tell people who work for me that if they are unwilling to take reasonable risks, they won't be working here long. We don't want people who do an average job and keep on doing it the same way. "There is always a better way," is one of our corporate mottos. The other is to "Do whatever it takes."

   Examine yourself—what do you fear most: The unexpected? Uncertainty? Change? Failure? Success? What others will think or say? That someone will be hurt and no longer be your friend if you should succeed or fail?

I wanted to be a speaker and was offered an opportunity to deliver a speech early in my career. The only time I had spoken in front of a group of people was in grade school when we did "Show and Tell." As soon as I got off the stage, I headed straight for the ladies room and lost my lunch. That was the last and only time that ever happened. I am now a professional speaker and recognized by the National Speakers Association (www.nsaspeaker.org). I score in the top five percent consistently. If I had never tried that first speech because of my fear of failure, I might have never realized my dream of being a professional speaker.

Everyone should seize opportunities they don't think they can handle. It is good to push yourself into situations that make you nervous or fearful as long as they don't put your life at risk. Stay alert for challenging opportunities.

8. **Get real and stop whining.** Identify your strengths and discover your opportunities for improvement (not weakness). It's okay to be confident about the things you do well but get real about the things you need to improve and do it. No whining allowed. Check your mindset and attitude regularly. Stop being a victim or martyr and stop making excuses why you can't succeed.

9. **Live success in your mind and avoid poverty thinking.** See yourself being successful and experiencing your dream. How does it feel; what do you smell, hear, etc.?

Have a positive mindset. Ingrain thoughts into your subconscious mind that you were born to succeed. You become what you think about most of the time and learning how to control your thoughts can help you maintain a positive state of mind. Using Neuro-linguistic Programming (NLP™) to guide your subconscious mind can work well.

Avoid poverty thinking and having a defeatist attitude. Are you giving up too soon? Scott Sulak offers a content rich Web site loaded with resources for modifying the thoughts in your mind. He teaches how you can understand how to make changes for good. (www.changeforgood.com)

10. **Use Quantum Physics—Vibrating strings of energy.** Leverage your unique talents and your pure, intuitive intelligence. True leadership can be administered through feel by connecting to people at an uncommon and unfamiliar communication level. "Feel" energy. Relate with others better by "hearing" the unspoken words and "reading" the unwritten messages to take your leadership skills to a more advanced level. Non-verbal remarks can send a powerful negative message and discourage success.

I enjoyed the book *Quantum Success: The Astounding Science of Wealth and Happiness* by Sandra Anne Taylor. This revealing look at the science of success shows you the formula for abundant living and is actually based on the principles of quantum physics. It describes how you can tap into these powerful forces to make your dreams be realized. Do a web search on "Quantum Leadership" for more information.

11. **Be "fully" present.** Give respect, gain trust, and don't dampen the enthusiasm of yourself or others. People matter and sharing a piece of your time with them can be life changing for both of you.

12. **Be tenacious, don't give up, and be tough.** Donald Trump is a positive influencer for me. I have almost every one of his books and use them as guidelines and inspirations when I need a jump-start or reminder of the possibilities that can be realized. One lesson I've learned from reading about Donald Trump is that tenacity is absolutely necessary for success. This means that every day you apply 100 percent focus and nothing less. (www.trumpuniversity.com/connect/newsletters.cfm)

My father taught me to be tough. Donald Trump believes in being tough too. Tough is what you are when you refuse to give in or give up. Mr. Trump's recent book, *Think BIG and Kick Ass in Business and Life,* contains a gold mine of inspiration.

You have to fight for what you believe in. There are few things of worth that are easy to achieve. Never lose sight of your dream and do what you gotta to do to get what you wanna get because no one is going to do it for you.

Success Exercise:

Take a few minutes to be in the moment with yourself. Answer the following questions honestly using your own intuition and experiences to guide you. Give yourself credit where appropriate. Then, decide which areas require greater focus in order for you to achieve greater success.

Am I a good listener?	Yes	No
Can I hear what isn't being said?	Yes	No
What's it like to know me?	Yes	No
What's it like to work for me?	Yes	No
What's it like to work with me?	Yes	No
How effectively do I communicate?	Yes	No

Do I have goals and aspirations?	Yes	No
Do I positively impact those around me?	Yes	No
Do I try things that are out of the norm or considered a risk?	Yes	No
Can I realize success?	Yes	No
Am I ready to get started?	Yes	No

When will I take the first step? How about now?

Which areas do I need to focus on most?

_____

When will I start improving these?

_____

Need more help? Email solutions4U@hthts.com.

"*The road in life that will bring you the most satisfaction and fulfillment representing the greatest success is based on your deepest passions. You are in charge of your future and need to resolve to succeed to realize your dreams.*"

—Ivy Meadors

ABOUT THE AUTHOR

Why is Ivy any different from any other woman who grew up in a small country town without a college education, technical background or worldly visions and yet ended up a success story? Would you listen to what she has to say about success?

Meet the founder and CEO of High Tech High Touch Solutions, Ivy Meadors, who shares her life-learnings through conferences, consulting and mentoring, contributing to people's ability to be successful in business and life. Her dynamic and charismatic imprint has been felt among Fortune 500 corporations, US Government agencies, universities and non-profit agencies worldwide.

Ivy has accumulated thirty years' experience in customer service and support and developed a platform of excellence upon three pillars: customer service, communication techniques, and progressive deployment of technologies. Her career with U S West Communications and IBM contributed to her advanced development. Ivy transforms businesses, Help Desks and Call Centers by "seeing" things that are not so obvious to others.

Ivy is likely the only female conference producer in technology. She is the owner of the Signature Customer Service and Support Professionals Conference (helpdeskconference.com) and the Government Customer Support Conference (governmentconference.com). An authority on leadership, she is also a dedicated advocate for developing young leaders and abused women.

As a speaker, Ivy engages and educates by delivering presentations that are powerful affairs, teaching people and businesses how to exceed and excel. Ivy gives her audience sound business solutions, imparts a passion for action and challenges them to commit to success, transforming the lives of thousands. She holds the credentials of a professional speaker recognized by the National Speakers Association.

Free resources on her website include an information-packed newsletter plus topics on leadership, speaking, mentoring, customer service, technology and more. Please visit the website for resources and sign up for the newsletter at www.hthts.com or www.ivymeadors.com.

SUCCESS IS A STATE OF MIND 2

An interview with…

Deepak Chopra

David Wright (Wright)

Today we are talking to Dr. Deepak Chopra, founder of the Chopra Center for Well Being in Carlsbad, California. More than a decade ago, Dr. Chopra became the foremost pioneer in integrated medicine. His insights have redefined our definition of health to embrace body, mind and spirit. His books, which include, *Quantum Healing, Perfect Health, Ageless Body Timeless Mind,* and *The Seven Spiritual Laws of Success,* have become international best sellers and established classics of their kind. His latest book is titled, *Grow Younger, Live Longer: 10 Steps to Reverse Aging.* Dr. Chopra, welcome to *Success is a State of the Mind.*

Dr. Deepak Chopra (Chopra)

Thank you. How are you?

Wright

I am doing just fine. It's great weather here in Tennessee.

Chopra

Great.

Wright

Dr. Chopra, you stated in your new book that it is possible to reset your biostats up to fifteen years younger than your chronological age. Is that really possible?

Chopra

Yes. By now, we have several examples of this. The literature on aging really began to become interesting in the 1980s when people showed that it was possible to reverse the biological marks of aging. This included things like blood pressure, bone density, body temperature, regulation of the metabolic rate and other things like cardiovascular conditioning, cholesterol levels, muscles mass and strength of muscles, and even things like hearing, vision, sex hormone levels, and immune function. One of the things that came out of those studies was that psychological age had a great influence on biological age. So you have three kinds of aging, chronological age is when you were born, biological age is what your biomarker shows, and psychological age is what your biostat says.

Wright

You call our prior conditioning a prison. What do you mean?

Chopra

We have certain expectations about the aging process. Women expect to become menopausal in their early forties. Everyone thinks they should retire at the age of sixty-five and then go Florida and spend the rest of their life in so-called retirement. These expectations actually influence the very biology of aging. What we call normal aging is actually the hypnosis of our social conditioning. If you can bypass that social conditioning, then you're free to reset your own biological clock.

Wright

Everyone told me that I was supposed to retire at sixty-five. I'm sixty-eight, and as a matter of fact, today is my birthday.

Chopra

Well happy birthday. You know, the fact is you should be having fun all the time and always feel youthful. You should always feel that you are contributing to society. It's not the retirement, but it's the passion with which you're involved in the well being of your society, your community or the world at large.

Wright

Great things keep happening to me. I have a forty year old daughter, but I also have a thirteen year old daughter. She was born when I was fifty. That has changed my life quite a bit. I feel a lot younger than I am.

Chopra

The more you associate with young people, the more you will respond to that biological expression.

Wright

Dr. Chopra, you suggest viewing our bodies from the perspective of quantum physics. That seems somewhat technical. Can you tell us a little bit more about that?

Chopra

You see, on one level, your body is made up of flesh and bone. That's the material level but we know today that everything that we consider matter is born of energy and information. By starting to think of our bodies as networks of energy information and even intelligence, we begin to shift our perspective. We don't think of our bodies' so much as dense matter, but as vibrations of consciousness. Even though it sounds technical, everyone has had an experience with this so-called quantum body. When for example, you do an intense workout, after the workout you feel a sense of energy in your body, a tingling sensation, you're actually experiencing what ancient wisdom traditions the "vital force." The more you pay attention to this vital force inside your body, the more you will experience it as energy, information and intelligence and the more control you will have over its expressions.

Wright

Does DNA have anything to do with that?

Chopra

DNA is the source of everything in our body. DNA is like the language that creates the molecules of our bodies. DNA is like a protein making factory, but DNA doesn't give us the blueprint. You know when I build a house, I have to go to the factory to find the bricks, but having the bricks is not enough. I need to get an architect, who in his consciousness or in her consciousness can create that blueprint. And that blueprint exists only in your spirit and in consciousness, in your soul.

Wright

I was interested in a statement from your last book. You said that perceptions create reality. What perceptions must we change in order to reverse our biological image?

Chopra

You have to change three perceptions. First you have to get rid of the perceptions of aging itself. Most people believe that aging means disease and infirmities. You have to change that. You have to regard aging as an opportunity for personal growth, spiritual growth. You also have to regard it as an opportunity to express the wisdom of your experience and an opportunity to help others and lift them from ordinary and mundane experience to the kind of experiences you are capable of because you have much more experience than them. The second thing you have to change your perception of is your physical body. You have to start to experience it as information and energy, as a network of information and intelligence. The third thing you have to change the perception on is the experience of dying. You know, if you are the kind of person who constantly is running out of time, and then you will run out of time. On the other hand, if you have a lot of time, and if you do everything with gusto and love and passion, then you will lose track of time. And when you loose track of time, your body does not metabolize that experience.

Wright

That is interesting. People who teach time management don't really teach the passion?

Chopra

No, no. Time management is such a restriction of time. Your biological clock starts to age much more rapidly. I think what you have to really do is live your life with passion so time doesn't mean anything to you.

Wright

That's a concept I've never heard.

Chopra

Well, there you are.

Wright

You spend an entire chapter of your book on deep rest as an important part of the reverse aging process. What is deep rest?

Chopra

One of the most important mechanisms for renewal and survival is sleep. If you deprive an animal of sleep, then it ages very fast and dies prematurely. We live in a culture where most of our population has to resort to sleeping pills and tranquilizers in order to go asleep. That doesn't bring natural rejuvenation and renewal. You know you have had a good night sleep when you wake up in the morning, you feel renewed, you feel invigorated, and you feel refreshed like a baby does. So that's one kind of deep rest. That comes from deep sleep and from natural sleep. In the book I talk about how you go about making sure you get that. The second deep rest comes from the experience of meditation, which is the ability to quiet your mind so you still your internal dialogue. When your internal dialogue is still, then you enter into a stage of deep rest because when your mind is agitated, your body is unable to rest.

Wright

You know, I have always heard of people who had bad eyesight and really didn't realize it until they went to the doctor and were fitted for lenses. I had that same experience a couple of months ago. I had never really for several years, enjoyed the deep sleep you're talking about, so the doctor diagnosed me with sleep apnea. Now I sleep like a baby, and it makes a tremendous difference.

Chopra

Of course it does. You now have energy and the ability to concentrate and do things.

Wright

Dr. Chopra, how much do eating habits have to do with aging? Can we change and reverse our biological age by what we eat?

Chopra

Yes, you can. One of the most important things to remember is that certain types of food actually contain anti-aging compounds. There are many chemicals that are contained in certain foods that have an anti-aging effect. Most of these chemicals are derived from light. There's no way to bottle them; no pills that you can take that give you these chemicals. But they're contained in plants that are rich in color and derived from photosynthesis. Anything that is yellow, green, and red or has a lot of color, such as fruits and vegetables, they contain a lot of these very powerful anti-aging chemicals. In addition, you have to be careful not to put food in your body that is dead or has no life energy. So anything that comes in a can or has a label, qualifies for that. You have expose your body to six tastes, sweet, sour, salt, bitter, pungent, and astringent because those are the codes of intelligence that allows us to access the deep intelligence of nature. Nature and what she gives to us in bounty, is actually experienced through the sense of taste. In fact, the light chemicals, the anti-aging substances in food, create the six tastes.

Wright

I was talking to one of the ladies in your office and she sent me an invitation to a symposium that you are having in June, in California. I was really interested. The title is *Exploring the Reality of Soul.*

Chopra

Well the symposium is going to be mediated by me, conducted by me, but we have some of the world's scientist, physicist, and biologist who are doing research in what is called, non-local intelligence, which would be the intelligence of soul or spirit. You could say the intelligence that orchestrates the activity of the universe the god for example. Science and spirituality is now meeting together because by understanding how nature works and the laws of nature work, we're beginning to get a glimpse of a deeper intelligence that people in spiritual traditions call divine, or God. I think this is a wonderful time to explore spirituality through science. If anyone is interested in coming to this symposium, then they can go on our website, www.chopra.com and get the details.

Wright

She also sent me biographical information of the seven scientists that will be with you. I have never read a list of seven more noted people in their industry.

Chopra

They are. There's the director of the Max Planck Institute, in Berlin, Germany, where quantum physics was discovered. Dr. Grossam is a professor of physics at the University of Oregon, and he talks about the quantum creativity of death and the survival of conscious after death. It's an extraordinary group of people.

Wright

I think one was Hans-Peter Duerr, nuclear physicist and philosopher that sounds as if it's going to be really great. Is it over two days?

Chopra

Well, actually the first day is an evening reception, so it's only one day.

Wright

Dr. Chopra, with our *Success is a State of the Mind* book we're trying to encourage people to be better, live better, and be more fulfilled by listening to the examples of our guest. Is there anything or anyone in your life that has made a difference for you and has helped you to become a better person?

Chopra

Well, I have to be honest; the most important person in my life was my father. Everyday he said, "What can I do in thought ward indeed to nurture every relationship that I encounter just for today." That has lived with me for my entire life.

Wright

What do you think makes up a great mentor? Are there characteristics mentors seem to have in common?

Chopra

I think the most important attribute of a great mentor is that they teach by example and not necessarily through words.

Wright

When you consider the choices you've made down through the years, has faith played an important role?

Chopra

I think more than faith, curiosity, wonder, a sense of reference and humility has. Now if you want to call that faith, then, yes it has.

Wright

In a divine being?

Chopra

In a greater intelligence. Intelligence that is supreme, infinite, unbounded and too mysterious for the fine mind to comprehend.

Wright

If you could have a platform and tell our audience something that you feel would help them and encourage them what would you say to them?

Chopra

I would say that there are so many techniques that come to us from ancient wisdom tradition that allow us to tap into our inner resources and allow us to become beings that have intuition, creativity, vision and a connection to that which is sacred. That in finding that with in ourselves, we have the means to enhance our well being. Whether it's physical, emotional or environmental, we have the means to resolve conflicts and get rid of war we have. We have the means to be really healthy. We have the means for economic upliftment that says knowledge is the most important knowledge that exists.

Wright

I have seen you on several prime time television shows down through the years where you have had the time to explain theories and beliefs. How does a person such as me experience this? Do we get it out of books?

Chopra

Books are a tool which offer you some road map. But I think that if you sit down every day, close your eyes and put your attention in your heart and ask yourself two questions, who am I and what do I want, then maintain a short period of stillness and body and mind as in prayer or meditation, the door will open.

Wright

So, you think that the intelligence comes from within. Do all of us have that capacity?

Chopra

Every child that is born has that capacity.

Wright

That's fascinating. So, it doesn't take trickery or anything like that?

Chopra

No, it says in the bible in Psalms, *"Be still and know that I am God."*

Wright

That's great advice. I really do appreciate you being with us today. You are fascinating. I wish I could talk to you for the rest of the afternoon, I'm certain I am one of millions that would like to do that!

Chopra

Thank you, sir. It was a pleasure to talk to you!

Wright

Today we have been talking to Dr. Deepak Chopra the founder of the Chopra Center for Well Being. More than a decade ago, he became the foremost pioneer in integrated medicine. We have found today that he really knows what he's talking about. After reading his book *Grow Younger, Live Longer, Ten Steps to Reverse Aging,* I certainly hope you'll go out to your favorite book store and buy a copy. Dr. Chopra, thank you so much for being with us today.

Chopra

Thank you for having me, David.

ABOUT THE AUTHOR

Deepak Chopra has written twenty-five books, which have been translated into thirty-five languages. He is also the author of more than one hundred audio and videotape series, including five critically acclaimed programs on public television. In 1999, *Time* magazine selected Dr. Chopra as one of the Top 100 Icons and Heroes of the Century, describing him and "the poet-prophet of alternative medicine."

Dr. Deepak Chopra
The Chopra Center at La Costa Resort and Spa
Email: info@chopra.com
www.chopra.com

SUCCESS IS A STATE OF MIND 3

An interview with...

Sela Pearson

David Wright (Wright)

Today we are talking with Sela Pearson. She is the owner and featured speaker for Akanke Creations. She is a motivational speaker, storyteller, poet, author, and healthcare educator. Her personal life experiences coupled with her health care experiences lend authenticity to her speeches. Through Akanke Creations, she seeks to inspire, encourage, motivate, and empower others toward positive personal growth.

Sela does workshops and keynote addresses in Nashville and other major cities. As a popular speaker, she is sensitive and empathetic to many because the experiences she shares are heartfelt. Her counterparts say that Sela is enthusiastic, sincere, insightful, and a pleasure to know. She is a leader in her field.

Sela, welcome to *Success is a State of Mind.*

Sela Pearson (Pearson)

Good morning and thank you very much. I am honored to be here today.

Wright

Akanke is a unique name. What does that mean?

Pearson

Akanke is a name from West Africa that means *to know her is to love her*. A coworker gifted me with that name about twelve years ago. Whenever I think about that name connection, I like to think that when people meet and greet me, the energy that builds is based upon unconditional love and that as time progresses those who stay in touch find it to be a statement of truth.

Wright

It is great to know that people think that highly of you also; you have to live up to it every day. It is like being named the king—you have to be the king every day.

Pearson

Yes, you have to live up to that name in a manner of speaking. I try to treat everyone I meet in a manner that reflects how I would like to be treated. It is a great honor and I am so blessed.

Wright

"Rise*Up"—is that a slogan, a speech title, or a workshop title? What does it stand for and how will others benefit from it?

Pearson

"Rise*Up," is used as a slogan and as a workshop title; I use it in both of those capacities. It stands for "Radiate Inner Self Esteem*

Unleash Potential. You Are Greater Than You Think!" It reflects the genius of self-potential. We are all truly greater than we think; we just do not allow ourselves to let our light shine.

I ran across a quote, and people who may be familiar with Marianne Williamson or possibly saw the movie, *Akeelah and the Spelling Bee,* have seen or heard the quote: "Our deepest fear is not that we are inadequate. Our deepest fear is that we are powerful beyond measure. It is our light not our darkness that most frightens us. . . . And as we let our own light shine, we unconsciously give other people the permission to do the same. As we are liberated from our own fear, our presence automatically liberates others."

When I read that quote from Marianne Williamson it made me think about the creation of "Rise*Up," We have all this potential within us. We do not free ourselves to do and become all that we are created to be in this life—in this world. We need to break through those barriers of fear to become the best that we can be.

Wright

Would you share with our readers a little bit about your health care background and how has it helped you in creating and delivering speeches?

Pearson

I am a graduate of the University of Phoenix where I obtained my Master's in Business Administration degree with emphasis in Healthcare Management. I have a BS degree in Community Health and I am a Certified Health Counselor. I have also worked in the capacity of a nurse over the past thirty-nine years.

In speaking about increasing self-esteem in people, I look to redirect feelings of worthlessness. My extensive healthcare background can assist people in fostering positive beliefs and overcoming symptoms of depression that may manifest in physical form.

My healthcare background is a big plus in helping to motivate people to adapt positive attitudes. The avenues of nursing I worked in included populations in prison settings, pediatrics, and senior citizens. I have worked extensively with people living with AIDS and cancer. My expertise has fallen under the category of crisis counselor. I facilitated alcohol and substance abuse groups, as well as victim abuse groups.

I have personally experienced a lot of grief through the passing of many family members and friends. I feel that through personal and professional experience I am equipped to assist people in handling crises. Having survived situations of battering and victimization, I am able to help people to break free of those chains that bind them.

Wright

Being a graduate of the University of Phoenix in your major, how do you see that affecting your life in the speaking field?

Pearson

I have always been interested in speaking. I was blessed to be the student speaker for the graduating class of 2007. Les Brown delivered the commencement address. I was afforded the opportunity to view a video of Les Brown In 1995 and admired his passion and motivation in speech form. I was a member of Toastmasters International at the time, and in 1996 I quit my job to follow my dreams, but unfortunately, the timing was off. I spoke on a smaller scale, holding tight to my day job, fearing to let go. On graduation day from the University of Phoenix I had the opportunity to meet Les Brown in person. Celebration was in order because he hugged me after I delivered my speech and proceeded to refer to the essence of my speech in the delivery of his own—a definite honor.

My MBA degree with emphasis on health care management will give me the opportunity to keep abreast of management trends in healthcare. People are experiencing a lot of stress today and healthcare workers are no exception. I look forward to providing solutions and assist in relieving those stressful situations. Having completed the University of Phoenix curriculum, I feel well equipped to pursue avenues of speaking and workshop presentation that will prove quite beneficial in the future.

Wright

As we are talking here today, I am experiencing some of the things that you have experienced in your life—one of the beloved members of our family just passed away two days ago. I understand that six of your immediate family members have passed on since April 2000. How has this affected your life, your beliefs, and your motivation?

Pearson

Two brothers have passed away, two sisters, my son, and my mother. They were all very creative, each in their own way. A lot of that creativity I find within myself.

My father, Thomas Razor, passed away in 1993. The process of speaking began with him and a reel-to-reel tape recorder when I was ten years of age. I did not realize until thirty years later that public speaking was what I felt drawn to do. It was actually the beginning without realizing that it was a beginning.

My father was a person who encouraged all of his children to read and to study. He was always telling us that just by picking up books and reading them we would acquire a lot of knowledge and wisdom in life. That has been an important factor throughout my life.

I take the precious memories of my family and hold them close to my heart. That has helped me survive the passing of those family members. Each one instilled something beautiful in me and I give thanks daily for their having blessed my life, no matter how short lived.

My son, Nassar, was a precious young man who believed in my dreams far more than I did. He encouraged me and tried to help me work at making the dream a reality. Every time I start a new project, I give honor to him. When I returned to school, it was in honor of his memory.

My mother, Thelma Razor, was "Mom"—what does one say and how does one honor the person who birthed you into the world? Through her bout with cancer, my sister, Liya, helped to create the Sisters Network in Buffalo, New York. Susan G. Komen's Race for the Cure honored her in 2005.

When my sister, Nisa, passed away in January of 2007, she was on the verge of completing a doctorate program. As you can see, we are a family who followed my father's advice and steeped ourselves in knowledge. I consider myself blessed to be carrying this torch forward in honor of my family.

Wright

What is your definition of success? Who or what has been instrumental in your life toward developing a speaking career?

Pearson

Success is moving from one day to the next with grace and ease. I used to measure success by the number of dollar bills I had. Then one day all of that was gone. I have learned that through grace I am able to move into the next day without fear of what lies behind me or before me.

A few years ago I wrote a poem called *Fear*. Writing the poem helped move myself past the point of allowing fear to completely overtake and shadow my life. The slogan "Rise*Up" was born from that poem. I realized that we are greater than we think. I began to accept the notion that I am greater than I think because of some of the circumstances that I have gone through in my life—the battering, the victimization, and things of that nature that put me in places of depression where I could see no way out. In writing the poem, *Fear,* it helped me to release that and it gave me permission to love myself. What I do through my poetry is to release a lot of anxiety. This is the poem:

Fear

I have always looked upon you as an enemy of mine;
but now I know and understand that you were a friend in kind;
For you loomed so above me making me cringe inside.
The echo of your harsh words caused me to lay all my plans aside.
So I closed off all avenues that foretold of my dreams in life,
never realizing that I would confront you at some point and time.
So confront you I did and when you raised up your head,
I quickly pounced on it dismissing you as a cause for harm,
for it was as if we both knew that it's a mightier force than you,
who sets me on the path and controls my every move.
So my dear friend, as I cast you from my side,
please know that we will always be friends,
for you have given me back my life.

When I witnessed Les Brown's video and saw how passionately he delivered his speeches and how motivational he was, it impacted on my life.

I recently completed reading a book by Deepak Chopra titled *Peace is the Way.* It instructs us on how we can create peace in our life and in the world by starting with ourselves. We create peace for ourselves and then it moves out from there.

I have read and reread *As a Man Thinketh* by James Allen. It is one of many favorite books. The writings of Kahlil Gibran are of great interest and inspiration.

Alice Walker's *Temple of My Familiar* is another powerful book. I would be amiss to not include Susan Taylor of *Essence Magazine* for such thought-provoking words of wisdom. I am presently reading a book by Eric Butterworth titled *The Universe is Calling* and it is powerful.

Those are some of the people who have impacted my life.

Wright

People are intrigued by what stimulates one in life. What has been a great motivator for you? We know that you are an avid reader; would you share some of the books you have read and their impact on your life?

Pearson

In 1979 I worked for an insurance company called Combined Life Insurance Company of New York. W. Clement Stone owned that company. One of the philosophies was, "whatever the mind of man can conceive and believe, the mind of man can achieve for those who have PMA, which is a Positive Mental Attitude." We had to read Napoleon Hill's book, *Think and Grow Rich.* That book allowed me to stand up for myself and honor my truths. Those types of books have made a big impact on me.

Over the years I have read many self-help books. They help condition and stimulate your mind to move in positive directions. I have learned to associate with people who move in positive directions, doing worthwhile activities, and who are working to turn those dreams into reality.

Wright

How do you tie poetry into your speeches? Do you have a favorite poem?

Pearson

I incorporate poetry into my speeches because it is an outlet—a release. Some people go to the psychiatrist's office and sit on the couch—I take pen to paper and write. I give written expression to whatever I am feeling. I have learned how to take those thoughts, write them into journals, and then create poetry of my innermost feelings. Reviewing poems that I have written years ago that may have sounded okay then, are so powerful now. They become my backbone in life.

There are several poems I have written and reread that are very special, and *Be Still Our Hearts,* is one of my favorites.

Be Still Our Hearts

Listen to the silence
casting a spell upon us
as the echo of the wind
lashes about our ears.
Be still our hearts and listen

to the distant sounds of life
floating on a breeze
causing waves to rock inside.
Quiet little murmurings
stirring within our souls
making us want to jump with joy
for we are acknowledging God.
Feel the presence of the Almighty
as our hearts sing out loud
of the stillness and peace
that is focused on the inside.
Let's take that calm and peacefulness
and hug it to our sides
then allow for the stillness
to become a part of our lives.
Go about your day
free from restlessness.
Secure in the knowledge
that to reach your God
you only have to still your heart.

We get so busy and so bogged down that we forget to take that moment of silence, still our hearts, and just be in that moment. The poem reminds me that no matter what I am doing I need to take the time to still myself. As you rush about during the course of the day forgetting things, losing things, turning back to go home to check on things, know that those are the times to still yourself, and in that moment of quietness allow God to operate in your life knowing that the answers are right there for you.

Wright

Is there any form of music or dance that elicits a creative flow for you?

Pearson

I love all types of music. I love to listen to classical music because I can take the time to be peaceful and to meditate. I think that meditating—being still and being quiet—is very beneficial in life. It allows you to take time out from the busy world that we live in.

I love African drumming as well as Native-American drumming and flutes. Sometimes it is so intense that I can feel the heartbeat of the music. There are African drums that when I hear them I can hear words being processed through the drum, and the vibrations sing to my heart. There is a connection and honoring of my African and Native American roots.

I love to dance. I think that movement is important, if we are physically able to move. I love to be able to copy the birds with my arms outstretched and spinning around as if I am flying. It is a feeling and sense of soaring that gives me a great feeling of release. I never need any particular style of dance; it is just that freedom and liberation that is allowed when in that mode.

Wright

Walk with us through your typical day. How do you start your morning? Does it create the momentum for the day? Do you maintain it, and how can this help others to view their lives as a success?

Pearson

A typical day includes waking up and greeting and embracing the power of that morning. Next, I do some form of prayer, usually affirmations of thankfulness and love. I give thanks for life, limbs working, loved ones in my life, and an alert mind.

I have also learned to honor people in my life. There are many people who, through the course of the day, the week, the month, I call upon to help me in various ways. These people include: my sons, Anwar (his wife, Stephanie, and their three children, Ruqiyyah, Hamid, and Karimah), and Jonathan. My sisters: Yasarah, Thomasina, and Ronda, are a big help in my life. My nieces and nephews, especially John, are very supportive. Devoted friends like Joshua, Gloria, Delores, Della, Michele, Jean, Jennifer, Bridgette, Ms. Nance, Trina, Bernadette, Lynn, and the Campbell family are also in this list. I have supporters like Janice of the Antara Center, Diana, Montanez and Paula of Interplay, and Delsenia of Bridge Your Soulful Journey. Toastmaster comrades such as Brenda and Dennis (they are just phenomenal people) are always asking me, "What is your dream? Is there any way I can help you make that dream a reality?" Also, business colleagues, Craig of WestbrookStevens.com and Gwynelle and Thandiwe of Women to the Nth Power, offer much support. Reverends Cheri and Karl of First Church Unity offer much wisdom in weekly sermons and workshops. (To those I know who may be reading this chapter: this list is extensive and please know that if your name is not listed you are still loved and I am thankful for your presence in my life and your never-ending support.)

When I think about life and people, I know that this book, *Success is a State of Mind*, will touch many lives. Everyone everywhere has dreams to share and stories to tell about what motivates them in life. What makes us unique is that the dreams are all different just as we are all different. Some of us sit on our dreams and we allow those dreams to fade away into the sunset. Others of us work at our dreams for a moment and then with deep sighs we relinquish them and allow them to turn to dust. A small percentage of us (I now place myself in this category) allow those dreams to consume the very fiber of our being. We allow those feelings to ignite at the very core of our being and light up every cell within our bodies. We radiate that energy and unleash that passion into the world.

When I talk about "Rise*Up" it is meant to be shared—take the knowledge that we have and share it with others so that they too can realize that they are greater than they think.

Part of my day consists of thinking about what I can do to help someone move forward in life. People look for success stories that credit someone with twenty billion dollars and another with one hundred million dollars, but there are success stories every day in our lives. There are people who come through who just have a smile to share or a witty story to tell. There are people who might not have much of anything, but who are willing to share whatever it is with others. They are willing to share from their heart because they know that at that moment, the person they are reaching out to is in need. Those are success stories for me.

I try to be helpful to people. One of the things that I always do before I leave home is to put myself in a *positive* frame of mind by doing affirmations every day. I used to work at a job where I had to be at work at 6:00 AM. People would ask me how I could come to work smiling and be so cheerful when they barely wanted to be there. The difference is how you start your day and the thoughts that you imprint in your mind before you leave home and embark on the journey to work.

I always try to be a positive influence in people's lives. Many times people have remarked to me that with all that is going on in my life how do I keep my smile? I can help turn their day around and my world could be crumbling. My reply is that sometimes it is that spirit you have to carry, whether you call upon God, the universe, Mother Mary, Jesus, or in your own defined way. You have to put joy in your life every day. That is how I begin my day and that is how I end my day.

I've learned from people I've been associated with who have had severe illnesses and I've learned by seeing the lives of my family pass away. In addition to the close family members I have mentioned, there have been several close friends and other family members.

I've learned that laughter is good medicine for the soul. We have to find ways to help ourselves relax. We have to find ways to make ourselves laugh throughout the day. I am hearing new information about smiling and how you can burn off calories with laughter and how good laughter is for you. It takes just as much energy to make that frown as it does to make that smile. If you realize that when you smile, it uplifts everything—your whole body seems to be uplifted. I think to myself, why walk around with a frown when I can just as easily turn that frown into a smile? Walk through there, have that positive mental attitude, maintain it through the day.

As a salesperson, I was taught to go through the day singing little kids' songs like, "If you're happy and you know it clap your hands." They were very simple songs, but they are so impactful in our lives because they help to bring us back to that moment so we can put a smile on our faces. That is what I have learned to continue doing in my life.

Wright

What a great conversation. I really appreciate all this time you've taken with me this morning to answer all these questions. I have learned a lot and I know that our readers will.

Today we've been talking with Sela Pearson. She is a health care educator, an author, a poet, a storyteller, and she is also a motivational speaker.

Through her company she seeks to inspire, encourage, motivate, and empower others toward positive personal growth. I think that we've learned this morning that she's really good at it.

Sela, thank you so much for being with us today on *Success is a State of Mind.*

Pearson

I thank you. I will conclude with this one remark: I would just like for everyone together to affirm, "I am greater than I think," and yes, you are!

Thank you, David.

ABOUT THE AUTHOR

Sela Pearson holds a MBA degree with emphasis in Healthcare Management. She has a BS in Community Health and she is a Certified Health Counselor, a Licensed Practical Nurse, an author, poet, storyteller, and health care educator. She is owner and featured speaker for Akanke Creations. In 2007 she received the Outstanding Student Award from the University of Phoenix (Nashville) and was also the student commencement speaker that year. She is an independent contractor with Westbrookstevens, LLC. People-to-People Ambassador Programs honored her to act as a delegate to South Africa, Egypt, and China. She is listed in: *Marquis Who's Who in the South and Southwest* and *Who's Who among American Women, Madison's Who's Who, Strathmore's Who's Who, International Who's Who in Poetry,* and was Ambassador of Poetry in 2006. She is a member of Toastmasters International, Nurses Association, Spirited Divas of Nashville (Red Hat Society), Board Member of Antara Center, and is active in the Leadership Program of InterPlay (Nashville). Sela is also an active member of the Cherokee Wolf Clan.

Sela Pearson
P.O. Box 111341
Nashville, TN 37222
Phone: 615.365.3187
E-mail: selapearson@bellsouth.net
www.akankecreations.com
www.westbrookstevens/sela pearson.htm

An interview with...

Dieter Pauwels

David Wright (Wright)

Today we are talking with Dieter Pauwels, a professional coach, trainer, and speaker based in St. Louis, Missouri. Dieter believes that the beliefs we hold serve as the guidelines by which we live our lives. Some of these beliefs, he says, may empower us, while others prevent us from getting what we want and deserve. When we understand how specifically our chosen beliefs influence our thoughts, feelings, and actions, we can discover how to reinvent ourselves, not in accordance with the standards of others, but in accordance with our own desires and goals.

Understanding the structure and power of our beliefs can make all the difference in our ability to attract and create the lives we want.

Dieter, welcome to *Success is a State of Mind.*

Dieter Pauwels (Pauwels)

Thank you, David. I'm delighted to be a part of this project.

Wright

So why do people come to you for coaching, Dieter?

Pauwels

People seek me out for a variety of reasons. Most often it's because they would like to change, achieve, or create something in their personal and professional lives. From the outside looking in, they might appear to have it all together, yet they feel something is missing or they are not getting the results they want. This desire for change is often the result of a perceived gap between where they are today and where they want to be at some point in the future. This might mean a more rewarding relationship, better health, a more exciting career, more business success, or a new sense of fulfillment and balance in their lives. They choose to work with me because they want the structure and support personal coaching provides.

Wright

How then do you define coaching?

Pauwels

I see coaching as a partnership in which I guide and support clients to a higher level of personal and professional standards and achievement. Together we create a road map for success. My coaching methods are very outcome-oriented and highly solution-focused. Coaching increases the number of choices and options a client has to accomplish what he or she wants. It offers the opportunity to explore what is really possible, and the development of the means and resources to achieve that. I find it brings out the best in people and inspires them to appreciate and support the best in others.

Wright

How important are a person's beliefs in the coaching process?

Pauwels

The ability for clients to recognize and accept their beliefs is essential to an effective coaching relationship. Beliefs, together with values, greatly influence the goals clients set for themselves and the actions they will take in pursuit of these goals. What you believe has a profound effect on how you go about achieving what you want. Limiting beliefs will hold you back; empowering or positive beliefs move you forward.

I want to know what my clients believe about success and failure because often our definitions of success and failure are distorted.

Changing limiting or erroneous beliefs is probably one of the most powerful interventions I facilitate as a coach. Sometimes when people feel stuck, I've found the problem is often not what they initially recognize as the problem, but rather some belief they maintain about themselves or about the possibility of getting what they really want. When I'm able to assist people in solving a problem and changing the beliefs that first led to the problem, I can then create new possibilities and experiences for my clients, even outside the initial context of the problem. That's very powerful.

The beliefs you hold about yourself, other people, and the events that have shaped your life have consequences for every aspect of your career, financial success, relationships, even your health. After all, the most significant difference between underachievers and high achievers is not just talent and competence, although these components are important. The most important difference is the set of beliefs achievers hold about themselves and others as they pursue their goals.

Beliefs create a structure of right and wrong, which includes what others expect of you and what you expect of yourself. Your beliefs shape your life to the degree that they determine what seems possible, acceptable, achievable, or whether or not you deserve something.

Most of us spend our lives trying to justify and validate our own concept of ourselves and others. We play our roles to the best of our ability and with the best of intentions.

What ideas do you have about money? Do you believe you have to work hard to make a lot of money or do you believe money comes easily to you? What do you tell yourself about love and relationships? Do you believe that members of the opposite sex cannot be trusted? Do you believe relationships are hard work? Do you believe that you will find your soul mate? What do you believe about success? What assumptions are you making about success that you may not be aware of?

Because we accept our personal assumptions and the beliefs that support them as if they are true, we seek out experiences in our lives to justify what we have agreed to believe. Our internal beliefs become self-fulfilling prophecies. If you believe that life is unfair, you're not smart enough, attractive enough, or if you believe that true love is just an illusion, or that you will never achieve financial independence, then by default you will always worry about relationships, money, and your career. Worse, you will unconsciously keep creating the same situations over and over again to validate what you believe. In other words, more and more situations will show up to give you more and more reasons to worry and experience the same negative emotions and results.

Our beliefs are not always logical or rational. They tend to operate beneath the surface of our conscious awareness. If beliefs were formed at the conscious level, it would be easier to change them.

Wright

How would you define "beliefs"?

Pauwels

Beliefs are the assumptions, judgments, or agreements you have made (mostly subconsciously) about yourself, others, and the world you live in. Beliefs are thoughts that have become true for you. When you believe something to be true, you have no doubts; the belief becomes a fact.

Beliefs are thoughts and thoughts are energy. Consider that energy flows where attention goes. In other words, the beliefs you hold become strong attractors for certain experiences. When you believe something, you'll automatically start looking for experiences that validate and reinforce what you believe to be true. Beliefs, therefore, shape your reality.

Wright

Is there a difference between what you believe to be true and your values?

Pauwels

That's a great question. I look at values and beliefs as two sides of the same coin called motivation. Values are basically ideals that are important to you in your life. They are usually expressed in abstract terms such as respect, success, health, freedom, loyalty, love, honesty, integrity, and so forth. Your values, together with the beliefs you hold about yourself and others, provide the inner motivation to take action toward your goals. Values and beliefs create a perceptional filter through which you experience life. While one person might believe that being successful is making $250,000 per year, another person may believe that success means the ability to make a difference in someone else's life. Each will therefore choose different strategies and do different things to achieve their objectives.

At a deeper level, what you value and believe gives you a sense of identity—a sense of self-worth. It is from this unique point of self-reference that you see and interpret the world around you. Most people live their lives consistent with their self-image and will do almost anything to operate within the boundaries they have created. They cannot change any of the behaviors, habits, or beliefs that hold them back without changing the image and assumptions that they hold about themselves.

Every positive act of change in your life is fostered by a change in self-perception. This means that what is standing between you and your goals, dreams, and aspirations are not circumstances but the assumptions you have made about yourself. Think for a moment about something you really want, but for some reason have not yet achieved or experienced. Now think of what's preventing you from getting what you really want and ask yourself, "Who would I be without that thought?" It is in the answer to this fundamental question that you will start to discover that you might become more of who you want to be by adopting new and more empowering beliefs.

I coach many creative, intelligent, skilled, and passionate people who, despite having clearly defined goals, are not achieving the success of which they are truly capable. It's not that they fear failure; it's not that they don't have the know-how. It's because they unconsciously find a way to sabotage themselves. They don't allow themselves to succeed. What all these wonderful people have in common is a negative self-belief. Unable to give themselves permission to value themselves, they cannot achieve the success they deserve.

One of my coaching clients, a young and vibrant entrepreneur in his mid-thirties, started coaching with me because he wanted to take his business to the next level. He told me that for the last couple of years his business had remained stagnant and he felt himself procrastinating to make decisions needed to grow his business. I asked him what would stop a smart and creative young man from achieving the success he really wanted. "I don't know," he replied. "But sometimes I feel that achieving success means that I'm selfish, and I feel really guilty about that." When I inquired more about his feeling of guilt, he mentioned that a voice in his head kept telling him that he should just be happy with where he was, that he didn't need any more than what he had already.

I think we all have such voices talking to us. Like bullies, they try to intimidate us and keep us from achieving the success we want. They tell us that if we want too much for ourselves we're self-centered or selfish, or that one day others will find out that we're not that good, or that success is for others but not us. When we listen to these voices, and it's hard not to, things can get pretty dark inside our heads.

In coaching we sometimes refer to these little voices that hold us back as our "gremlins." Recognizing these little creatures for what they are is a first step toward taming them. A playful, yet effective way we can deal with them is to personify our gremlin by giving it a name, some characteristics, and perhaps a personality.

I've always had this little voice—this little gremlin—in my head that I call Peter Perfect. He is a smart and witty creature who always tells me that unless I can do something perfectly, I shouldn't do it. But instead of hoping that one day he would go away, I have come to understand that in recognizing Peter Perfect for what he is, I diminish his power to run my life and hold me back.

Clients who want to succeed in life must first give themselves permission to succeed. This means they have to develop a positive inner dialogue that is congruent with their true intentions. To determine whether their inner thoughts are supporting or limiting them, they need to ask themselves, "Would I say the same words to a friend, a family member, or colleague who needs my support?"

Wright

So where do our beliefs come from?

Pauwels

Our beliefs emanate from many different sources of influence including our parents, our family, teachers, friends, books, and media, among others.

Numerous studies have indicated that many of our beliefs are established between our third and eighth birthdays. Certainly we acquire many of our beliefs from our parents or early caregivers. Because we depend on them for survival, they have great influence over us; as a consequence, we sometimes learn the wrong things from our childhood experiences. We create generalizations about behaviors that become formed in repeated patterns, believing that this is just the way life is, based on what we observe growing up. Some beliefs are held from generation to generation; some of them are blessings, others are like a family curse.

Examples of generalizations I acquired growing up are that you have to work hard to make a living and you have to put your work before your family in order to be successful. It's easy to judge or criticize parents with the benefits of hindsight. I know that my parents and their parents did the best they could to live by what they knew and believed at the time. They created their own perception of reality based on their beliefs. This doesn't make them wrong, but it doesn't always make them right either.

People often resist changing beliefs because they don't want to question or dishonor what has been an important part of their personal history. But we can choose to leave the past where it belongs—in the past—and create a new and compelling vision for the future.

Wright

Why are beliefs so powerfully connected to personal achievement?

Pauwels

Our beliefs have a profound impact on our self-confidence, capabilities, and personal achievements. There are thousands upon thousands of self-help and motivational books out there, each promising answers on how to become successful, lose weight, gain financial freedom, or how to live a life filled with abundance and joy, and so on. We're led to believe that living a successful life is simply a book away.

While I do not discount any of these books or the strategies they provide, I do find that the tools they suggest don't always stick. People have been flocking to motivational seminars for years looking for solutions to their problems outside of themselves. Yet within a few weeks, many find themselves repeating the same behavioral routines by which they recreate past experiences over and over again.

So what's preventing them from breaking those old habits? What's the real secret behind "The Secret"? The secret lies in understanding the power of your beliefs. On one hand, positive beliefs enable you to access many of your own inner resources, talents, skills, and even dormant capabilities. On the other hand, your beliefs become a powerful attractor for creating positive new experiences.

Most everyone knows the story about Roger Bannister who became the first athlete to run a mile in under four minutes. Before he did this (in the spring of 1954), running a four-minute mile had been believed to be impossible and beyond the physical limits of the human body. Now, did Roger Bannister possess a superhuman quality or ability? No. He succeeded because he set aside the widely accepted belief that it wasn't possible to run a mile in under four minutes. He decided it was possible, and the rest is history. What's even more interesting, within seven months after he set this amazing record, thirty-seven others followed him, and within the following three years, another three hundred athletes ran the mile in under four minutes. Once disproved, the old belief of what was possible no longer limited those who followed after Bannister.

Beliefs represent the means by which we create our own reality. Expect success in any given venture and you're more likely to achieve it. Expect to fail, and most certainly you will. Taking the time to understand the true power of some of our long-held beliefs allows us to discover that we have the ability to create any point of view we choose. We can create new and compelling personal expectations by breaking through the limiting boundaries we've been convinced we could never change.

Wright

Why do we hold on to beliefs that might limit us?

Pauwels

To answer that question let's talk for a moment about why we create and adopt beliefs in the first place. Usually, we adopt a particular belief with the best of intentions and hold on to it as a means of taking care of ourselves. Such beliefs become the framework of our emotional comfort zones. Another reason we hold on to beliefs is that as human beings, we need some sense of certainty in our lives. Beliefs can become so much a part of our reality that we accept them as fact. I'm sure you have heard people say things like, "Well, that's just the way it is," when in reality, it's just the way it is for them.

People have a unique desire to explain or justify things. I think each of us wants to be right. To explain various events or issues in our lives, we start making assumptions and thus we create beliefs. The things that we know, or think we know, together with the assumptions we have made and the beliefs we've adopted become our frame of reference. Because we view all information through this lens, we are inclined to generalize, distort, or delete information on the basis of whether or not it matches our perception. We see what we believe because we always look for evidence to reinforce beliefs we have already adopted. As a consequence, beliefs become our self-fulfilling prophecies.

We're all creatures of habit. We hold on to what is familiar and comfortable. We somehow resist the flow of life's creative energy, and deny our innate ability to change. We not only hold on to the possessions we have accumulated—material clutter—but more significantly, we hold on to our emotional clutter, which includes the assumptions, beliefs, and perspectives we've carved into our psyches.

When we tell ourselves we are too old to learn a new skill, we are effectively holding on to clutter that hinders us from changing and growing. Choosing to embrace change means continually sorting through our baggage and pitching the stuff that no longer works for us. When our closet is full, we have no room to hang new clothes. So we need to check our minds—our psychological "closets"—and throw out all the limiting beliefs, ideas, and emotions that hold us back so that we'll have room for new, empowering beliefs and patterns of behavior.

Wright

How important is faith in creating beliefs?

Pauwels

Faith is a kind of energy that can drive the creative process. Many people have wonderful ideas but lack the faith to make them real in their lives. Just think about the great creators, like Thomas Edison, Leonardo da Vinci, or Albert Einstein. While they did not have any evidence to prove their beliefs, they had faith that their beliefs would become reality. When you have a strong enough faith, there is no doubt in your mind. The level of conviction determines the probability of manifesting your creation.

Wright

If beliefs are such a powerful force in our lives, how do we recognize them?

Pauwels

Your outer reality, based on life's experiences, reflects your inner reality, which includes beliefs, thoughts, and attitudes. When your inner reality is filled with negative self-thoughts (such as you're not good enough) or you harbor negative emotions such as anxiety or fear, you'll find that you will attract and create experiences that will reflect and reinforce those thoughts, beliefs, and emotions. The deeper the beliefs, the stronger the emotional investment we make in them. Our emotions are very much a reflection of our beliefs. So when you find yourself responding emotionally to a certain event or situation, it's important to be aware of any underlying beliefs you might hold about yourself or the situation that triggered your response. This is not always easy, since the relationship between your beliefs and your experiences may not seem obvious at first or even logical.

One way to discover limiting beliefs is to focus on negative patterns of behavior because people will behave congruently with what they believe. We all make bad choices, but if you find yourself always being late for appointments or procrastinating about certain tasks or not being able to keep a job for more than six months or you find yourself staying in an unhealthy relationship, then you need to recognize and re-evaluate the underlying beliefs triggering the behavioral choices you are making.

Another way to discover limiting beliefs is to think about something that would really make a difference in your career, relationship, finances, or in your life in general.

I had coaching client who indicated that getting a promotion would really make a difference in her career and would also put her in a better financial situation. She felt that as a single mom, she would feel more secure in taking care of her son if she could gain a promotion. So I asked her what was preventing her from getting that promotion. She thought about it for a while and said, "Well, I guess I just have to schedule a meeting with my boss and ask." Then I asked her what was preventing her from setting up a meeting with her boss and asking for a promotion. The moment I asked that question, her physiology completely changed. Her shoulders dropped, her breathing became shallow, and even the color in her face changed. She told me that she had been with this company for only a year and that she had taken an entry level position with the hopes of eventually moving up and proving to herself that she could work her way up and get a better paying position.

Again I asked, "What's preventing you from asking your boss for a meeting, and asking him for a promotion?"

She responded, "I don't think I have what it takes to succeed."

This is a perfect example of how limiting beliefs can prevent you from taking action. In a situation like this, you sometimes don't believe you can do something because you just don't know yet what is needed to move forward. Saying you haven't done something is no justification for not being able to do it. Once she got clear on what would be expected of her in her new role, we created an action plan that would allow her to acquire some additional skills. Six months later, no longer believing she had to prove herself and feeling confident she had the necessary skills to get a promotion, she got the interview, asked for the promotion, and got the new position.

While I'm coaching, I tend to listen very carefully to my clients' self-talk. Over the years I've found that most of our self-talk comes from our parents. Once you get curious about the voices in your head, you can start to identify some belief patterns. Some of them help us move forward, others keep us stuck in the past.

I was working with another client who came to me to improve his communication skills so he could be more effective in his job as a regional sales manager. He believed that he always had to be right and have the last word. He felt that it was his responsibility to have all the answers. During our coaching conversation, I asked him if he really believed these things to be true. Hesitating, he said, "Well, I guess that's something my father would have said. My dad knew everything and I always looked up to him when I was growing up."

The fact that he could recognize that belief enabled him to think about new ways of communicating.

Wright

What about positive thinking, and the people who use positive affirmations in their lives?

Pauwels

The mind is such a powerful tool. Think of your mind as having two parts: one part representing your conscious awareness, your current thoughts, and attitudes, and the other part representing your subconscious mind, which holds your belief structure. While positive affirmations have an effect on how you feel, your thoughts guide and focus your attention. Positive thoughts will be more likely to attract positive experiences, and negative thoughts, negative experiences.

Positive thinking alone, however, cannot accomplish the results you want if your inner belief system doesn't support your positive self-talk. Trying to make positive changes in your life despite negative beliefs is like trying to plant seeds in non-fertile soil. The seeds don't have a chance to take root and grow. Unless your belief structure supports your positive self-affirmation, you will only create more inner conflict and turmoil.

Wright

Do we *choose* our beliefs?

Pauwels

The answer to that question has the power to change your life. If you insist that you have no choice in your beliefs, you will remain disempowered. This is a typical victim mentality within which you live your life reacting to what life throws at you.

This perspective denies you the responsibility of your own experiences and prevents you from enjoying the power to choose that which is rightfully yours. When you feel that you have no choice, and therefore no options, you get stuck in one perspective.

I believe that we choose our beliefs, and we do so for very good reasons. Our beliefs serve us in some way or have benefited us at some point in our lives. But to gain inner power is to accept that you are not a powerless victim of external forces, that you can take responsibility for the circumstances of your life.

When you are free to choose what you believe, you become not a victim but a victor, and that is very liberating and exciting. There is power in choosing. By doing so, you give yourself permission to be open to other possibilities. You can choose to let go of the beliefs that no longer serve you or honor you, and create new empowering beliefs aligned with your values, your goals, and your heart's truest desires. When you change the way you look at the world, then the world you look at will change.

Wright

Can you change limiting beliefs? If so, will you share the process?

Pauwels

Yes, you can. Remember, if you accept the fact that you choose the beliefs you have adopted, you can also choose to let go and change the beliefs that no longer support your goals and inner desires. Beliefs are fluent and changeable.

I remember as a child growing up in Belgium and believing in Saint Nicholas. We didn't have a red-nosed reindeer, but we did have Saint Nicholas. The night before he came, we would put out some carrots, leather, and sweets in front of the chimney, hoping that he would bring us some toys. One St. Nicholas Eve, before he was due to arrive, I decided that instead of going to bed I would sit on the steps and wait. After a while, I noticed that it was my mother, and not Saint Nicholas, who was actually delivering the presents. After a moment of disappointment, I accepted the new evidence, and let go of my old belief.

Similarly, what you believed about relationships when you were fifteen, I hope, is a little different than what you believe about them as an adult. When you were ten years old, you probably believed your dad knew everything. At twenty years old, well, suddenly he didn't know everything anymore.

My role as a coach is to create new possibilities for my clients by offering different perspectives and sometimes challenging and questioning their beliefs. It's interesting that sometimes you need a different point of view just to understand your own. It's as though you're a fish swimming in the water. The water is your reality—the way you see the world. You're in it every day and it's all you know. You want someone on the outside to look in and provide you with a different perspective.

The first step in changing a limiting belief is creating awareness of the beliefs that you hold. This is probably the most difficult step because limiting beliefs are like blind spots—you don't see them. As a coach and observer, I shed light in those areas to illuminate self-imposed limitations and their impact. Let me use another example to illustrate the different steps in changing limiting beliefs.

A client came to me because he wanted to make a career change. He had interviewed for a few positions, yet was never hired. During our initial coaching conservation, we discovered a limiting belief. He said, "I believe I need a college education to make lots of money and be successful." He believed this so strongly that for him it was a fact.

The second step in changing a limiting belief is to acknowledge and accept it. Acknowledgment is saying, "Yeah, that's what I believe, it's true for me." Once you acknowledge a limiting belief you hold, even when it is outdated and no longer supports you, it is important to accept it for what it is. When you acknowledge and accept it, it opens up the possibility to move forward.

Part of acknowledging a limiting belief is to identify the positive purpose or reason for holding on to it, such as a need for security or to avoid feelings of pain, failure, or abandonment. It is so important to acknowledge and honor the positive intention of holding a belief, because when you update or change a belief that has been limiting you, you want to keep that positive purpose intact. Failure to do so is like throwing out the baby with the bath water.

Let's go back to my client. He had been working different jobs over the last couple of years that, because they paid so little, only reinforced his belief that he needed a college degree to earn a good salary. He also acknowledged that by staying in these low paying jobs, he felt that he couldn't fail. Because this limiting belief gave him a sense of security that felt valuable to him, he held on to it.

The third step is to redefine your old belief and reinvent a new and empowering belief. Coaching offers a wide variety of strategies by which to establish new beliefs and reframe limiting or erroneous ones.

One powerful method I recommend is to come up with counter-examples. Counter-examples are like exceptions to the rule. While they do not negate the belief, they offer a wider frame of reference, thereby enabling you to create new possibilities. It wasn't too difficult to come up with a few counter-examples to my client's belief that he needed a college degree to earn a lot of money and be successful. Richard Branson, Bill Gates, and Steve Jobs—just to name a few—didn't have a college degree and became very successful entrepreneurs. This realization became a source of motivation for my client to consider and create new possibilities. So we established a new belief saying, in effect, "I can create anything I want and I'm successful." We then created an action plan for him to move forward and succeed.

Wright

What are some of the key beliefs relevant to personal achievement?

Pauwels

Your beliefs constitute the primary source of motivation for personal achievement. First, you have to believe your goal is worth achieving, but at the same time, it has to be something you really want. All too often, people try to make changes in their lives or achieve goals in order to live up to the expectations of others.

Second, you have to believe that it is possible for you to achieve your goals. When you believe that something is not possible for you to achieve, even if you think it might be possible for others, you're probably not going to commit much effort and means to accomplish it. Henry Ford said that whether you believe you can or you can't, you're always right.

Third, you have to believe that achieving your goals will have no negative consequences. I worked with one client who wanted to move into an outside sales position in his company, but something kept preventing him from pursuing his goal. After exploring his motivation strategy, as well as his beliefs, it became apparent that he believed that moving into an outside sales position would mean more travel and time away from his wife and kids. Once he came to terms with that, he was able to redefine his goal according to his true priorities.

And finally, you have to believe that you are fully and truly deserving of reaching your goal and the success that follows.

Wright

What impact do beliefs have on the workplace?

Pauwels

People seek employment in the workplace because they believe it will help them meet life's basic needs. Job security, after all, means personal security too—food, shelter, clothing, transportation, and so on. But over time, we've come to expect that our professional work will meet our basic human needs for personal growth and social contribution as well. For many of us, the traditional motivational concept of the carrot and the stick no longer seems so appealing. We want more from our jobs than just money.

This phenomenon may explain why more and more people seem willing to work harder in jobs that pay less but offer more personal fulfillment. With the amount of time we invest in our jobs, and in our careers, we want our work to be meaningful—something we can really believe in. For people who believe their work is meaningful, coming to work is less about collecting a paycheck than about participating in something larger than themselves and making a contribution of benefit to others. When people are engaged in work that reflects their values and beliefs, they tend to be more committed and productive.

I strongly advocate a company management style incorporating new ways to meet employees' needs for personal fulfillment and social enhancement, even relevance. Personal development leads to business development.

Wright

Any final thoughts?

Pauwels

I believe that personal success lies in living the life you were born to live—to its fullest. Therefore, we must challenge ourselves to stop believing in what we think is true and start believing in what we really want. By accessing the power inherent in positive beliefs, we can overcome outdated thinking to pursue goals that are congruent with our deepest desires.

Wright

Dieter, thank you so much for joining us in *Success is a State of Mind,* and sharing these profound ideas about the affects our beliefs have on so many aspects of our lives. I've really enjoyed this conversation, and appreciate your willingness to spend time with us.

Pauwels

Thank you, David.

Wright

Today we've been talking with Dieter Pauwels, who believes that when you understand how your chosen beliefs influence your thoughts, feelings, and actions, you can reinvent yourself to live a more authentic, successful, and fulfilling life.

ABOUT THE AUTHOR

Dieter Pauwels is a Certified Professional Coach, speaker, trainer, and author. He works one-to-one with individuals and professionals to help them better identify and achieve the results they want in their professional and personal lives. His main focus is on life, career, and business coaching.

Dieter has more than fifteen years' experience in the personal development field. He has had the privilege to study and mentor with leading industry experts, such as Jim Rohn, Bob Proctor, and Anthony Robbins.

His experience in sales and executive management positions with leading organizations in the United States, Europe, and Asia has given him a unique, cross-cultural perspective into the dynamics of personal development and professional success.

Dieter's international and varied life experience enables him to have an open-minded approach to provide the attitude, mindset, and skills needed to empower others to create the results they want.

Dieter is a Certified NLP™ Coach from the NLP™ and Coaching Institute of California and professional member of the International Coaching Federation (ICF). Dieter holds a bachelor's degree of Business Administration and a bachelor's degree of Information Sciences from the University of Antwerp, Belgium.

Dieter Pauwels

Dieter Pauwels International
6340 Clayton Road, #404
St. Louis, MO 63117
866.207.3588 (toll free)
Office: 314.646.0133
dieter@dieterpauwels.com
www.dieterpauwels.com

SUCCESS IS A STATE OF MIND

5

An interview with...

Sue Melone

David Wright (Wright)

Today we're talking with Sue Melone, an authentic and dynamic leader who helps businesses deliver record-breaking results. She is the President of Boldtrek, Inc., a cutting edge business performance improvement company based in Portland, OR. Sue has transformed poor performing businesses into world-class organizations by building leaders and teams that can collaborate, execute, and deliver results never thought possible. Currently, she is on a mission to revolutionize the way leaders create extraordinary results by igniting what matters: the application of the bold, untapped talent in each of us.

Welcome to *Success is a State of Mind.*

Sue Melone (Melone)

Thank you so much, David.

Wright

Let's begin by building a frame of reference. What is a "success" state of mind?

Melone

The word "state" is an interesting one in and of itself. By definition, we take "state" to mean a mode or condition as in a state of confusion or a state of well-being. At some level these conditions are associated with some sort of boundaries to help us define what it means to be in a state of X. So for example we may be able to characterize a person in a state of anxiety as someone who displays apprehension and fear, uneasiness and self-doubt. Physiological signs may result as part of being in this state of anxiety: sweating increased heart rate and the like. The "state" you are in defines what you are being at any one time. We may observe a person who is anxious and conclude that this person is in a state of anxiety or observe a confused person and conclude that a person is in a state of confusion. When we see a state of anxiety or a state of confusion we can identify it using a generally accepted set of characteristics. In sum, we know it when we see it.

The "success" state of mind does not fit this conventional definition on every dimension. Yes, the success state of mind is about being…it is about who you are being…how you are showing up for the present, this very moment in time. The paradox here is that a success mindset is not really set at all. It is not a steady or static state nor is it one that can easily be defined by a generally accepted set of characteristics. Indeed, for every person asked to define "success" there is likely a different definition. Think of some of the books out in the market today: *The Success Principles, Success is a Choice, Success Built to Last, Quantum Success*. Definitions and advice emerge from the realms of sports, religion, business, self-help, talk show hosts and grandmothers. The synthesis of my experiences and my thinking and learning about success can be summarized simply: the definition of success is fluid. Success is a state of being without easily defined boundaries because just as soon as boundaries are defined the kaleidoscope of reality changes. Success is always in the present. It is not about the past and it is not about the future. A success mindset exists in the now. You cannot plan to get in the state of success for some period of time like for your upcoming math exam, the big game against a rival, or a meeting with your boss. Can you study, practice and prepare? Of course. Still, no amount of study, practice or preparation delivers a guaranteed result. Success is in the moment and it requires being fully present and taking action from a level of awareness that we cannot easily define. So when someone asks me what my definition of success is I refrain from throwing out terms like happiness, wealth, power, and balance because by my definition the answer to the question "what is your definition of success?" would be "I don't know". Ambiguous? Absolutely! Stick with me for a minute.

The world as we know it can be simply drawn like this: a small circle, perhaps the size of a penny is a space defining what we know. A larger circle, perhaps the size of a desert plate, is a space defining what we know we don't know. The rest of space, out beyond your pad of paper, your desk, planet Earth and the universe as we believe it to be, is a space defining what we don't know that we don't know. This space is infinite - Universe with a capital U. Many people don't venture out past the penny-sized space and may measure their success within the boundaries of what they know. For example "I have my MBA and 10 years of experience in sales and marketing". What they know defines their success. Others may view the desert plate-sized space and see obstacles or shortcomings: "I don't know accounting" "I don't know how to speak Spanish" and measure their success accordingly. What about the big space, the Universe space? What would it be like to define success in that space? To stand in success in a space that has no reference to space except for "here" and no reference to time except for "now"? What if a success mindset existed only in the Universe, out beyond what you know and know you don't know? I submit it does.

Wright

So, in order to have a success mindset you are saying that we have to be in this space where we don't know what we don't know. How do we get there?

Melone

Well, it would be nice if a solar powered, high speed train pulled up in front of our home or business and took us there but it's not quite that simple. Getting there requires radically different thinking…extremely radically different thinking. The spaces filled with what we know and what we know we don't know are finite. I could make a list of one million things and I could go down the list one by one and check "know" or "don't know" next to each item. How to ride a bike: know. How to perform a tibial osteotomy: don't know. But what would the list of "don't know, don't know" things look like? Wow, well…eh, I don't know. This is the infinite space of incredible possibilities. The success mindset exists in this space…this fluid, scary, bold, boundless space. Success requires different thinking. Albert Einstein nailed it when he said: "The significant problems we have cannot be solved at the same level of thinking with which we created them." Einstein was a brilliant "different thinker" who often ventured into don't know/don't know space…not seeing things for what they were but for what they could be. This is huge. His examples of applied different thinking generated new possibilities and results that changed the way we see the world today. Huge!

A success mindset exists in the present space of possibility. It is about creation in the now. Different thinking, again, radically different thinking, enables creation…creation of what is possible now. It is difficult for most of us to get into and stay in this mindset because we are staring reality in the face (or so we think) and reality is based in those two tiny spaces of know and know I don't know. We think, decide and act in the shadow of reality and this is immeasurably limiting. While we may see the very limitations we stand in, without a different thinking mindset we are destined to remain in the boundaries of reality that we have drawn. Consider another bit of insight by Einstein: "reality is merely an illusion, albeit a very persistent one." The old "it is what it is" mentality keeps us in the dark. People with a success mindset are thinking and moving freely one may say "in spite of reality" or beyond reality. They see possibilities. There is nothing fixed about their thinking or their being in the moment. In a Universe of constantly changing variables they stand in what is possible. This is their signature being. The success mindset can change the world. It already has.

Wright

How does different thinking translate into success?

Melone

This is the critical point, the game changer, the competitive gap that eludes many individuals, teams, and organizations. This is the work I am so passionate about. It is the difference between a double digit growth business plan on paper and the execution of such a plan, a 5 star chef's recipe and the making of such a culinary delight in your kitchen tonight or simply declaring that you are going to be the country's next music sensation and making a new album that breaks all previous sales records. It is about action. Not just any action. Different thinking drives different action which, in turn, delivers different results. The success mindset is not set! It's not fixed! It is constantly moving, redefining what is possible and creating in the present. This is a holistic event. People with a success mindset invite the heart, mind, body and soul…and they expect them to show up. Inherent in this mindset is action. Action transforms different thinking into different results.

Let's look at some examples of how this plays out. Michele Kwan, a world-class skater with years of skill development and mental rehearsing under her belt, brings even more to the rink when she competes. During her powerful programs she purposefully brings together every aspect of her being into focus. Michele describes this state as "when I am out on the ice the only thing I can hear is the beat of my own heart." You have heard this called "the zone" by countless other athletes - the space where mind and body meet in action that allows them to perform their very best. Some, like Tiger Woods and Michael Jordan, exist in "the zone" more consistently than other athletes. They bring a sharply heightened awareness to the present moment which enables them to lock out distractions, engage all of their talents (known and unknown) and be the best possible self they can be right there in the now. They are not thinking about falls or misses in the past or the next jump shot they will take. Everything…everything is in the present.

The success mindset in action is a talent multiplier. I once heard someone being interviewed describe an athlete as someone who had "played above and beyond her God-given gifts." What else is coming into play here? The success mindset ignites possibilities at a level and frequency that most others cannot even fathom. This mindset in action translates possibilities into success.

The business world has ample success stories as well but in my view we don't even scratch the surface of what is possible here. We know about the mindset of CEO heroes like Bill Gates and Anne Mulcahy...people who stand in possibilities...and how their different thinking and different action has translated into incredible results. No doubt countless others across every industry have combined a success state of mind with talent to deliver a measurable advantage over the competition. Fantastic! Still my mind wanders to imagine what kind of mindset millions of American workers bring to their organizations every day...and what if just 10% of them were able to be "in the zone" today...to "be" in a mindset of success. What would be possible?

Wright

What differentiates those with a success mindset and those without? Can anyone possess a success mindset?

Melone

None of us know how good we can be. What is possible is unknown, untapped, undiscovered. Curiosity and a will to win propel me as a leader and a human being to explore what is possible for me and those I lead. I don't mean discovering if Al, one of the mechanical engineers on my team, can perform his job a tiny bit better. I mean unleashing big, bold Al to create what is possible...a moving-and-learning-with-zest Al! Each one of us has a journey of possibilities at our feet. It is the steps that can be tricky.

The body of multidisciplinary work attempting to define the attributes associated with successful people could fill a small library. Is it attitude? Choice? Luck? Socio-economic status? Studying the possible effect of many of the popular variables expands my thinking.

Recently, I have been immersed in the work by Malcolm Gladwell, Jim Collins, Warren Bennis, Seth Godin, and Dr. Carol Dweck. One common theme shared by these brilliant thinkers is that successful leaders are on a journey of constant learning. Dweck's research examines two potential views individuals may adopt that can dramatically affect the steps taken in life. The first, a fixed mindset, is defined as belief that an individual's qualities and abilities are set and their work in life consists of confirming these attributes. The other mindset is a growth mindset, which is based on the belief that basic qualities can be developed through targeted efforts. Enter passion, learning, moving. People who are present, who are actively engaged in the moment, who passionately pursue what is possible and who learn and improve from every step along the way…these are people with a mindset of success. They are in charge of their own process of thriving. Set minds are owned by those who are fixed on what they view as current reality with limited possibility. They minimize mistakes and risk. These are people who are not learning and not moving and who are, at best, maintaining and surviving. They are comfortable within the confines of the penny-size space. It is what is it is, they know what they know. Period.

Contrast this mindset with the mindset that applies different thinking, takes different action, gets different results, learns, improves, expands, stretches…it is about move, move, move! A success mindset translates to: thrive in the moment. *Success is about the relationship you are having with the present.* It doesn't carry the burden of mistakes from the past and it doesn't project into the future. It is thriving in the moment.

Can anyone possess a success mindset? Yes. I am going way out past the desert plate here and standing in the place that every single individual has the capacity to thrive moment to moment…regardless of past circumstances, innate talents and abilities, previous assumptions or judgments. It is possible. Imagine the power of dozens, hundreds, thousands of people thriving moment to moment inside a single organization. The promise of this idea alone is the driving force behind my work.

Wright

What is standing in the way of organizations creating environments where individuals can thrive?

Melone

The enemy of possibilities for an individual, a team, or an organization is business as usual. Status quo. Immobility. Decades-old command and control leadership snuffs out creativity and disables talent. Here risk is rarely tolerated. We hire people like ourselves. We have the same meetings week after week. Fierce conversations are outliers. Intertwined with the day to day execution of business are distractions, egos, politics, mixed messages, labels like "bad move, bad idea, bad choice", advice like "don't rock the boat", "keep your head down" and "pick your battles"…the list continues. I think one of the most debilitating circumstances organizations can create is an environment of fear. Think about what an environment filled with fear supports. It's all about survival. Remember Cannon's fight-or-flight response? Fear plays right into a fixed mindset. People freeze up. Emotions take over. Mistakes and fears from the past are remembered. What will it feel like when I fail? It is a fight in the mire of failure. Unfortunately, organizations are often places where failure is avoided at all costs and fear rules. If a person is already living with a fixed mindset, fear is just going to cement boundaries into place. It is survive mode. It is how business as usual perpetuates and pervades our organizations.

Wright

How do some people break out of "business as usual"?

Melone

Those who enter situations filled with fear, formidable obstacles, or impossible odds with a success mindset stand out. Think about the opening minutes of the movie, *Saving Private Ryan*. Think about the stories you have heard about heroic actions, kids who navigated hell-on-earth circumstances and lead incredibly productive lives, and people who produced extraordinary results despite the most challenging of environments. These people are not simply employing survival skills. They are applying something more.

People who are working with a success mindset are focused on "what is true now". They take action from a place of centered focus. They get right in the tempest of ambiguity, sleeves up, guts out. They learn. A quote from Theodore Roosevelt that I have carried with me for decades paints this picture well: "the credit belongs to the man who is actually in the arena, whose face is marred by dust and sweat and blood; who strives valiantly; who errs and comes short again and again, because there is no effort without error or shortcoming; but who does actually strive to do the deeds, who knows the great enthusiasms, the great devotions; who spends himself in a worthy cause; who at best knows in the end the triumph of high achievement, and who at worst, if he fails, at least fails while daring greatly so that his place shall never be with those cold or timid souls who know neither victory nor defeat." Those are such powerful words: "great enthusiasms, great devotions"…almost like there is something magical about putting yourself out there in the throes of possibility to learn, to "spend" yourself even when the effort may not deliver the results you expected. The success mindset does deliver unexpected results- extraordinary results that may show up as successfully building the number one software company in the world or as failing to create an engine that runs on water on the 117th try. Here, and this is a huge point, failure is accepted with gratitude. Every experience more clearly defines what is true now and launches those with a success mindset into the next slice of the journey. They are richer in the present as a result of their different thinking. They are unstoppable.

Wright

As a business leader and coach, what would you share with other leaders who want to help their teams become unstoppable?

Melone

If we look at the success mindset from a business perspective, the possibilities are unfathomable. Never before in the history of civilization has the pace of development and change been so rapid. Technology is redefining the definition of global markets, communication, and community every day. The Center for Creative Leadership recently published a paper about senior executives' views on trends of the future. Not surprisingly, themes like increasingly complex challenges, pace of change, need for innovation, need for talent, and need for authenticity surfaced at the top of the list. The writing is on the wall. It's in huge 72 bold font. We must learn. We must fail. Faster. Faster. Faster. We must draw from that place of don't know / don't know. We need different thinking and different action. We need to look inside ourselves and become more of who we are. The success mindset frees us to be in this place.

Wright

So where do we start? How can we achieve this mindset on a scale that can help us thrive in the future?

Melone

We all have a role in this on two main fronts. First, on an individual level, we each have the ability to stand in a success mindset, albeit some more easily than others. By increasing our awareness we can look inside ourselves and discover what is possible in the realm of the present...which is constantly changing. Ultimately, different thinking happens when each one of us lets go of our personal boundaries of "who I am" or "how it is around here" and stands in possibility. Not future possibility...dreams, wishes, and the like. Possibility in the now...in action. That is the mindset of success. It starts with us.

The second front is the environment in which we exist. Each one of us affects the space outside of ourselves. Indeed, we are all connected and part of the Universe. Possibilities abound in terms of what this connectedness, what this environment looks and feels like at any given moment in time. As a parent, colleague, teacher, foreman, stranger, human you are an element of the environment. You are a creator. Who you are being in the present is connected to and impacts others. Create. Create. Create.

Let's look at the world through a business lens. Organizations by their nature create what we call work environments or work cultures. It's a collective space created and nurtured by those in it. Work cultures are as unique as the individuals who comprise them. Many are seemingly counterproductive. Think Dilbert. Some are on the cutting edge, pushing the discovery of what is possible. Think Whole Foods and W.L.Gore. Much like a success mindset serves as a multiplier of an individual's talent...remember heart, mind, body, and soul multiplied by a success mindset equals extraordinary...the work environment is a formidable multiplier for individuals, teams, and organizations. Leaders can create collective space that is THRIVE space. It is simple, bold, and sadly uncommon work. The gas pedal that can radically change the velocity with which a team, a department, or a business can grow and thrive is right below our feet yet a rare few leaders put the pedal to the metal. Note: this is not your incremental, continuous improvement velocity here. This is beyond-rocket-ship-speed, dare-I-say magical velocity because it is the exponential effect of many people with different thinking and different action coming together to collectively tap the unknown. Want to blast your business into the extraordinary? Push this gas pedal: create an environment where people can zoom.

Sound scary? The remedy for fear is action. The first simple bold step for leaders is to enable the journey for others. My core belief is that you are successful when you help others become successful. As a leader, how can you enable a success mindset, a desire to thrive, and an ability to zoom in every individual you lead? It starts with you. Stand in possibilities. Lead from not knowing. Go to the places where you don't have the answers. Think differently about what is possible and show it through your actions. Help your team members learn and make mistakes faster, gravitate to that unlimited space of don't know-don't know and abandon business as usual. Know the great enthusiasms and the great devotions of creating in the now. Enable the journey of success… the sleeves up, guts out relationship with the present.

How? "Thrive" leaders ask: what is success now? What did we learn? What's next? What's possible? They build confidence in others by standing for their growth. This isn't fluffy soft skill stuff. This work elevates the game of business to a new level. Business guru Marcus Buckingham states, "…competitive advantage is helping individuals become more of who they are." Competitive advantage? I find this true yet so incredibly understated. The leaders and businesses that actually do the work of enabling what is possible in others will leave the rest so far back they will be a mere speck in the rear view mirror. We don't know what we don't know about how successful we can be.

What can we learn from the present? We need to learn more about leading. Faster. We have come up woefully short in terms of tapping even our known resources and peek ever so infrequently at what is possible beyond what we know. Consider the data that the Gallup organization gathered regarding the engagement level of employees. On average less than 20% of employees are highly engaged, that is: passionate about their jobs and their organizations. Consistently, only a minority of them feel their opinions count. At any one time, like right now, at least half of the people in your organization are not actively engaged in their work. It's not just "them", it's us. Engagement levels are not radically different across industry or job level. Approximately one in five entry-level employees are actively engaged. Nearly the same hold true at the executive level. Does the definition of actively engaged equate to a success mindset? Perhaps. What we can conclude is that when employees are not actively engaged they are not fully in the moment, they are not in growth/thrive mode, and they are not experiencing a sleeves up, guts out relationship with the present. We are leaving so much untapped. To consider what is beyond, what is undiscovered is just mind-blowing. It has been the root of many a sleepless night for me.

Wright

So what's next?

Melone

The world is beckoning a new leadership paradigm. Not a micro shift or adjustment. Something bold and beyond current solutions and thinking. Something that even redefines the way we innovate and create – a metaparadigm. We live in a disruptive age. We have spent the past several decades trying to convince people that they need to change, assume new skills and behaviors, and break out of business as usual. Meanwhile change is being redefined in terms of speed and complexity every second of every day. It is leaving us in the dust.

Here is a very simple example: think about the term "multi-tasking". Think back to about 5 years ago. What did it mean to "multi-task" then? What about 10 years ago? What will it mean next summer? Speed and complexity are eventually going to rip our hands right off the hold we have on business as usual, thinking as usual, and results as usual. That said, what action can we take today? I am reminded again of Einstein's message: it's going to take a different level of thinking to solve this problem of trying to keep up with the speed and complexity of change in our world. We need to get to it.

There are many hints that the time for an emerging metaparadigm is now. Among my favorites are: *The Age of Speed* by Vince Poscente, work by Theodore Modis, Marshall Goldsmith's *What Got You Here Won't Get You There,* everything by Tom Peters, and Gary Hamel's *The Future of Management.* There are a zillion things telling us that what worked in the past is not likely to serve us in the future. Caution: the future is here. If we are to lead successful businesses and successful lives today we must think differently right here, right now.

We must be able to thrive on ambiguity. Anything can happen. Anything. Situations beyond "rational" can be exacerbated by the speed and complexity of our world. The likelihood that we can know enough or plan enough for everything decreases exponentially by the second. This sheds a whole new light on the term "readiness".

Wright

How do we prepare ourselves and others to be successful in the storm of ambiguity?

Melone

Years ago when I was in graduate school preparing for a teaching assignment at West Point, I drafted a theory connecting leadership, readiness, ambiguity and success called "flexionality". I have been refining it ever since in my work with soldiers and business leaders of all levels. In short, flexionality addresses the need for something beyond training and experience – something that enables the infantry private, the shift leader on graveyard shift, or the Chief Operating Officer to be "ready" to successfully navigate each second of ambiguity. That something is happening in the present – at the core of every human being who stands in the open field of don't know/don't know. It is success on the battlefield, the shop floor or the boardroom being defined by the person's relationship with the present. In the moment, that relationship shows up as "I have been here" not in the sense of "I know what is happening and what to do because I have been in this exact situation before" but in the sense of "I have been here in the don't know/don't know. I am enough now." The different thinking here is not simply applying what you know but drawing from what you don't know that you don't know in that calm, centered moment. Different thinking in the present that taps the unknown differentiates a flexionality mindset from a traditional readiness mindset. To be successful today requires us to draw from more than our training and experience. We must be able to stand in the present and the unknown.

Success, what is possible for each of us, will elude us as long as we are stuck in our current thinking. We have to create that which we have yet to imagine. Leaders can be the spark, the ones who run with the torch into "what is possible" space and discover untapped talent, resources, and possibilities. This is not work for the fake or faint-hearted. I named my company "Boldtrek" to reflect the kind of leadership I am referring to and the kind I am seeking to create:

leadership that is authentic in its pursuit of what is possible for others. This is leadership that is in action, out past the edge, creating new realities, breaking performance records. I believe that when we see the present world through a success mindset, we can lead ourselves and others to crush what we currently know as possible.

I think Gary Hamel is really on to something. His recent book, *The Future of Management*, is a call for a leadership revolution now. He says we need to leap. Fast. He doesn't toss us yet another solution for incremental leadership development. Hamel fiercely contends that the future of management has yet to be created. Hamel's request is for leadership "that truly elicits, honors, and cherishes human initiative, creativity, and passion – tender essential ingredients for business success in the new millennium." Here, here. I say we grab a torch and make a break for the bold untapped space of possibility. The time is now. Success is now.

ABOUT THE AUTHOR

Sue Melone is the President of Boldtrek, Inc., a business performance improvement company based in Portland, Oregon. She has extensive experience as a business leader in operations, sales, manufacturing, training and development, and consulting.

A student-athlete to the core, Sue helps businesses deliver record-breaking results by providing professional coaching and training services to leaders and teams delivered with authenticity, commitment and zest. She has coached clients in a diverse range of industries including Internet technology, manufacturing, sales, legal services, education, construction, and logistics. Sue is a gifted coach whose unique blend of business leadership experience and ability to bring forth talent in others has ignited soldiers, sales teams and machine operators to deliver results never thought possible.

Sue has invaluable experience as a leader in government and Fortune 500 companies that spans over 25 years. She served as an active duty Army officer for more than 10 years with such leadership highlights as Company Commander and West Point Faculty selectee. For more than 12 years she has lead a variety of business teams for Fortune 500 companies in the forest products and building materials sectors. The common thread through all of her assignments has been the immense impact she made by engaging and developing talent and bringing that great human power to bear on the business of delivering results.

Sue holds an undergraduate degree from Yale University and did her graduate work at the University of Maryland. She is a certified business coach and leadership instructor. Weekly, she serves as a development coach for children at Self Enhancement, Inc. a Portland-based youth development organization, and she is the founder of The Torch Fund, a scholarship fund supporting low-income students who are the first in their families to attend college.

Sue Melone
Boldtrek, Inc.
4110 SE Hawthorne Blvd. #196
Portland, Oregon 97214
Phone: 503.206.5831
E-mail: sue@boldtrek.com
www.boldtrek.com

SUCCESS IS A STATE OF MIND

6

An interview with…

Jim Accetta

David Wright (Wright)

Today we're talking with Jim Accetta, a personal life and relationship coach, a certified trainer of Neurolinguistic Programming (NLP™), an inspirational speaker and published author of the book: *Getting What You Want: The Art of Living on Purpose.* Jim has over twenty-eight years of experience working with people in diverse and varied walks of life. He has been quoted for his coaching and training expertise in the *Boston Globe, Fitness Magazine,* and in *Crain's Chicago Business.* Jim operates Truly Human Coaching a Personal and Professional Coaching Company with the mission of helping people to live the life they truly want and the vision of creating a world in which people want to belong. Jim works with business professionals and entrepreneurs across the nation from his home in Mundelein, Illinois, creating change through the magic of words.

In his free time he loves and enjoys his time with his loving wife Connie, along with his children and two dogs. Jim also enjoys reading, writing, meditating, exercise, grocery shopping, cooking, and spiritual development.

Jim, welcome to *Success is a State of Mind!*

Jim Accetta (Accetta)

Thank you!

Wright

You're the first man I've ever heard of who actually loves grocery shopping.

Accetta

Yes, that usually does bring a comment or two! The shopping is part of what I refer to as "Designing Your Life"—doing and honoring what feels good. Often this means stepping out of culturally assigned roles. I'll discuss this more further on in this chapter.

Wright

So tell me, what is "Truly Human Coaching"?

Accetta

Truly Human Coaching has to do with living truly human. It is my company name as well as a set of beliefs and strategies that focuses on helping people to connect with their true humanness and live the life they love.

Being truly human has to do with truly knowing one's self, one's wants and needs, one's true motivations, and values. Two of the things that have been greatly ignored in our culture and many cultures are the emotional and spiritual aspects of our being. In the hurry of daily life people are so involved in doing and they leave these vital emotional and spiritual aspects of our humanness behind.

My work with clients focuses on getting back in touch with the many parts of their self that they have marginalized, forgotten, or ignored. I help my clients to connect to their true desires and their true passions. Then connecting with their passions, they can celebrate and even prosper by doing what they truly love, and paid for it!

We all have natural gifts, things we love to do that often provide great value to others. In our socialization process we as people have been directed onto a prescribed path instead of being guided to discover our gifts, to discover our true potential and to be the truly human divine beings we are meant to be.

Truly Human Coaching has to do with learning to slow down our lives enough to truly know one's self, uncovering beliefs and choices that were "given" to us by our parents, relatives, teachers, and society at large and learning our true yearnings, uncovering our true gifts, and making conscious intentional choices to adopt empowering beliefs and live the life we love.

Regarding the spiritual aspects of our being truly human, we start by honoring and then building or rebuilding the relationship one already has with a 'higher power' or God/Goddess/All That Is. Our spiritual life, albeit often ignored, is important to our daily well being and vital to our continued growth. Being truly human has to do with inviting and honoring 'all parts of ourself', not just the ones that our culture or society has deemed valuable.

Wright

What do you mean by "live the life you truly want"?

Accetta

Living the life you truly wants starts with the question, and then the answer of first knowing what one wants. How do we know what we want? Where does one's desire or conception of desire begin?

Think for a moment: as an infant, we want for basic necessities including all that brings us pleasure. Next, we are offered information from our environment, our homes, technology, culture, and family beliefs and values—all information and lenses that both enable us to makes sense of the world we live as well as limit what we perceive. This is really a topic that entire books are written about—a subject that I introduce in a three-hour workshop titled: "Introduction to Neuro-Linguistic Programming: The Study of Subjective Experience."

Early in life people are taught as children what pleases their parents. In order to receive love and feel safe, people learn how to perform:—they can't do certain things and they can do other things. As hard as parents might try, they forget about any disapproval or approval that really shapes their children, and so there are grown up people running around the world doing what they have been taught is the "right" thing to do and the "proper" thing to do, and what the "proper" path to happiness is. For more, see my article on Socialization at my Web site: http://www.trulyhumancoaching.com/ -newsletter.aspx#LifePurpose.

Living the life you truly want first starts with answering the question on a consistent basis, "What do I want?" while at the same time answering the question, "What have I learned that I wanted from parents, teachers, and society at large?" Said a bit more crudely, what are we doing to be good little boys and girls, good workers, good husbands and wives, good parents, good people? The more important question that I will continue to refer back to is: "What do you want?

Go ahead and ask yourself, for any life area: "What do you want now?" A couple of other common questions I will ask new clients are: "How do you feed your spirit?"; "How do you nourish yourself? What do you do that feels deeply soulful to you? In other words, what moves you?

Too many of us have become separate from what is truly human in each of us—our feelings, our desires and yes, even our dreams and ability to manifest those dreams. My coaching helps people to reconnect with their desires, their dreams, and what truly stirs them. We then become involved together on a path that begins to make all the things happen they truly want!

The questions what do I want, what feels good to me, what sparks my interest, and what tickles my fancy, are so rarely asked! I want my clients to regularly ask themselves, on a soulful level "What do *I* want?" Try it again, now, for your most intimate relationship, or your sexual life, what do you truly want? What do you desire? Knowing our true desires by asking this great question is key in getting what you want; it carries great gravity and power. Napoleon Hill speaks of this 'knowing' and then imagining, expecting and desiring in his book "Think and Grow Rich" (1937)... I have created useful adaptations to this procedure in chapter 2 of my book, *Getting What You Want: The Art of Living on Purpose*. This is very much along the lines of the more popular "Law of Attraction" as discussed in "The Secret."

The next step in our coaching is allowing and experiencing those things that tickle our fancy, that stir and excite us, that bring us to a place of joy. Talk about living richly! To choose to enjoy simple pleasures *and* do what you love in the world is to truly experience humanness. So I think connecting with our passion while living in the world and being very present is what being truly human is about . It is in the 'being present' that is is lost for too many people. Unbeknown to themselves, these folks (and there are many) are caught in their own schedules, their ongoing to-do lists: "I have to do this next. I have to do that next."

Being "Truly Human" is the difference in choosing to be, rather than choosing to do. It means responsibly owning our personal power and then consciously choosing—choosing to be and choosing to do.

Wright

How does your approach differ from other coaches and other forms of counseling and therapy?

Accetta

My approach provides sustainable lasting results, period.

There's a wide variety of coaching and therapy models. I think a better way to define what do is that I *specialize*. Each coaching or therapy model starts with a basic belief about people and about what makes us tick. Here is mine.

I believe that people are naturally creative, resourceful, and whole, not ill and in need of being fixed. People learn over time how to "live in the world." We develop adapted patterns of thinking, feeling, and behaving that at some time in our lives were useful—until they become no longer useful. These patterns of thinking, feeling, and behaving become "natural" and largely unconscious and end up "running the show" much like the man behind the curtain in *The Wizard of Oz*.

My approach is in helping my clients to become observers of their own life—observing their outward behaviors and the impact they are having on others, observing the choices they are making each day, and uncovering the often limiting beliefs that determine those choices. My clients and I also use a great deal of time in the discovery of their own values, their gifts, what they truly love, and helping them to honor and incorporate these gifts and values into their daily life.

Once aware of these often unconscious values, choices, and beliefs, we work together in changing the limiting beliefs and create new empowering choices that enable them to honor their values and live the life they love.

You ask how my approach differs from other forms of therapy. That is a very large question. Over the past twenty-eight years, I have studied a myriad of therapies and approaches. They range from the cognitive models, behavioral models, psychoanalytic models to hypnosis, coaching, family therapy, narrative therapy, brief solution oriented therapy, and more. To answer your question about how I differ would require another book entirely!

Let me say that the common theme among most or all of the therapies I have studied is the importance of the therapeutic relationship over time. A recent reading shows study after study that one of the most important aspects of change in coaching or therapy is the relationship between the people involved. Good therapists and good coaches know the importance of this relationship. (The Working Alliance: Theory Research and Practice: Horvath, Adam O. & Greenberg, Leslie S. Ed. 1994)

In summary, my overall approach with each client rests in my confidence, and trust that each one of us can have whatever he or she wants—that we are fully capable, creative, and resourceful. Somewhere the beliefs, attitudes, and behaviors that were once useful for them in their family or community are no longer working or rather are no longer providing the outcome they desire. They are stuck in their own patterns. Our work together consists of my clients becoming aware of these obsolete patterns and any together to reprogram these beliefs, attitudes, and behaviors toward empowerment, choice, and possibility.

Wright

What is your background?

Accetta

My background is a mixture of consistent personal and professional development. My entire training and education background are in the areas of working successfully with others to create change with them and the systems they live in. I was intentional in my early studies, focusing on the areas of counseling psychology, developmental psychology, sociology, and anthropology. In these areas, my primary focus was interpersonal communication and the helping relationship. It was during that time when I developed my focus on the importance of the helping relationship and my beginning learning and skills in the areas of Gestalt psychology and the field of NeuroLinguistic Programming (NLP™). I am currently one of the few experts in the field of NLP™ in the U.S. which clearly differentiates me and my coaching from their coaches. .. Being an expert in the field of NeuroLinguistic Programming affords my clients with a vast pool of resources from this field of communication excellence.

My own passions fuel my coaching. I love learning! It natural for me; it excites me and drives me to learn more. As a social worker I served as a family therapist and an addictions specialist, utilizing a brief solution-oriented approach working with families and individuals in groups. Currently I use a mixture of Ericksonian Hypnosis, NeuroLinguistic Programming, Transactional Analysis and Narrative Therapy. I continue to incorporate these knowledge and skills in my coaching with a great mixture of spiritual and metaphysical work. As a coach, I am consistently "working my stuff," "walking my talk," and delving into even more learning to expand my knowledge and effectiveness. By the way, *I offer a complimentary trial coaching session for free* in order to show people considering hiring a coach just how extraordinarily effective Truly Human Coaching is! I offer all those interested in coaching to 'try me on as your coach' by participating in a sample coaching session with me. You can signup on my website at www.trulyhumancoaching.com.

Wright

What are "moments of truth"?

Accetta

Moments of Truth are the moments we create—each and every moment we have lived and will live. When I refer to moments of truth, I am referring to the great ability we have to create excellent moments, over and over again—to create great moments of love and joy, peace and contentment, intimacy and connection, and presence and spiritual connection.

Of course other moments of truth come in different, sometimes unfriendly or clearly hostile forms: a snide comment made to a co-worker, angry words toward a spouse, a misdirected comment to a child, or simply creating havoc with a bad temper. All of these people create; they also are moments of truth.

We all have the ability to create moments—to create the lives we want. Each moment is another opportunity to choose to create the moments of truth we want in our lives.

Companies and associations hire me to speak about "time management' and how we use our time with my talk: "Moments of Truth." The talk is great for professionals, managers, any service personnel, and of course, people who are interested in creating moments of truth in their life. During this presentation I connect the "moments of truth" that occur when you first meet someone, during interactions, when presenting yourself or your business. Within the first thirty seconds there are hundreds of moments of truth that occur. Moments of Truth are lasting impressions that really do occur! So I offer participants great tools to be present, to be genuine, and to build excellent moments of truth!

We all have 168 hours of week in which we live. Every one of those hours and minutes are moments of truth or opportunities for choices—we choose how we use them. Each moment we have the opportunity to create greatness and create great memories. People forget that every chance they have with someone they love, every chance they have to stop and smell or look at a flower or cook a great meal (instead of just a fair meal), to enjoy delicious food, to enjoy your partner in great sexual union all are chances to create greatness and create great memories. But people usually just don't believe they have time to create great moments. It's not a matter of having time—we all have the same amount of time. Each moment is a moment of truth. What do you want to do with *your* moments of truth? What moment of truth do you want to create?

One of my favorite quotes magnifying the preciousness of each moment comes from the wise and wonderful Judith DeLozier:

"You only have so many heartbeats,

how do you want to use yours?"

SO... how do you want to use yours?

Wright

What is NLP™?

Accetta

Neuro-Linguistic Programming (NLP™) a field of the study of excellence in communication as well as is an attitude—a way of thinking and living in the world. NLP™ helps you focus on your thoughts, feelings, behaviors, and beliefs to reach your goals and achieve amazing results.

NLP™ has to do with three things:

- **Neuro**: Nervous system through which experience is received and processed through the five senses

- **Linguistic**: Words, language, and nonverbal communication systems through which neural responses are coded, ordered, and given meaning.
- **Programming**: The ability to organize our communication and neurological systems to achieve specific desired goals and results.

Richard Bandler, co-creator of NLP™ and John LaValle, President of the Society of NLP™ offer the following definitions:

"Neuro-Linguistic Programming™ (NLP™) is defined as the study of the structure of subjective experience and what can be calculated from that and is predicated upon the belief that all behavior has structure. People such as Virginia Satir, Milton Erickson and Fritz Perls had amazing results with their clients. They were some of the people who's linguistic and behavioral patterns Richard Bandler built formal models of. He then applied these models to his work."

John LaValle adds: "Neuro-Linguistic Programming was specifically created in order to allow us to do magic by creating new ways of understanding how verbal and non-verbal communication effect the human brain. As such it presents us all with the opportunity to not only communicate better with others, but also learn how to gain more control over what we considered to be automatic functions of our own neurology." (quoted from www.pureNLP™.com)

Here is a story I often use to illustrate what NLP™ is:

A boy asked his mother, "What is NLP™?"

His mother said, "I will tell you in a moment, but first you have to do something so you can understand. See your grandfather over there in his chair?"

"Yep," said the boy.

"Go and ask him how his arthritis is today."

The boy went over to his grandfather. "Granddad," he said, "how's your arthritis today?"

"Oh, it's a bit bad, son," replied the old man. "It's always worse in damp weather. I can hardly move my fingers today." A look of pain crossed his face.

The boy went back to his mother. "He said it was bad. I think it hurts him. Are you going to tell me what NLP™ is now?"

"In a minute, I promise," replied his mother. "Now go over and ask Granddad what was the funniest thing you ever did when you were very young."

The boy went over to his grandfather. "Granddad," he began, "what's the funniest thing I ever did when I was very young?"

The old man's face lit up. "Oh," he smiled, "there were lots of things. There was the time when you and your friend played Father Christmas and sprinkled talcum powder all over the bathroom pretending it was snow. I laughed, but I didn't have to clean it up." He stared into the distance with a smile.

"Then there was the time I took you out for a walk. It was a lovely day and you were singing a nursery rhyme you had just learned. Loudly. A man went past and gave you a nasty look. He thought you were being too noisy. He asked me to tell you to be quiet. You turned around and said to him, 'If you don't like me singing, you can go and boil your head.' And then you carried on even louder." The old man chuckled.

The boy went back to his mother. "Did you hear what Granddad said?" he asked.

"Yes," his mother replied. "You changed how he felt with a few words. That's NLP™." (Used with permission from: Joseph O'Conner, *NLP ™ Workbook.*)

Robert Dilts offers one of the most comprehensive definitions of NLP™ I have seen:

"NLP™ stands for Neuro-Linguistic Programming, a name that encompasses the three most influential components involved in producing human experience: neurology, language, and programming. The neurological system regulates how our bodies function, language determines how we interface and communicate with other people, and our programming determines the kinds of models of the world we create. Neuro-Linguistic Programming describes the fundamental dynamics between mind (neuro) and language (linguistic) and how their interplay affects our body and behavior (programming).

"NLP™ is a pragmatic school of thought—an 'epistemology'—that addresses the many levels involved in being human. NLP™ is a multi-dimensional process that involves the development of behavioral competence and flexibility, but also involves strategic thinking and an understanding of the mental and cognitive processes behind behavior. NLP™ provides tools and skills for the development of states of individual excellence, but it also establishes a system of empowering beliefs and presuppositions about what human beings are, what communication is, and what the process of change is all about. At another level, NLP™ is about self-discovery, exploring identity and mission. It also provides a framework for understanding and relating to the 'spiritual' part of human experience that reaches beyond us as individuals to our family, community, and global systems. NLP™ is not only about competence and excellence, it is about wisdom and vision.

"In essence, all of NLP™ is founded on two fundamental presuppositions: 1) *The Map is Not the Territory.* As human beings, we can never know reality. We can only know our perceptions of reality. We experience and respond to the world around us primarily through our sensory representational systems. It is our 'neuro-linguistic' maps of reality that determine how we behave and that give those behaviors meaning, not reality itself. It is generally not reality that limits us or empowers us, but rather our map of reality; 2) *Life and 'Mind' are Systemic Processes.* The processes that take place within a human being and between human beings and their environment are systemic. Our bodies, our societies, and our universe form an ecology of complex systems and sub-systems all of which interact with and mutually influence each other. It is not possible to completely isolate any part of the system from the rest of the system. Such systems are based on certain 'self-organizing' principles and naturally seek optimal states of balance or homeostasis.

So, what is NLP™? It is the study of the structure of subjective experience and the practice of modeling behavioral excellence. NLP™ is magic in action!

Wright

What do you have to offer people?

Accetta

I offer people the opportunity to change something in their life that the truly want to change. I offer an answer, a path, a way home. I offer life-altering moments, a connection for clients to realize their deepest desires, soulful intimacy with others, true happiness, and sustainable life changes.

During my talks and during my coaching, in day-to-day interactions I offer acceptance and celebration, curiosity and discovery, joy and learning, and of course, hope and fun! Simply said, change happens when people are around me.

During my professional keynote speeches people come away with real skills they can use immediately to build better relationships and to create excellent moments of truth in their lives wherever they want! After only a forty-five-minute talk, the kinds of changes that can take place are really amazing.

Many people hire me when they feel like there's something missing in their life. They are doing all the "right things" in school, at work, in their family roles, with friends—and still something is missing. Some clients have waited a bit too long and show up feeling hopeless or full of despair about the place they have landed in their life; they are just not happy. A common statement might be, "No matter what I do, it doesn't seem to work." They say things like, "I'm just not happy," or, "I just don't feel like I am on top of things." Some even feel desperate. For these wonderful souls I immediately offer hope—hope that things will get better, they will find a way out. I just always know hope and the possibility of change are present. I live in a world of infinite possibility. It is the major focus of my first book: *Getting What You Want: The Art of Living on Purpose.*

There is so much greatness in every person. People have just forgotten that how truly beautiful and magnificent they are. They've learned to criticize themselves, to beat themselves up and chide themselves about how they live and what they are supposed to be doing. Many folks are trying to measure up to something and they're not even sure why!

Two of my central themes in coaching and speaking are full acceptance and working with our shadow selves. We have so many parts of ourselves that we have marginalized over the years. These parts tend to show up in different ways if not honored.

Together, my clients and I get to know these forgotten marginalized parts; part of the learning is loving and honoring these parts. Many people say, "Well, I don't like that part. I don't like it when that part shows up!" "I don't like acting that way." Many folks simply deny that they are even acting certain ways, until, of course, the people closest to them begin pointing out these other selves. When we are open to this feedback from those closest to us, we are inviting a great opportunity for change.

We might not like the affect that we have on the people in our lives, but in order to honor that part of us, we need to accept it as our own. We need to own it, honor, it, accept it, learn from it and them become responsible with it! We need to find out what we are angry about, what we are sad about, what we are defensive about, and learn from these parts. In the awareness and learning comes choice, that way our behavior or shadow self doesn't have to come out on other people. We then begin to have a relationship with these parts of our self, honoring them, learning about them, and then creating the changes in our lives that we truly want.

I really help people to become observers of their own life by helping them to slow down. People are moving so fast "getting things done" that their emotions and so many other parts of themselves are shut down or simply not given space. These marginalized parts are still operating below one's level of consciousness and at *the same time these parts are determining the persons thoughts, feelings, and behaviors!*

During coaching, people start learning to slow down. They begin paying attention to the voices, pictures and emotions that are going on inside, to slow down some of their inner voices, to create and attend to images that are empowering and begin to eliminate neural and behavioral patterns that are no longer useful. My clients are able to learn who they are and begin making the right choices for themselves through the building of healthy relationships with their many selves. That's where some of the hardest and most rewarding work begins. Once they begin learning who they are and they begin to become aware of the limiting and often self-defeating patterns that they once felt caught in, they can then begin to have choices they never thought possible.

So the gifts available and what I have to offer are hope, sustainable healthy changes, as well as a great spiritual life and ongoing emotional growth. I offer people endless possibilities, paths of great growth filled with intimacy, wonder, joy, and fulfillment. I offer great magic. I offer my clients opportunities to have choices about how they want to live, ways to discover what they want and what's truly human in each of them.

Wright

What do you mean when you talk about "Walk the Talk"?

Accetta

"Walk the Talk" is a term I learned in some of the coach training I've participated in through The Coaches Training Institute (www.thecoaches.com).

I developed this into a tool I use with clients and with mentee coaches. As a client tool, *Walk the Talk* is a structure for a client that keeps him or her in action, creating balance, leading to the fulfilled great lives the client deserves. It is a checklist of items for the client to focus on various areas in which he or she may be procrastinating; perhaps, a desired quality of life shift or simply practices the client wants to include in his or her life.

A few questions I use when designing a *Walk the Talk* list with a client are:

- What do you do that is self-nurturing?
- What practices do you want to make a regular part of your life?
- What would give you joy once you complete it?
- What is the quality-of-life shift you long for?

We then might design around any of these questions or simply focus on major life areas and design practices for the client to walk in his or her daily life. Such life areas we might include are career, spouse/relationship, personal health, friendships, finances, etc.

The second area I use the term "Walk the Talk" is in reference to personal integrity. I have always believed that one's integrity—one's word—is to be held in high regard. There is a personal responsibility that one assumes in the role of a professional healer, and that responsibility is to start with healing thyself. I have met many coaches, therapists, healers, speakers, doctors, nurses, etc. who although they "talk a good game," they do not live by the principles and practices they talk or look to improve. I am so sorry to see them still performing in their roles, disconnected from their very being. Too often they are interested in living out stories that they do not even realize that they are the star and director of. As I mentioned earlier, like many of us, they are not yet conscious of the many beliefs and choices that are "running the show" from behind the curtain. Yes, just like the *Wizard of Oz*.

I mentor a local networking group here in the Chicago area and I coach individuals on various boards and associations. As a therapist, manager, hypnotist, trainer, and coach, it has always been important to adhere to a standard that I consider "walking my talk." It is vital that any person helping others to "live big" or "live the life they want" are in fact living this way themselves!

A primary personal quality of a "good mentor" is one who serves as an example and role model for others. I define "role model" as a person who acts as an example for a particular task or set of values. If you are considering hiring a coach, I urge you choose wisely. Ask the coaches you are considering how they celebrate their lives, how they live big or have designed their great life! In other words, are they walking their talk?

I invite you to visit my Web site: www.trulyhumancoaching.com, or write me at: jim@trulyhumancoaching.com. I will be happy to help you to "walk your talk" or to find out if the person you are considering helping you with your life is truly "walking his or her talk."

I live in a world with infinite possibility. Anything is possible if you truly want it *and* you truly believe it. I offer this to clients, to members of my audience, and to my readers. Part of walking my talk is the work I have done in regard to my own shadow selves and limiting beliefs—those very things that hinder too many relationships and abilities for helping professionals. As so many of us great coaches will testify: "Do your own work, love yourself, love others, and the rest will follow."

Wright

In "walking your talk," what is most important to you?

Accetta

We all have our own sense of personal integrity, who we are, how honest we are with ourselves and with those in our lives. I hold integrity as one of my highest values. When I refer to "walking my talk," I'm referring to living a life I propose and declare I am living. When you work with a coach, therapist, healer, or any professional regarding your life, these people operate through their own socio-cultural and very personal psychological filters. By knowing our values, we are aware of the filters or screens that will bias our perception, whether we are aware of them or not. I want to share with our readers some of what is important to me—some of what I love.

I declare and propose to others to "live the life you love." I continue to create the life I love. My personal life is most important; in fact, it is sacred. My personal and spiritual development, my wife and our relationship, my children and our relationships, these are most important. As part of this sacred life with my loved ones, as well as with clients and all other places in the world, I enjoy creating and contributing to an environment of love and acceptance, of fun and learning, of exploration and success.

I wish for each person to live the life he or she truly loves. What that looks like for you or for any of my clients or for my wife and my children, I don't know. I know the life I want for *me*, and I know how to help you and other people like you to discover the life you love that is uniquely yours. As your coach, helping you to live the life you love is my first and only priority. Living your greatest life, whatever that looks and sounds like for you, whatever really feels right, becomes my focus. Continuing to explore and help people move further along their path is one of my greatest honors.

I delight in discovering the many gifts others have. I value celebrating our gifts and delighting in ourselves and in our lives—being able to be as full and big and genuine and as comfortably vulnerable as we can be with the people we love most. I enjoy sharing that joy and discovery in the world with as many people as possible. I especially delight in attracting people who have their toys out and are ready to play!!! Anyone just itching to play out there?

In my introduction during my presentations, I talk about the world being a place where people want to live. I dream the dream of everyone waking up in the morning with great joy and gratitude, celebrating their life each day and saying things like, "Mmmm, another great day to be alive!" And then moving through their day feeling at peace and in love with their lives, with the people in their lives and in the magnificence and beauty of living in the world. I enjoy people doing things they love, growing and thriving as they do them, and simply basking in the enjoyment of each day. Then, when they go to sleep at night, going asleep comfortably tired and contented, at peace with themselves and in love with themselves and the world, restful, and looking forward to another day. How does living such a contented day sound to you?

Through the self-knowledge gained through our work together, my clients experience huge gifts and great rewards, great inner richness and spirituality as well as real world enjoyment, fun, and adventure—whatever really tickles each person's fancy. I help people live the life they love as long as it doesn't impose on the will of other people. Simply put, to live well and harm none.

Wright

What do you love?

Accetta

Hmm, great question! I am a very passionate and sensual person. I love great food, intimacy, sex, learning, and delight—delight in the world, the delights of nature, and of people. I love working with clients who really want more for themselves, who enjoy the notion of taking full response-ability for their lives—people who want to be conscious of and intentional in the design of their moments.

My work with clients is phenomenal! I love working with clients and love the experience of being with them in the full richness of who they are. I love that in my own life, I walk my talk—waking up and really being sensually full and present each day, looking at the gifts that are in my world, leaning into these gifts that I have created and continue to create in each day. I love discovering and celebrating the gifts that other people have to offer. I love delighting in the delight of people, and anything that feels really good.

Wright

What do you mean when you talk about "limitless possibilities"?

Accetta

We live in a world of limitless possibilities. Too often what appears to be possible is severely hindered by familial and cultural filters. So many truly creative people (e.g., Albert Einstein, Martin Luther King Jr., Michelangelo) have all stepped outside what most or all people thought impossible in order to create the possible. It is in their dreaming, their believing, and their acting that great things were created in the world. It is about possibility—limitless, infinite possibility.

In my first book, *Getting What You Want, the Art of Living on Purpose,* I repeatedly ask the question, what do you want? I believe that any answer there is great. So many people limit themselves before they even allow themselves to dream, that they don't go after things that could bring them so much joy and enjoyment and fulfillment. And so, I encourage everyone to think of limitless possibilities of greatness. A simple example is asking a person what he or she would love to do. The first answer is normally, "Oh, it's not realistic." Some people tell me, "Here's what I can't do, here's what I don't want to do." So just getting to what they want sometimes is a little bit challenging.

A lot of people just don't allow themselves to answer that question and to check in and go, "Hmmm, what *do* I want here?" Regarding one person I asked, I said, "No, even if you could have it, even if it wasn't realistic, what would it be?"

"I'd love to live in Tahiti," she replied.

I thought to myself, a lot of people live there so that's pretty possible, what could it take? $5,000 to $10,000? I asked, "So why don't you go?" and she said it would cost too much.

"How much does it cost?" I asked. She said she didn't know. *She didn't know—she had never made the effort to find out!*

I don't know how many years she said she couldn't live her dream because of cost, but I'm sure there are more reasons there than that— fear, cynicism, self doubt, other limiting beliefs, or more. In this simple conversation, she used a limiting belief as a reason to simply stop dreaming, to give up, and to believe her dream was impossible. So if you really want to go to Tahiti, it's just that easy. You go! You get your money together and you go. You save over time and you do what it takes! (I discussed motivation and goals in detail in my January 2008 newsletter., visit my website as www.trulyhumancoaching.com see the article entitled "Meeting Your Goals-Guaranteed!) Because she didn't allow herself to dream—to just explore adventure and allow it to be— she just didn't allow it to happen.

So, limitless possibilities? If one thinks that one's dreams are not possible, are they impossible? When you believe your dream is possible, you envision it, and know now that you deserve it. What is possible then? Much more, I promise you.

Wright

What is your definition of success? Or what do you consider success?

Accetta

Success is defined individually for each person. We all must come to know our own "success." My definition of success has to do with true happiness, a soulful peace, inner contentment, *and* outward rewards. A large part of such success has to do with knowing one's self, and I mean *truly* knowing one's self. Until each person has an awareness of self and a beginning love and honor and compassion of one's self, then true success is still out of reach. I also lean into a more metaphysical definition of success. In this definition, there are 7 components of true success, they are:

1. Access to Resources: These resources include money, emotional resources, spiritual resources, knowledge, skill, people, opportunity....virtually any resources.

2. Intimacy with our raw materials and tools: Briefly put, intimacy and relationship with the following parts of ourself:

   a. Tools: Desire, Imagination & Expectation
   b. Raw Materials: Beliefs/Attitudes; Thoughts/Feelings/ and Decisions/Choices

3. Knowing the wonder of fun & happiness
4. Feeling Deserving (the most charged and most powered)
5. Knowing the wonder of power
6. Intimacy with talents
7. Access to spirituality

*The metaphysical definition of success, tools and raw materials are from Lucid Living material (www.lucidliving.net) and Lazaris (www.lazaris.com)

The definition of success by how many "things" we have is a much more common practice in our society. Most often this is associated with people's worth as a person to themselves, their families, and their communities. The more commonly agreed upon definition of success is having a certain amount of money, a certain kind of clothes, a certain kind of education, a certain kind of haircut, a certain kind of skin color, a certain kind of gender. Such definitions often are associated with feeling better than or less than others. This "better than or less than" is just one set of beliefs that are given to us by our family, school, media, and culture at large, or what I refer to as the "consensual reality."

Let me give you an example. You might recall the dog food commercial: "My dog's better than your dog" or all the commercials praising fancy cars, certain clothes, lifestyles, all as "better than—" Being "better than" is a primary motivator for consumers in our economy!

Beliefs and choices that were made far before we were aware of them are loudly operating under the surface. Some of these are the beliefs we have been given about success; some are the beliefs that our parents handed down about our self-worth, as well as a myriad of others. Until we have understanding of and relationship with the parts that we might be marginalizing, those shadows are going to keep showing up. If we are operating out of beliefs that are not congruent with the self, a true sense of happiness and success will not be achieved. To be successful means to be at peace with one's self in the world in a way that feels right for each person.

To achieve 'true' success, we need to know ourselves, our wants, desires, gifts, dreams... This includes the awareness that is gained through our own personal work with ourself... or more aptly put, our many selves.

The great psychiatrist and author, Carl Jung, referred to shadow selves. Jung believed that a human being is inwardly whole, but that most of us have lost touch with important parts of ourselves. Through listening to the messages of our dreams and waking imagination, we can contact and reintegrate our different parts. The goal of life is individuation, the process of coming to know, giving expression to, and harmonizing the various components of the psyche. If we realize our uniqueness, we can undertake a process of individuation and tap into our true self. Jung stated that each human being has a specific nature and calling that is uniquely his or her own, and unless these are fulfilled through a union of conscious and unconscious, the person can become sick. And of course, by "sick" I'm sure he was referring to "dis-ease," the many diseases (dis-eases) that so many struggle with. Much of the work I do with clients has to do with their owning and beginning relationships with what some refer to as their "shadow selves.

"We all are born whole and, let us hope, will die whole. But somewhere early on our way, we eat one of the wonderful fruits of the tree of knowledge, things separate into good and evil, and we begin the shadow-making process; we divide our lives.

"In the cultural process we sort out our God-given characteristics into those that are acceptable to our society and those that have to be put away. This is wonderful and necessary, and there would be no civilized behavior without this sorting out of good and evil. But the refused and unacceptable characteristics do not go away; they only collect in the dark corners of our personality." (Robert A. Johnson, author of *Owning Your Own Shadow: Understanding the Dark Side of the Psyche*. San Francisco: HarperSanFrancisco, 1991.)

Johnson observes that we devote the first half of our lives to the cultural process—gaining one's skills, raising a family, earning a living. In the second half we work to restore the wholeness—making holy—

of life. Theologians point out that the word "religion" stems from rejoining, reunion. To Johnson, the process of re-joining with our shadow side is a religious experience. In a sense, I like to use the term "spiritual." When we join together in sweat lodges, go on vision quests, or delve into the mythopoetic side of the "men's movement" we are delving into the spiritual dimension.

Johnson points out that no one can escape the dark side of life, but we can "pay out" that dark side intelligently. The dark side will come out, whether we want it to or not. To honor it is to prevent it from blowing up in our faces. An example is when we unwittingly take it out on other people. This shadow work is a large part of what we do in Truly Human Coaching.

I want to add a bit more about our work with our shadow selves. Here I am quoting from "Lazaris-Working with Your Shadow: An Imperative on the Spiritual Path 1995, NPN Publishing Inc.""The Shadow is made up of all the stuff that you have denied, that you discount, that you defend yourself against, that you distract yourself from—all the aspects of you that you pretend don't exist—or (if they do exist) are "no big deal." The Shadow is made up of all the stuff you learned to resist and that you refused to accept.

As a little kid you learned: You shouldn't be so selfish, you shouldn't be so greedy. You should do this, you shouldn't do that, you shouldn't do the other. You shouldn't question so much, you shouldn't you shouldn't, you shouldn't.

And as a good little boy or a good little girl trying to become "idealized," … trying to win favor, trying to survive … (laughter) … you did what you were told. And you shoved your shelfishness and your greed and your self-centeredness behind you, pretending it did not exist. "In what hand? What are you talking about? Well, it doesn't matter." You discounted and you defended: "I am not, I am not, I am not."

But you didn't just stuff the dark stuff, the ugly stuff, the stuff that society says is bad and wrong and sinful and terrible and immoral and all that. You also denied the good stuff because of the messages that you got: Don't be so curious, don't be so inquisitivie, don't be so honest, don't be so in touch with your feelings, don't be so creative, don't daydream like that, don't be that inventive, don't ask questions.

And you got all of those messages not just from mothers and fathers and siblings and extended family, but also from society of television, a society of education, from a society of religion.

And all of these things—dark and light—got shoved behind you into what is called the shadow." (pp. 7-8)

Let me ask you, how can we know if we are "successful" if we are not sure what we truly want? How can we know what we want if are living inconsciously within the matrix of the consensus reality? We can have a lot of things, but if we're frustrated about things, situations, or people in our lives or we are mad at ourself or marginalizing or putting parts of ourself aside and they are showing up in different places, then how can we truly be happy or successful? Again, these frustrations, anxieties, fears, and more are really an aspect of ourselves—perhaps a shadow self, perhaps a value we have that has been discounted or rubbed against. Knowing these parts of ourselves helps us to make choice, to choose the success that is right for each of us.

Wright

What do you mean by "we create our own reality."?

Accetta

I think Abraham Lincoln states it much simpler: "People are about as happy as they make up their minds to be."

What happens is that if a person has some feelings or emotions, they may point to the outside world and say, "Oh, because of that I feel this way." There is a lot of blame and victimization that goes on when we blame others or outside circumstances for what or how we feel. Feelings, emotions, and thoughts, start inside us. They are some of the primary filters we use to perceive the world!

A real difference and shift begins here when we start to operate from the framework that all the feelings we experience are already in us. We create different situations in the world to support stories that we have inside of us. Such scripting was referred to in early therapy methods, specifically Transactional Analysis work (see Steiner, Claude: *Scripts People Live, 1974*). We have genuine feelings and emotions that are in us and stirred or impacted by the outside world. Our experiences are screened or filtered by our beliefs, values, and attitudes; screened and filtered through our cultural and familial lenses, all those many things we learn during our socialization process. When we experience emotions we are really experiencing things that are already there; our feelings are stirred in us by what we perceive in our internal world and seemingly by our external world. It's not a matter of what is making us feel a certain way, but the stirring that is in each of us. It's part of the self-awareness that I spoke of earlier, it's part of the self-knowing.

The drama triangle[1] that was originally described in the field of co-dependency has much wider application than originally thought.[1] I have witnessed this pattern in most human relationships in our culture. The drama triangle positions people or parts of themselves into three positions: victim, persecutor, and rescuer. This is another culturally bred and supported phenomenon that so many people get caught up in *and they don't even know they are in it!* My work with

---

[1] The author and relationship expert Harville Hendrix, Ph.D. discusses how co-dependency is rampant and 'normal' in our culture; in fact that not being 'co-dependent' is the expection rather than the rule!
Getting the Love You Want: A Guide for Couples, Henry Holt Company 1988

clients around this focuses on identifying their personal responsibility and choice in every matter. They can no longer be a victim when it's always their choice. It's always up to them, and I really want people to know that and make each and every choice for themselves.

We create the world that we see every day. Every day I create intention and I encourage my clients to create intention about who they want to be, what they want to be in the world that day, how they want to feel, and the impact they want to have on other people. So much of what I do has to do helping others consciously create the world that they want to live in—creating the moods and attitudes, the actions and the impact they want to have on others; because it *is* all up to each of us—it is all up to each one of us to create the life we want every day. It is magick, pure and simple![2]

Wright

What do you find important about honoring all parts of yourself?

Accetta

Self-love is a way to inner peace and interpersonal harmony. Honoring all parts of ourselves means honoring and delighting in our thoughts, emotions and desires that show up—as well as *not* making ourselves wrong or feeling bad about thoughts or feelings we have.

Certainly we might not like a behavior or certain ways that we act, but with self-knowledge we can stop behaviors we would rather not do. What too often happens is that people end up shaming

---

[2] According to Wikipedia: "Magick is the broadest sense , is any act designed to cause intentional change. To change nothing into something and something into something else." The definition goes on to read: "Magick is not capable of producing 'miracles' or violating the physical laws of the universe (e.g., it cannot cause a solar eclipse), although 'it is theoretically possible to cause in any object any change of which the change of that object is capable by nature." http//en.wikipedia.org/wiki/Magick.

themselves about a behavior or berating themselves about it, and it gets them stuck in that behavior instead of helping them to change. A much better and more effective way to view the behavior is to say, "Okay, what did I learn from this? And how *do* I want to be in the world?" I help my clients to take personal responsibility as an adult in the world and make a decisions that are in alignment with their true desires and who they want to be.

This is very much like the NLP™ presupposition "there is no failure, only feedback." In other words, we are not wrong or bad and have not failed when we do things we don't want, or don't achieve the outcomes we want. All the supposed wrongs and failures are really feedback. They are information that we can learn from!

How does the story of Thomas Edison go? He was on light bulb attempt ninety-eight. It didn't work and someone commented on his number of failures. His response? "They are not failures, I have found ninety-eight things that did not work; I'm getting closer!"

It's important to know what you want to do, and if there are feelings or thoughts or beliefs that are getting in the way then becoming aware of them, taking the time and effort to sort them out and getting to know what's wanting in you is key. There are hidden parts of our self that "show up" and it's a matter of really listening to the feelings and emotions; the voices or the pictures that one becomes aware of. And then inviting this awareness with discovery, with full acceptance and love, a full honoring of these parts of you. It all has to do with honoring yourself. You don't have to have a "good" or "bad" reason for thinking or feeling any particular way, but we've been taught that some are right and some are wrong. They are not—it really depends on what we decide to do with them.

It's always a matter of choice—a choice that many people are not even aware of as possible, yet. A choice that most people living in the matrix of the consensual reality are not aware of, nor are they ready to take responsibility for and make. Allow me to end with a quote from my first book: *Getting What You Want: The Art of Living On Purpose* (2003):

"I suggest that we live in the world as if there are endless possibilities. If you must talk about what you cannot do, or believe you are unable to do, add the word *"yet"* to the end of your sentences. "Yet" presupposes that the possibility exists that you have found out how to make it occur; how to reach your goal; or how to live your dreams…yet"

Wright

What a great conversation, Jim. I really appreciate the time you've taken to be with me today to answer all these questions! I have learned a lot, and I know our readers will too.

ABOUT THE AUTHOR

Jim Accetta is a personal life and relationship coach, a certified trainer of Neurolinguistic Programming (NLP™), an inspirational speaker, and published author. He has been quoted for his coaching and training expertise in the *Boston Globe, Fitness Magazine,* and in *Crain's Chicago Business.*

Jim is President of Truly Human Coaching where he provides personal and couples coaching for individuals and couples seeking very personal and intimate change and growth.

For the last twenty-eight years, Jim has helped thousands of people to live more of the life they truly want. From social service to business management and from family therapy to training professionals, Jim has helped people create meaningful connections with others, including the most meaningful of connections—with themselves.

In his free time, Jim loves deep intimate times with his beautiful wife, Connie, quality time with his children, as well as writing, reading, meditating, exercise, marital arts, spiritual development, cooking, and grocery-shopping.

Jim's professional speaking topics include: "Moments of Truth," "Instant Rapport: Building Rapport in 60 seconds or less!" and, "Getting What You Want: The Art of Living on Purpose."

Jim Accetta, MA, CPCC
Truly Human Coaching
240 Jeanette Place
Mundelein, IL 60060
Phone: 847.566.3122
E-mail: jim@trulyhumancoaching.com
www.trulyhumancoaching.com

An interview with…

Mark Victor Hansen

David Wright (Wright)

Today we're talking to Mark Victor Hansen. Some call him America's Ambassador of Possibility. In the area of human potential, no one is better known or well respected. For over 26 years, Mark Victor Hansen has been helping people from all walks of life reshape their personal vision of what is possible. You may know Mark as the "Chicken Soup for the Soul Guy." If so, you will be surprised at the many successes that have propelled him into the world spotlight. Mark, welcome to *Success is a State of the Mind*.

Mark Victor Hansen (Hansen)

My great pleasure. I couldn't be happier to be here.

Wright

Mark I've heard about as many different definitions of success as people I've asked. Since it seems to mean different things to different people, what does success mean to you?

Hansen

Success means realizing your dreams, making a difference and leaving a legacy.

Wright

In that order?

Hansen

Heard that before? I just made it up today just for you. I thought I'd come up with a brand new definition. I thought I ought to meditate, cogitate and ruminate on this and come up with something new. I tried to say how you could do it comprehensively so it would cover all success. I mean, realizing your dreams in marriage or at work or spiritually—it fits. If you can make a difference in each one of those dimensions, with your family, your kids, your business, your life or your charity that means you leave a legacy, and that's really good. Our poster boy is Paul Newman. Here's a guy who everybody loved his dressing. He created Newman's Own and now he's giving $125,000,000 to charities like Hole in the Wall Gang and Make a Difference Day, which is held by *USA Today*, and Make a Wish. I'm saying that every one of us can do that. It's not just Paul Newman. You can do it in your own inimitable way and I'll gladly talk to that if you want.

Wright

You know, back when I was younger my first, middle and last thought was always of myself. As I get older, that legacy thing is really becoming more and more important to me. I have three children and it really is important.

Hansen

I've got two kids and a great wife. I'm going to deal a seminar called, *Residual Philanthropy*, which means you work once for the philanthropy, but you get paid back a thousand times. I can give you the Paul Newman example. In the book business you've got Dave Barry—who I think is the funniest guy writing today—and Steven King and Amy Kent, and they got together and did the Rock Bottoms Remainder Group. They charge $100 a ticket. They say they're no good, but everybody will come out because they're famous. One day a month they all perform in their band. If they came to Knoxville, TN., you'd probably pay $100 for you and your wife to go see them.

Wright

Oh yeah.

Hansen

And I would too. They raise $1,000,000 a year to end illiteracy. The naysayers say, "Well, you want to end illiteracy so that more people will buy your books." No, these guys are fed. The deal is you get your future days paid for so that you can really leave a legacy that serves everyone. I believe that most baby boomers are saying, "How do we get everyone educated? How do we get healthcare for everyone? How do we really take care of our fellow human beings?" That is the high level of success. That is the high benchmark; it seems to me, on a go-forward basis.

Wright

You know, because of the phenomenal success of the *Chicken Soup for the Soul* series, many people think you're an overnight success.

Hansen

I am.

Wright

Well, I know you've been teaching, training and helping people for over 26 years. How did you get started, and what is the focus of your career?

Hansen

Well the focus keeps modifying. Today the focus is on leaving a legacy of creating 7,000 professional speakers. We have a population on the planet of about 7 billion right now. What I want to create is 7,000 speakers because I believe leaders are born at seminars. Have you ever been at somebody's seminar that just caught you on fire inside and turned you on your ear? All of a sudden you were saying, "I can do this and take a new vector." Has that ever happened to you?

Wright

The man's name is Paul Meyer.

Hansen

Paul and I are good friends. As you know he did *Chicken Soup for the Grandparent's Soul* with us. Paul and I have been at tens of meetings around the country together and do a lot of business. I think Paul is just a genius. So did his stuff do it for you or did he?

Wright

Actually, he did a lot of things for me personally. He took me under wing when I was a kid. He took me from a million-and-a-half company to about 40 million in five years. It was basically his advice.

Hansen

Can I hear what that advice was?

Wright

He put me on a goal-setting system. Every time he would write a leadership program—he had a company called SMI in Waco, Texas—I would go down twice a year for the executive seminars. In addition to that, I was on a list that every time something new came out they didn't have to ask, they just mailed it and I paid for it.

Hansen

That's the way I think every person who wants to grow should be with my stuff, your stuff, and Paul's stuff. What I'm saying is that if we had 7,000 superstar speakers at my level or above, you could literally get to 7 billion people. We could get the people out of the ghettos, we could get to the people who aren't fed and don't have a glass of water or a bite of food—which is just ridiculous because we have a planet that can do plenty. We just have vested political interests and other kinds of interests that are keeping people enslaved. What I want to do is end that mental tyranny once they change their picture and idea—like you 40x your idea by getting under the tutelage of our friend Paul. I'm saying everybody can do that. If you do multiple people, like if you get under Paul and Mark and Dave and whoever else it is, if you get in front of 100 of them, one of them will just take you. If each one of them multiplied you just once that would be great, but some of them are going to multiply you 10 and 100 times. Yesterday I took an intensive training with one of my peers, just he and I. One idea he gave me yesterday is going to be worth $50 million. He showed me how to do something I didn't know I knew how to do. He said, "Look, here are the seminars you are doing, this is how big they can become if you'll just do one more thing." I went, "Dang, that's so easy. I can do this."

Wright

Time Magazine calls *Chicken Soup for the Soul* the publishing phenomenon of the decade with over 80 million books sold in North

America alone. You've now had years to reflect on the success of the book. Have you come to any conclusion as to why it was so successful?

Hansen

Yes. What we teach at our Mega Book Marketing University, which we hold once a year at our Mega Speaking University, is that to be successful with my book or the book that you are writing here, you've got to have instantaneous behavioral change. That happens in books like, *Who Moved My Cheese?* We wrote *Chicken Soup for the Teenage Soul.* Our publisher says, "I've got teens and they buy cd's, concert tickets and clothes. You blew it this time, pal." We sold 19 million teenage books. If you and I are 15 and we go, "What's happenin' man," or whatever we say to each other, we don't go deep, but if you will read out loud a story to me like, I Wish I Had a Brother Like, what it does is open up your heart and soul and then we have a heart to heart, soul to soul, core essence to core essence experience with one another. It's no longer "Hey, man that was a cool movie." Now it's "I'm a real human being and my brother isn't treating me quite like that," or sister or father or whatever. Does that make sense? So because of instantaneous behavioral change, and because we did it bite sized, while we were rejected by 33 publishers, our agent fired us, and we had 133 more turn downs from Jack and I going to the Book Expo ourselves. We decided to suck it in and tough it out and now we've got 72 different copies of *Chicken Soup* out in one decade, which nobody else has done that many best sellers in a row, ever. The *Guinness Book of World Records* says we're the world's best selling non-fiction authors right now.

Wright

Well I'm one of those clod dads who should have written you a thank you note. I've got a 14-year-old daughter. About a year ago I went into her bedroom, which I'm only allowed in if I beat three times and announce myself first. But she was sitting on the bed crying and I looked and she had *Chicken Soup for the Teenage Soul* in her hands. I started questioning her about it and she was so moved by those stories. If it didn't change her life it certainly did change a lot of her actions. So I really appreciate you guys writing that one.

Hansen

Well, let me do three things with you. Number one is I'd ask you to buy the whole series. There are five of them now. Make sure she gets the teen journal because we ask the questions. We tested it against 6 million teenagers—thanks to our partner Nickelodeon—and we found the questions that kids want. The reason we did it was that Jack and I had kids calling us and saying, "Mark I've got a gun in my oven and I'm going to kill myself if I don't get to talk to Mark Victor Hansen or Dr. Jack Canfield." I went, "Holy smoly." Neither of us are psychiatrists. But these books open their hearts and they figure the guys who could write a book that has such depth of feeling and emotion like what you saw in your daughter—that, by the way, happens to everybody because we have found the classic stories. The story has to cause a heartfelt tear. That's why we did the book, of course. A prisoner wrote us, "Dear Mark and Jack, I've been in prison five years contemplating killing the guy who put me here. Then my sister sent me your book and I read it six times. When I get out in five more years, I no longer want to kill the guy who put me here.

Don't you wish you were the judge who was going to get dusted and say, "I want that book given to every prisoner." It's not because it's Mark and Jack, it's because we found a zone that no one's ever touched before. I'm saying that everybody has a book in them. Everybody has a story. What our books do, and I may be over answering your question, but it goes along the zone of what your book's doing, and that is you've got to read somebody else's story to sharpen yours. Dreams sharpen dreams, stories sharpen stories, and we're in the first time in history where the game is changing so fast that you've got to keep reinventing yourself. Isn't that what you've had to do lately?

Wright

Absolutely.

Hansen

You didn't have to reinvent the business once and blow it to $40 million. You invented the business once and then you keep reinventing and reinventing.

Wright

You know, a few weeks ago my family and I were kicking back in Florida watching the ocean. I was channel surfing and caught you on a religious television program. It was a large audience and you were teaching principles of faith. How important has your faith been to your business, as well as your personal life? Do you think faith and success are connected in any way?

Hansen

One of my favorite lines in the Bible is Hebrews: 11. What it says is faith is substance. *"Now faith is being sure of what we hope for and certain of what we do not see."* You saw that $40 million before it came to pass, correct?

Wright

Right.

Hansen

I saw that for Jack and I—and I'm the visionary of the two of us and Jack agrees with that, but he's a genius. I'm so lucky to have three genius partners, if you count my wife. If you get one friend that gets to exercise his or her genius with you it makes life better, but I've had three and I'm sure I'm not done because I'm going to live to be 126 with options for renewal. So, faith has been critical to me. When I was bankrupt and upside down luckily I went to see Dr. Norman Vincent Peele at church, and two guys said, "We're going to take you up to Harlem to see this guy Reverend Ike." We went to him and every Sunday from then on I went to two churches. Now my wife goes to one church down here and I go to a giant church up in LA with 9,000 per service, and I'm on the board of directors at Agape.

Wright

Wow.

Hansen

The fact is that I'm poured full of, not religion, but spiritual understanding because I want to have spiritual discernment. I believe we're all spiritual beings in a spiritual universe. If you will acknowledge that you will get to have a profound, blessed spiritual experience. Could I go a step further?

Wright

Absolutely.

Hansen

The book I'd ask you to read that fits that little model I shared, which is instantaneous behavioral change. It is *Prayer of Jabez*. Have you read my friend Bruce Wilkinson's book?

Wright

Absolutely. Yes.

Hansen

Well, I do that every morning when I wake up and before I go to sleep because the anecdote he shares is that if you don't ask for your blessings, you don't get them. Duh! I've got a 15-year-old at home who goes, "Duh, Dad." Does yours do that?

Wright

Absolutely.

Hansen

If I am blessed, not only do I have a blessing, but I can show you where the blessings are so that you can get blessings too.

Wright

Tell us about your new book *The One Minute Millionaire: The Enlightened Way to Wealth*. Do you really think that it is possible to inspire the creation of one million new millionaires in 10 years?

Hansen

Unequivocally, yes. The way we're doing it is that the book is a rocking best seller. Every week we've been in the *Wall Street Journal*. It came out October 17 and we went to number one, and stayed there for a long time. We're trying to make it number one again for this Christmas. Then, we'll get a sequel behind it called *The Last Minute Millionaire: When You Need Money and You Needed it Yesterday*. Notice the *One Minute Millionaire*'s subtitle is, *The Enlightened Way to Wealth* because we want rich people to come out of enlightenment, which means they come from abundance and create massive value for other people and leave a legacy. That's what it looks like to us. Our fastest millionaires so far are Karen Nelson Bell and her husband

Duncan. They have gone from 0 to $1,000,000 in four months and nine days. They both got fired from good jobs, said that they were going to read this book of Mark and Bob's and we're going to go to their seminar. They went, "who, Las Vegas." We teach four ways to do it. You can do a Real Estate Money Mountain, a Business Money Mountain, an Investment Money Mountain or Internet. We don't care which way you do. There are some basic principles. One is you've got to live below your means and another is that you've got to save 10 percent of your income. Well, if you just save one dollar a day, over a lifetime that's $25,000. With 10 percent interest its $2,750,000 and at 20 percent interest do you know how much it turns into? One billion dollars.

Wright

Wow.

Hansen

Now, can you get your kids to start saving like I've got mine saving? The answer is yes. We're saying that it is a fundamental principle that everybody has got to make themselves wealthy. You've got to become self-reliant to action.

Wright

You know, when you appear on such shows as *Oprah*, *CNN*, and *The Today Show*, you assure people that, and I'm quoting you now, "You can easily create the life you deserve." Can you tell us what you mean by that?

Hansen

Well, first of all I don't think anyone should live in poverty housing anymore. Next year, October of 2004, I am on of the spokespeople for Habitat for Humanity and we're going to end poverty housing in America. Our vision is to create 30,000 new homes. We ask everybody in the audience to go to our website and ask everybody to contribute. What's amazing is that we've got the little soccer leagues that are contributing, the little football leagues and the carpenters and the plumbers are contributing, no one ever asked them. Yet you and I grew up in a country that believes in barn raisings. Remember when 100 years ago? If a barn was going up and you were my neighbor, I'd ask you to come up and we'd whip this barn up. It was my barn, but I didn't pay you, we had a big party and everybody was happy? Well that's the same thing that Habitat is doing, except it's saying, "Hey look, the lowest element of society hasn't got a chance unless we give them a house. We're only short 30,000 houses. I'm saying I'm going to get 1,000,000 people to come out in October and play. No one has ever done that. It's not going to be fun, it's going to be exquisitely fun and we're going to solve the housing problem in America. Once you've got a prototype then we can go solve the housing problem in the rest of the world. Can we bring capitalism to the world? Yes. Can we bring enlightenment to the world and not eradicate illiterates, but eradicate illiteracy which we have a big problem with in America. I already told you that Dave Barry and the boys and girl are trying to do that, and I'm supportive of that. I'm saying that the big question that you are asking and that everybody reading this has to get is can you get your future days paid off? Meaning that once you're financially self-sufficient so you can go do something that's really important. Once you do something that's really important—what we're teaching in the book is that you've got to have multiple streams of incomes so that you never have to worry because everything changes and pulsates. My teacher when I was in grad school said, "There are no straight lines there is only wave propagation." So you've got to have multiple sources of residual income, meaning I worked once but I've been paid almost 100 million times on *Chicken Soup*. That's the right way to get paid.

Wright

Mark, you've been called one of the Top 10 Motivational Speakers. In the year 2000, the Horatio Alger Association of Distinguished Americans honored you with the prestigious Horatio Alger Award. Do you think success is more attainable for those who are entrepreneurs?

Hansen

That's a great question. Entrepreneur means a lot of different things. It means somebody that takes self-initiative to action, so the answer is yes. It means somebody that doesn't believe in entitlement, so the answer is yes. It means somebody that knows there is always a way to do it, so the answer is yes.

Wright

You're known as a passionate philanthropist and humanitarian working tirelessly for organizations that you've mentioned such as Habitat for Humanity, American Red Cross, March of Dimes and ChildHelp USA. How does helping others who cannot help themselves figure into the success equation?

Hansen

Well, the spiritual line is that to him or her much is given much is required. I wrote a whole book called *The Miracle of Tithing*. Anyone who goes to my website and wants it I'll sign it to them. But what we teach in it is different than anyone else. I think that God gave me the commission to teach people to give. How do you get people to give? I think there are for t's to get people to give. Everyone knows about

Treasures, but I think there are three that precede it. The first is that you've got to Tithe your thinking. If you have 10 great ideas are you willing to give one of them to a church or charity?

Wright

I've never thought about that.

Hansen

No one thinks about it. I'm going to tell you if you go to my website you can download it free. It's *Idea Tithing*. The other three are thinking, which is more important than the other three, I think, your Time, your Talent, and then your Treasures. I'm asking you to help with Habitat come next October, and you'll do it and bring your kids and it'll be a great time, but the thinking is where the deal is because the thinking is the ultimate leverage.

So the point is that when I was with the Red Cross they ran out of blood four years ago. Ms. Dole, Elizabeth Dole, says, "Look Mark, there's no blood. We need 300,000 pints." I said, "We'll have it in a week." She had to get the AMA to write it off and okay it because I went to the chiropractors, who I do a lot of work with and they've given me three honorary doctorates, and I did a fax blast to 60,000 doctors and said, "I want you to bring in 100 patients, adjust them for free, call 800-Give-Life (that's the Red Cross) and bring out a little blood mobile, and ask them for a pint of blood." I said, "If you ask they'll give it and have them bring in a friend, you'll have a new patient." Everybody's practice went up because people love people who give. I think that you and I and everyone were coded in our DNA and RNA to give. Now if you don't give—I'm writing a book with Art Linkletter now called *How to Make the Rest of Your Life the Best of Your Life*—and the biggest of the four big keys are that you've got to have a cause bigger than you are. In other words, if you retire to nothing you die inside. But if you start giving to a cause bigger than yourself, and I'm saying that idea tithing is a cause everyone is willing to give to because ideas don't cost anything, but that's all that anything is. This interview that we're doing was your idea before you called me.

Wright

It has been written that Mark Victor Hansen is an enthusiastic crusader of what's possible and is driven to make the world a better place. Of course, we've found that out in what you've said here today, but could you give our readers and me some practical advice how to join you in making the world a better place?

Hansen

I'm desperately trying to do that. What I want them to do is come to my live seminar, shake my hand, let me sign a book to them and give them a directional cue, whether it's Habitat or that I give blood every quarter. Now I've got my 16-year-old in high school signed up to give blood. She said, "Do you really do this every 56 days dad?" I said, "Yes. If I'm in the country I do." You know, if you go into China or some other countries you can't give blood until six months later. She said, "Do you want me to do that?" I said, "You're not doing it for me. The highest form of giving is anonymous and you're going to save the lives of people who will never know you." The bottom line is one of my idea tithes is that I hope you give your body parts away after you are done because someone needs your eyes, your heart and your skin. That's my belief.

There is another one that I'm fighting for. In America we don't do cadaver blood. You can write it on your license to take your cadaver blood; otherwise they throw it down the sewer. I don't know anything about you, but knowing the philosophy that you have, when you're dead you don't need it, right?

Wright

That's right. Well, what a great conversation. I want you to know how much I appreciate you taking this much time with me. I know how many activities you go through in a day and I want to personally thank you for being a part of this book, *Success is a State of the Mind*.

Hansen

I look forward to it. Thank you, David.

ABOUT THE AUTHOR

For over 26 years, Mark Victor Hansen has focused solely on helping people in all walks of life reshape their personal vision of what's possible for themselves. From Bangladesh to Birmingham, Mark's keynote messages of possibility, opportunity, and action have helped create startling and powerful change in more than 2 million people in 38 countries.

Mark Victor Hansen
www.MarkVictorHansen.com

SUCCESS IS A STATE OF MIND

8

An interview with…

Jake Rubin

David Wright (Wright)

Today we're talking to Jake Rubin, MA. Jake is an accomplished entrepreneur, CEO, and professional life and business coach. He is a graduate of the Co-Active Coach Training Program and is also a member of the International Coaching Federation (ICF). Jake earned a bachelor's degree in Psychology, with a minor in Business from UCLA, as well as a master's degree in Organizational Psychology and Behavior from the Marshal Goldsmith School of Management at Alliant University.

His clientele includes not only business owners, creative professionals, and high-powered CEOs, but also extraordinary people from all walks of life with the common desire to step out of the life that they're currently living and into the life that they were *meant* to live.

Jake, welcome to *Success is a State of Mind!*

Jake Rubin (Rubin)

Thank you so much David, it's a pleasure to be here.

Wright

So would you tell our readers what drove you to become a life and business coach?

Rubin

Sure, David. What gets me going and personally excites me is helping my clients to live their lives *fully* according to who they *truly* are. I get great satisfaction in helping people peel away layers of fear, insecurity, and doubt that inhibit them from going after what they really desire in life.

So many people go through their lives just settling for getting by. I often relate this to going through life in a sleepwalking state. The truth is we are capable of so much more than we choose to believe. We often feel a sense of comfort in limiting ourselves, in staying safe, and listening to that inner "saboteur" that tells us, "Who are you to live your dreams? Who are you to have an amazing life?" When in fact, deep down we know how truly powerful we are. We know we can make incredible things happen, yet many times we allow this inner "saboteur" to limit us and stifle our amazing gifts and passions.

What I enjoy most about coaching is being able to be a part of people's transformation into living lives of truth and honesty with who they are, helping them connect to their truly unlimited power to live lives of meaning, success, and fulfillment.

Wright

The title of this book is *Success is a State of Mind,* so how do you personally define success?

Rubin

Many people go through life trying to fit into society's definition of success. They look for external validation, and they look for material possessions that define their level of success. But these things are *not* what *true success* is comprised of.

Success is aligning yourself with your true purpose and continually striving to live that truth. It involves working toward goals that you feel are important, and doing things each day that bring you joy.

There is really one reason people want to be successful—what they *truly* want is to be happy and to feel alive. Why do some people want monetary success? Because they think that when they have the money to buy the things they want they will be happy. Some people want success so that they can feel fulfilled. Why do they want to feel fulfilled? Because fulfillment goes hand-in-hand with happiness.

One of the quotes that I have on my website is from author and philosopher, Howard Thurman, "Don't ask what the world needs, ask what makes you come alive and go do it, because what the world needs is people who have come alive." That is really the essence of why I'm a coach and why I enjoy helping people work toward success.

The truth is that success is a journey, it's not a destination. People think they can get to a point where they can finally say, "Okay, I've reached it. I'm successful. I can rest now." But it doesn't really happen that way, *success is the journey*. Success is striving toward things that you believe in. It's continually improving yourself. It's having worthwhile goals, and most importantly, success is being in a state of mind where you're able to share with others. To go for success as a personal endeavor without the desire to help others, is not going to be nearly as fulfilling as being in a place where you can share that success with others, where you can inspire others, and where you can help others on their own road to success.

Wright

In your extensive experience, what do you think are people's most common misconceptions when it comes to success?

Rubin

As I mentioned previously, I think people look to society to define what success is for them. As a society, we're inundated with images of material success, which we naturally associate with true success and happiness. While all those things are wonderful, and they are certainly by-products of monetary success, it's a mistake to assume that monetary success will give us happiness. Of course having a comfortable life and a decent income is an aspect of success, but when you limit yourself to that definition, you're limiting your ability to give to the world. Success is so much more than that. It's being in a place of living your truth and of giving your whole self with joy and happiness to this one life we all have.

Wright

You have written and spoken about intuition as playing a role in success; will you explain that a bit for our readers?

Rubin

Intuition is a fascinating subject. In fact, more and more attention has been given to it lately in the media. The main issue and question is: can we trust our intuition and how does it compare with more traditional decision-making strategies such as rational analysis or pro/con lists?

My feeling is, and research is beginning to support the fact, that intuition is our mind's higher intelligence processing hundreds if not thousands of bits of information and informing us through our body or our "gut" what the best decision for us is. Intuition is very powerful tool that we all have access to, but many times for many reasons, we shut it out and try to make a "rational" decision, even if that decision goes against our intuition. And more often than not, at least in my personal experience, in hindsight, my intuition was right on. But time and time again, we fail to listen to this very quiet voice within us. It speaks to us sometimes quietly and sometimes loudly, but in our society we are taught that we need concrete reasons for the decisions we make. We need to know why we made a certain decision. Saying "it just felt right" isn't very popular as a reason, especially in business. But I hope we are beginning to see a shift in trusting intuition as an extremely valuable tool in decision-making.

As a coach, I truly believe people *know* what they want to be doing, what is best for them, and what would truly make them happy. Yet, we choose to look and search outside of ourselves for the answers, when in fact, the answers are all within us.

Wright

Please explain the type of coaching you do in your company ClearQuest Life and Business Coaching? What would the experience be like for me as a client?

Rubin

Coaching is a process that helps you unlock your hidden potential. It helps you get "unstuck" and overcome the obstacles in your way. Your life becomes easier and more effortless as you learn to listen to your inner voice and evolve into who you truly are.

Furthermore, coaching is about self-discovery and about success measured by the degree to which you are actively creating the life you truly desire. As your coach, I don't simply provide you with the answers and direction. My job is to ask you powerful questions that will help you get to the core of what you believe and what you want for yourself. I will help you see the ways in which you sabotage yourself and teach you how to effectively deal with your own "saboteur." My goal is for you to be 100 percent clear about your personal truth and the values and goals that are important to you. As we do that, I help you begin to take action toward what it is you truly want for yourself and I hold you accountable for those steps, all the while supporting you and providing the space for your personal self-discovery and evolution.

Wright

It sounds like a very powerful, supportive relationship. Are the challenges different for your business coaching clients?

Rubin

The challenges certainly can be different with the entrepreneurs and business owners I work with. Most of them are really concerned about actively growing their businesses while still maintaining balance in their lives. Often they feel they're giving a lot of time to their business at the expense of all the other aspects of their lives including their own well being, health and time with family and friends. Other times, they're working *in* their business instead of on it, and it's not growing they way they would like it to. Most business owners have both of these issues and more. When this is the case, I work with them to find ways to help grow their businesses while still working toward balance in their personal lives as well.

Everything is interconnected; the way that you function in your workplace ties into how you function with others, into your family, into your balance, and into the success that you seek for yourself. So while the challenges are different they're still intertwined with the same basic principles of coaching and coaching people toward their success.

Wright

You mentioned a few moments ago, and it is also mentioned on your website, that you practice Co-Active Coaching. That's a term that, after all these years, I'm not familiar with. Would you explain that to our readers?

Rubin

Co-Active Coaching is a unique type of coaching that places the power not on the coach, but on the relationship. When an individual hires me as his or her coach, the client is in charge—the relationship is focused on getting the client the results that the client wants. The agenda is always coming from the client.

There are a few key parts to Co-Active Coaching I'd like to go over with you and your readers. There are three core aspects when it comes to Co-Active Coaching and those are: Fulfillment, Balance, and Process.

What is fulfilling for a client is intensely personal. My goal is to help clients value life today and to help them realize that fulfillment is always available and accessible to them. It's not something that we have to wait to achieve in the future. Fulfillment is possible today—right now—and so I help clients focus on what's fulfilling today, what's fulfilling right now in their lives, and living life with fulfillment right now.

As a coach I hear over and over, "I'll be happy when—," "I'll be able to relax when—" This is one of the biggest myths in life. People need to realize it's not the destination. We simply cannot wait until certain events happen to be happy and fulfilled; happiness is short-lived. Other challenges are always present as well and we begin to postpone our happiness until we can overcome those. It's a race we can never win. We have to be happy and fulfilled *now*.

The other concept I coach is called Balance. Balance is a dynamic concept. Achieving balance is difficult. As a coach, I explain to my clients that it's not a destination to be reached—we are either moving toward balance or away from it. So what I help clients do is look at the different perspectives of their lives or the situation that they're going through and help them choose the perspective they want to look at a given situation from. Clients learn that it is their perception and perspective of a given situation that is the most powerful tool they have in working toward balance.

The final concept is called Process. As human beings, we're always in the process of our lives. Sometimes it's smooth and graceful, sometimes it's a raging river, and sometimes it just seems really stagnant. What process is about is helping clients take an honest look at where they are in their lives—in this very moment—because if they're not honest with themselves, there's no way to move forward from that point.

Taken together, coaching Fulfillment, Balance, and Process creates a very powerful relationship that can help clients achieve the changes they truly want in their lives.

Wright

You also offer something called the ClearQuest Total Life Transformation in which your client receives both personal coaching and works with a personal trainer. Will you tell me a little bit more about that?

Rubin

This exciting program can truly enhance people's lives and take them to a whole different level. I know for myself when I am in good physical shape and take care of my body with exercise and proper nutrition, I feel much clearer and more focused. I feel that I'm in control and am honoring myself first in my life. The ClearQuest Total Life Transformation is an amazing process for clients in that they get coached to achieve both physical fitness and life and business success.

So what I've done is teamed up with a group of very select fitness trainers. We offer a package in which clients receive personal training, one to three times a week, including nutritional guidance and life/business coaching once per week. It's an incredibly powerful combination for people who want to take their lives to a whole new level.

The synergy of combining physical training, nutrition counseling, and life coaching is incredible. People are able to reach their goals rapidly. They feel much more fulfilled, and it's an amazing way for them to get where they want to go, much, much more quickly.

Wright

I own a business, and of course I have a personal life—family and friends and all of that. How do I know when I need a life or business coach?

Rubin

That's a great question. There are many points in a person's life when he or she could benefit from hiring a coach. For some, they've reached a point in life where they've achieved a certain level of monetary success but yet they still feel unfulfilled. Often, they feel that something is missing in their lives. For others, they are in a state of transition and perhaps are not where they want to be in their lives yet. Other times, people simply feel stuck. They may have many aspects of their lives in order, but there are one or two aspects that they know that they're not living fully.

As I mentioned, entrepreneurs often immerse themselves in their business at the expense of everything else in their lives. Since you are a business owner, your desire could be to grow your business to the next level, while still taking care of yourself and the relationships that are important to you. That would be a great time to work with a coach.

Wright

I've known very successful people; their businesses are going well and everything seems to be going well, but they're really just not very happy. Would that be a time for a life coach?

Rubin

Absolutely. That's a great time to work with a coach. There are so many reasons why people appear to be successful but they're unhappy. It goes back to the misconceptions of success I mentioned previously. People expect that monetary success will bring them happiness and fulfillment but they soon realize that's not always the case. Most likely, there is some aspect of their life they are not fully in touch with—that they're not living fully—and I think that's an excellent time to work with a coach. It happens at that point in life when you feel like, "I should be happy and I should be fulfilled, but something is still not happening for me, something is still holding me back from the level of happiness and success I want." The truth is, when we talk about success being a state of mind, all of it really comes back to happiness. It comes back to wanting to live lives of success because we want to be happy.

If you ask most of the spiritual leaders in this world, what the meaning of life is, they'll tell you it's to be happy. Why? Because when we're happy, we're able to give ourselves to others. We're able to be kind and we're able to be giving towards the needs of others.

Wright

Well, what a great conversation. I really appreciate all the time you've taken with me this afternoon to answer these questions. I have learned a lot and I am sure that our readers will.

Rubin

Fantastic, it's been a pleasure.

Wright

Today we've been talking with Jake Rubin. Jake is an accomplished entrepreneur, CEO, and professional life and business coach. In his coaching practice he is able to make a tremendous and positive impact on his clients' lives. His clientele has included not only world champion athletes, artists, and high-powered CEOs, but people like you and me and extraordinary people from all walks of life. He instills in his clients a common desire to step out of the life they're currently living and into the life that they were meant to live.

Jake, thank you so much for being with us today on *Success is a State of Mind.*

Rubin

Thank you David.

ABOUT THE AUTHOR

Jake Rubin, MA is an accomplished entrepreneur, CEO and Professional Life and Business Coach. He is a graduate of the Co-Active Coach Training Program, an ICF Accredited Program, and also a member of ICF, the International Coaching Federation. Jake earned a Bachelor's degree in Psychology with a minor in Business from UCLA, as well as a Masters degree in Organizational Psychology & Behavior from the Marshall Goldsmith School Of Management at Alliant University.

Jake's road to success began at the age of 22, when he co-founded Pro-Vision Productions while enrolled at UCLA. Today, Pro-Vision is an award-winning film and video production company that has produced top-notch works for a wide variety of clients, including BMW, UCLA and The History Channel. After the sale of his interest in Pro-Vision Productions, he founded GoMiata.com in 2002, an online retailer of factory & after-market auto parts and accessories for the Mazda Miata.

GoMiata's first year revenues exceeded each of the first year revenues of both Apple Computer and Amazon.com. With Jake's visionary leadership and the efforts of a devoted team of employees, GoMiata grew into a multi-million dollar enterprise. When his passion became coaching others to success and fulfillment, he sold GoMiata to a new owner and the company continues to prosper.

In his existing practice as a Professional Life & Business Coach, Jake is able to make a tremendous and positive impact in his clients' lives. His clientele includes extraordinary people from all walks of life with the common desire to live lives of true success, happiness and fulfillment.

Jake Rubin, M.A.

ClearQuest Life & Business Coaching
9777 Wilshire Blvd. Suite 707
Beverly Hills, CA 90212
Phone: 323-799-4321
Fax: 888-783-6379
E-mail: info@clearquestcoaching.com
www.ClearQuestCoaching.com

SUCCESS IS A STATE OF MIND 9

An interview with...

Dr. Jo Anne Bishop

David Wright (Wright)

Today we're talking with Jo Anne Bishop, PhD, founder and CEO of Crossing Bridges & Associates, a coaching, consulting, and conflict mediation company located in Honolulu, Hawaii. A motivational and inspirational speaker, Certified Professional Coach, licensed psychotherapist, and certified hypnotherapist, Jo Anne reaches a national and international client base in the banking, customer service, entertainment, and real estate related industries. Her coaching clients include CEOs, entrepreneurs, senior executives, and top producers. She specializes in conflict mediation in family owned businesses, as well as all levels of the corporate setting. She has also been a consultant and trainer to state, local, and federal governments.

Her mission is to empower each client with the ability to access their unlimited potential that lies within the conscious and subconscious mind. She believes that this potential is realized through harnessing the elements of passion, intuition, and creativity aligned with clear strategic decision-making, intention to succeed, and personal accountability.

She holds graduate degrees in Counseling Psychology and Public Policy and Administration. Her organizational memberships include the International Coach Federation, International Association of Coaches, American Society of Training and Development, American Association of Psychotherapy and Medical Hypnosis, Grow Institute, and the Hawaii Speakers Network.

Dr. Bishop, welcome to *Success is a State of Mind*!

Jo Anne Bishop (Bishop)

Thank you David, it's a pleasure to be here.

Wright

How do you define success?

Bishop

Each person defines success differently based upon his or her state of consciousness, values, upbringing, personality traits, and life experiences. In my view, there is no static definition of success; but rather, one that transforms itself as we grow and change. Many research psychologists believe that the process of defining success starts very early in childhood. Based upon our early successes in life, we make decisions about our ability to make an impact and influence the world around us. These decisions program both our conscious and subconscious minds and affect our decision-making throughout life.

Most people who are successful see that each level of learning brings challenges. These challenges are a foundation for their next level of learning and accomplishment and are seen as a developmental process. For me, success is a state of being that encompasses my passion, desires, and intentions and provides me with the ability to feel satisfied that I have done my very best. The byproduct of this process is a sense of self-validation in everyday life. Success is an attitude that I choose to create and experience daily.

Wright

Based upon your experience, what are the essential components for success and happiness?

Bishop

In my experience, the essential components for success and happiness are:

1. The understanding that we are unique individuals and that we cannot be compared to anyone else in success or life itself.
2. Knowing that our definition of success will change as we change our consciousness through growth.
3. Understanding that we are multidimensional beings in a state of flux and growth concentrates our attention to our overall accomplishments. We must recognize and acknowledge our daily victories in life while at the same time holding a vision for our overall success. This will help us be more realistic in our ability to validate our life process and will lead to a sense of satisfaction within ourselves and the relationships we hold dear.
4. Detaching from judgment; learning the skill of self-reflection which is a neutral position without judgment. This is paramount in letting our lives unfold by assessing the need for change. Judgment comes from the critical mind and limits our experience

and options by constraining our thinking to the linear dimension of right and wrong or either/or.

5. Developing a compassionate view of ourselves and the world around us allows us to see success as a fluid state of consciousness. When we can acknowledge that there is no right or wrong when it comes to success, our opportunities can expand as we embrace our unlimited potential. Success can be experienced in a variety of ways.

6. We must define our own individual meaning of success in order to ultimately feel successful. A definition of success provides a structure for goal setting.

As we look at history, we find people who have played a visible role on the world stage. These people have been great contributors to the advancement of humanity on many levels. They have effectively changed the world without feeling success or satisfaction within their lives. This is seen not only in industry leaders but also in spiritual leaders. What comes to my mind is the life of Mother Theresa. She gave many gifts to the world. Through her tenacity, courage, sacrifice, vision, and dedication, she became a living role model for the world by seeking justice, mercy, and attention for India's poor. Within her insurmountable mission, she felt that God had abandoned her, which led to a lifetime of mental suffering and anguish. She was not able to validate her contributions. Her definition of success was not based on her actions but rather through feeling the indwelling Spirit of God within her. Because this feeling evaded her, she suffered self-judgment through most of her life.

Even in this dilemma and challenge, she remained devoted and committed to her passion, goals, and intentions. Happiness and peace evaded her but did not stop her.

We must validate our success in order to feel the happiness that it can bring us. Usually the concept of validation is misunderstood. It leads to an incorrect notion of boasting. We were taught as children not to talk about our successes even in the privacy of our own minds. By owning our accomplishments through validation, we add to our security base of self-knowledge. It is not ego based but fact based. Success will not bring us peace if we continue to allow the critical mind to erode our self-confidence and self-worth. Our success must be viewed through a compassionate heart. This understanding creates self-value and produces the pathway to success as a state of being.

Wright

You just said that an individual's state of mind is a vital component in reaching success. Will you explain this further?

Bishop

Success is a state of mind that makes the process as important as the outcome. This state of mind embraces obstacles as opportunities and limitations as challenges, which allows us to become more than we were before we encountered the challenge. This state of mind contains a peaceful acceptance that we did our best in obtaining a goal. Successful people who experience success as a state of mind, demonstrate what can be possible when individuals pursue their passion for passion's sake.

Many people view success through comparisons such as wealth versus spirituality or power versus spirituality. They believe it is better to be spiritually successful rather than attaining success on the material plane. However, my belief is that this creates a dissonant feeling or a state of dis-ease that can never lead to happiness. The consciousness of success and happiness comes from an internal balance that finds peace with dissonance. This internal balance creates an atmosphere of acceptance that life is not always fair. Also, we move away from the concept of perfection and replace it with an understanding of challenges. Viewing success by comparisons such as wealth versus spirituality creates a state of conflict within us that can never lead to happiness. The consciousness of success and happiness is a balance within us that finds peace in dissonance and allows us to be acceptable human beings in light of our imperfections. This state of mind accepts that we are continually growing, evolving and progressing.

Wright

What is purposeful intention and how does it provide structure for success?

Bishop

Purposeful intention is the ability to be mindful and present within the moment of our experience. When we are present in the moment, our actions can be responsive instead of reactive. Responsiveness is a choice. Being at choice requires self-understanding and self-reflection. This state of consciousness releases the limitations that are self-imposed and brings options to problem solving. Purposeful intention is the ability to consciously choose our thoughts, actions, and behaviors. It integrates our desire to choose result-oriented living. It encompasses the notion that everything has a cause and effect. We become responsible and accountable for the decisions we make and how those decisions can affect our lives in the long-term, without blaming ourselves for not doing things perfectly. We can limit ourselves through our thinking or choose to move ourselves forward through positive self-regard. This provides a structure for success by bringing together our passion, commitment, and intention with strategic planning. Strategic planning includes goal setting, action plans, affirmations, and the ability to reevaluate that which is not working. Through this process, we continue to recommit to our goals and growth as we move along the continuum of life.

When our intention is purposeful, we give our full attention to incorporating all levels of our potential into action through choice. As we consciously chose our actions, we become aware of ourselves as multidimensional beings. This allows us to activate the subconscious plane where inner wisdom resides. We allow the conscious and subconscious to merge and choose to let our intuitive skills partner in our decision-making. We can then access a flow of energy which we can harness to reach our goals. I believe the more we use purposeful intention, the more powerful it becomes in our everyday lives. It takes a daily commitment to increase the skill and the empowerment it can give us.

Wright

You talk about making room for success. What does this mean and how can this promote a successful life?

Bishop

We do need to make room for success consciously, through a willingness to eliminate and release limiting thoughts, actions, and behaviors that will keep us from growth and expansion. Although this is a simple concept, it holds within it the concept of change. Change is challenging to all human beings and creates resistance within us, even if we choose to change.

Change takes us into the unknown. It can create a reaction of fear and overwhelm that can immobilize us. Many people feel they procrastinate when they want to take action with change. In my experience, procrastination sometimes evolves from a fear of starting the change process. People have come into coaching with the goal of resolving their procrastinating behavior. If we concentrate on the procrastination we will never be able to get to the root cause, which maybe both the fear of change and the fear of initiating the process of change through a declaration of intention.

In order to make room for success, we must own our fear of change.

Once we realize that we are afraid, we can use this fear and transform it into an action plan that will move us toward our commitments and goals. You can choose success and not make room for it. We have to remove the words "failure" and "perfection" from our vocabularies if we are to make room for success. These are fear-based words that only sabotage movement. The concepts of failure and perfection are end games. They move us into an immobilized state of fear which does not consider options and limits growth.

Fear is a universally felt phenomenon that occurs within the change process. Understanding and preparing for the sense of fear that will surely come will help us to prepare a plan of action to deal with overwhelm and immobilization. Consciously choosing to face fear and move forward is the most essential step in making room for success.

Wright

Your presentations include exercises on mindful consciousness and the power of knowing. How do these add to reaching a state of mind that promotes success?

Bishop

The definition of mindfulness is conscious awareness in the moment.

Mindfulness is a Buddhist concept and one of the pathways to enlightenment and the release from suffering. I believe we can use this concept in our everyday life by understanding the importance of focusing our attention on choosing how we wish to live our lives. Mindfulness allows us, from an internal point of view, to evaluate our state of being in the moment, which includes feelings, thoughts, and body sensations. Earlier, I talked about responsiveness versus reactionary behavior. Mindfulness allows us to pause and evaluate what is going on within us and activates an intention to choose our actions carefully based upon self-awareness.

Mindfulness is developed through a meditative state which includes the skill of self-reflection. It also involves the art of allowing our breath to move freely through our bodies without constriction. Many spiritual teachings and cultures regard the breath as the essence and power that connects us to the Divine. Through meditation, we allow the rational mind to rest and create an opportunity to bring forward from the subconscious mind information that can make our lives abundant with creative solutions and options that we could have never conceived with our rational mind. This allows us to move through barriers that might have stopped us in the past. Mindfulness celebrates simplicity; it celebrates life and breath as a gift. Through mindfulness we become thankful and appreciative of all the things that we are and will be. So through mindfulness comes the power of knowing that we are one with the Universe.

Wright

In many of your seminars, you allude to a process of utilizing intention, intuition, and universal energy in concert to successfully reach goals. Will you expand on this concept?

Bishop

My work with clients provides a framework to access their subconscious mind and reprogram patterns that created resistance to change. Through taking as little as ten minutes per day of quiet time, clients can allow their rational minds to rest and access their intuitive wisdom to come forward and integrate with the conscious mind. Building a bridge between the conscious and the subconscious mind allows them to choose to be responsive in decision-making instead of reactive from fear-based living.

The more we are responsive to obstacles and challenges, the more able we are to listen to the inner wisdom that is part of our intuition. Through responsiveness we can become "at choice" and become aware of the consequences of our thoughts, actions, and behavior. Intuitive responsiveness changes our brain cells and reprograms limited thinking to expansive options in problem solving. Like every habit we develop, it will either promote us or hold us in patterns that keep us at a standstill.

Conscious choice is the integration of self-reflection, passion, desire, and commitment. When these elements become integrated, we can access a flow of energy that can be considered universal energy or a higher power that is beyond the rational mind. This flow creates a sense of well-being and connection to the greater Whole. When we are connected to the universal energy, the feeling of gratefulness and thanksgiving prevails. This thankfulness is an essential component to a balanced state of well-being.

Wright

If success is a state of mind, can this be taught to others?

Bishop

Yes, I believe success as a state of mind can be taught to others.

There are a variety of learning options such as self-development seminars or use of a mentor, coach, or therapist. We can also learn through personal experience and self-reflection. We can seek out individuals that have gained our respect and possess the qualities for which we strive.

Essential to the process is the ability to self-reflect and self-validate what we have already accomplished. Success is a state of mind in which the individual chooses success through a developmental process, which gradually increases self-esteem, self-worth, and a sense of uniqueness. Uniqueness does not separate us from humanity but rather contributes to humanity. The process is influenced through mentors, modeling, experience, education, and self-care.

Wright

You comment on the idea of the virtue of perseverance as the most challenging component of creating a successful life. What makes you believe this is true?

Bishop

David, that's a very good question. Webster defines "perseverance" as steadfastness in doing something despite the difficulty. Single-mindedness is another definition for perseverance. Earlier in our discussion, I talked about mindfulness, which I described as an ability to be in the moment and be at choice. Mindfulness can also allow us to see our limitations and find ways and options around them.

Another definition for perseverance from Webster's dictionary is a continuous state of grace leading finally to a state of glory, which is the definition that I prefer. This definition integrates the mind and body and the concept of mindfulness. In Buddhist terms, mindfulness is the ability to be fully in the moment. Fully experiencing the moment releases the rational mind and puts us in touch with the flow of energy within us. We become one with this flow and this is sometimes considered a state of grace. When you allow yourself to be in the moment, you release the rational mind to the experience of being in your body as an integrated whole. This moment of experiencing the integrated whole is the act of mindfulness. A feeling of elation is sometimes the byproduct of mindfulness. Mindfulness then is perseverance in action through conscious awareness that we are evolving mentally, emotionally, and spiritually moment by moment.

When the elements of mind and body are combined, there is more of an opportunity to access the flow of universal energy, which I previously spoke about. This flow allows seeing obstacles and challenges as vehicles for growth. When we are in the flow, there is an opportunity to stand alone without the fear of being lonely. I think this is the challenge of perseverance. When we change, we not only face the challenge but so do our peers, family, and friends. Because of their fear of losing us to this change, they may pressure us to give up our goals and dreams. Through mindfulness, we can respond to their fear with compassion.

It takes courage to stand alone. Perseverance can be taught. Through prioritizing our goals and creating an action plan perseverance can be learned in stages. These stages help us to develop a tolerance for cognitive dissonance. Cognitive dissonance occurs when we are challenged by what we want to achieve and we are blocked by obstacles. It also can occur when we experience a difference between what we want and what others want for us. Perseverance needs to be fueled by our passion, intention and desire for change. We need courage to re-evaluate and reconsider decisions that we have made that really do not work and create new decisions without blaming ourselves. It also takes recommitment to the new plan that we have designed. We may have to repeat this many times to accomplish the desired result. Another way of thinking about perseverance is that it's a living affirmation of our intention to succeed. Perseverance is a habit that can be learned through daily application.

Wright

In your view, can success be measured?

Bishop

Yes, I believe success can be measured. Success is the experience of self-validation that brings us feelings of happiness, contentment, and joy a high percentage of the time. It can also be measured quantitatively through an increase in production, profit, sales, and the accomplishment of timelines and goals. Because the definition of success varies within each individual and organization, both must have their own metrics to measure success.

Wright

What a great conversation. I've learned a lot here today and I have you to thank for that. I really do appreciate all this time you've taken to answer all these questions.

Bishop

Thank you David, it's really been a pleasure to be here and speak with you.

Wright

Today we've been talking with Jo Anne Bishop, PhD. Jo Anne is a motivational and inspirational speaker. She's also a certified professional coach, a licensed psychotherapist, and a certified hypnotherapist. Her mission is to empower each of her clients with the ability to access their unlimited potential that she believes lies within the conscious and subconscious mind. She also believes that this potential is realized through the elements of passion, intuition, and creativity aligned with clear, strategic decision-making, intention to succeed, and personal accountability.

JoAnne, thank you so much for being with us today on *Success is a State of Mind*!

Bishop

Thank you, David.

ABOUT THE AUTHOR

Dr. Jo Anne Bishop is founder and CEO of Crossing Bridges & Associates. She is a Certified Professional Coach with a national and international client base. A top performer and leader in her field, she brings twenty years of expertise to coaching, communications, organizational psychology, and training development. She completed a highly successful psychotherapy and consulting practice in Beverly Hills and Long Beach, California, to create Crossing Bridges and Associates. A gifted speaker, presenter, and coach, she has developed dynamic, experientially based programs that propel clients to the leading edge in the competitive marketplace. Her programs integrate goal-setting, strategic decision-making, and accountability with the power of the intuitive/creative mind. Her credentials include graduate degrees in Counseling Psychology, Public Policy, and Administration. She holds certifications in education and clinical hypnotherapy. Dr. Bishop's professional memberships include: The American Association of Family Therapists, the American Association of Psychotherapy and Medical Hypnosis, the International Coach Federation, International Coach Association, American Society of Training and Development, the International Speakers Bureau, and the Hawaii Speakers Network. She and her husband reside in the beautiful Hawaiian Islands.

Jo Anne Bishop, PhD, MPA
Crossing Bridges and Associates
6800 Kalanianaole Highway, #126
Honolulu, Hawaii 96825
562. 760.3009 or 808.772.0266
crossingbridges@hawaii.rr.com
www.execandbusinesscoaching.com

An interview with…

Jean DiGiovanna

David Wright (Wright)

Today we're talking with Jean DiGiovanna, a personal and executive coach, speaker, and trainer, specializing in authentic leadership, effective teamwork, and professional and personal growth. She has a unique gift for shifting people's perspective of what's possible, empowering them to break through their greatest challenges to achieve what matters most. She is the Founder of ThinkPeople®, a coaching and consulting firm committed to making a difference in the way individuals and organizations think, work, and communicate. She coaches executives and their teams to achieve their highest potential and delivers comprehensive training courses in communication, coaching skills, and leadership to Fortune 500 Companies, small businesses, and start-ups. She has spoken both nationally and internationally on life and business strategies and her work has been described as "life-changing." She was recently named one of the Top Ten Coaches of Boston by *Women's Business Boston*. Her energy is contagious and her open, curious, and lightheartedness enables others to experience feeling fully alive.

Jean, welcome to *Success is a State of Mind*!

Jean DiGiovanna (DiGiovanna)

Thank you.

Wright

So what is your definition of success?

DiGiovanna

I've come to realize that my definition of success has changed over time. Years ago, I thought of success as achievement, getting to the top, having a certain financial status, and acquiring things that make me happy. While all of those are important, success is more than that. To me, success is about making a difference in the world; it's about uncovering my gifts and talents, and bringing them out into the world where the world most needs them. It's about making a difference in the work I do, the relationships I develop, and the communities I am a part of.

In years past, there were times when I was more concerned about myself, what's in it for me, sometimes at the expense of others. But, my definition of success began to shift as I started to recognize that there's enough for everyone. Abundance is all around us, and when I utilize my natural gifts to serve the world, anything is truly possible.

When I have the opportunity to impact another, such that their life or work is happier, that is when I know I've succeeded. Success goes beyond acquiring things and constantly being in a state of doing,

doing, and doing, to acquire more. It truly comes from who I am first, and then what I do.

So, to me, success is a way of being, it is a state of mind. Success is about being of service to others and then allowing life to unfold trusting it will all work out. It's about staying calm in the eye of the storm and moving forward in the face of fear, challenge, and the unknown.

As human beings we so crave predictability, yet wonder why life is not so juicy or exciting. It's really in the *not* knowing that you experience the riches of life. If you have every minute of every day planned out, where's the spark? It is in the unfilled spaces in our calendar that life most surprises us. Success is about being with the unknown and trusting and allowing miracles to happen, all the while keeping your intention of making a difference at the forefront.

Wright

What do you think is the biggest misconception about success?

DiGiovanna

I think the biggest misconception is that success is a place to get to. So often we say, "When I'm successful, then I'll be happy" or "When I get that promotion, then I'll be successful and that will make me happy." Until then, we live in a constant state of pursuing, achieving, and going after success. Why do we have to wait until we achieve or acquire things for us to believe we are successful?

What if success were not a place to get to; but instead, a state of mind or a way of being? What if success were possible in any moment? In other words I could choose success right now if I wanted. Success is possible in every moment if we shift our perspective on how we view it. How we relate to it makes all the difference in the world. It is our relationship to success that dictates how we achieve it, feel about it, and use it. If we relate to it as something in the future, we will be in a constant race to reach it, but if we relate to it as possible in any moment, so much more is available to us.

As Dr. Wayne Dyer, an inspiration of mine, so eloquently says, "Change the way you look at things and the things you look at change." Change the way you look at success, and begin to notice how success shows up for you. If we constantly believe that success is only attained by acquiring and achieving things in order to be happy, then we are actually depriving ourselves of happiness right now.

Wright

So, if success is a state of mind and available at any time, how would I tap into it?

DiGiovanna

Taking on the perspective that success is a state of mind or a way of being in the moment, the first step to recognizing it is to become aware of your state of mind in that moment. For example, if you're at work and beginning a conversation with your boss, are you going in frustrated, angry, open, or curious? Your attitude or state of being prior to that conversation will dictate how the conversation goes. First, become aware of your attitude in that moment. Awareness then creates choice. You now have a choice, prior to talking to your boss, about who you will be—your attitude. Choose a state of being that will forward the conversation and help you achieve what you want.

A great question to practice asking yourself is, "Who would I need to be to have what I want?" Then, determine that way of being that is most empowering and practice that prior to taking action. Going into a conversation with your boss being open and curious will reap a much different outcome than going in frustrated.

Change begins with you, and in the end you are ultimately the only person you have control over. Become more aware of your state of being prior to taking action and you will begin to shift your thinking in the moment. Over time it will become natural to you, but it does take some time. Raising awareness and shifting your thoughts is like building a muscle—it takes patience to strengthen it. In the beginning you may be out of shape and forget, but as my coach once told me, "It's not about how often you forget. It's how quickly you remember in every moment."

Wright

So, once you achieve success, how do you keep your momentum going and sustain it?

DiGiovanna

I get that question often from my clients. Success as a state of being like joy or happiness exists on a spectrum, and as humans we experience all parts of the spectrum. We can experience deep sadness to extreme happiness, deep failure to extreme success. I'm not saying it's not possible to be happy all the time or feel success all the time, but that extreme happiness and success can only be defined by the wide range of emotions we're able to experience. So, the wider the range of emotions or states of mind we can feel, the more alive we become.

Sustaining a state of success requires rigor in our way of thinking in every single moment. It requires recognizing our successes in the moment and appreciating what we have in the present, how far we've come, and what's good in our lives and in ourselves. The more we can appreciate the present, the more we're able to attract success and abundance in our lives.

Like the concept of a gratitude journal, I encourage my clients to keep what I call a "success" journal. In it you can track all the ways you were successful that day or enabled another to become successful, from the smallest action to the largest achievement. So, when you're having a bad day, you can open up your success journal and reconnect with the good in your life.

I encourage everyone to start a success journal. Sustaining success may also require reinventing ourselves. What fulfills us may shift over time and that may require us to take a hard look at what we are doing and who we are becoming in the world. It's not uncommon for any given individual to hold six or seven different careers in their lifetime. In addition, circumstances and relationships change in our life, causing shifts in how we feel.

What I ask individuals to do is become aware of what I call their "alive-o-meter"—how alive and energetic they feel. Your level of aliveness directly correlates to your fulfillment in life. If you feel your energy being drained or your level of aliveness start to waiver, take a look at who or what is working or no longer working in your life and begin to make changes that will free up more of your energy.

Sustaining success also requires learning from our failures. Ask any individual what their biggest lesson learned was, and nine out ten people will recall a lesson they learned when they did not succeed or achieve what they set out to. It is through our missed attempts, our risk taking, or stepping out of our comfort zone, that we are truly able to reap life's riches to be successful. It's about experiencing and appreciating the lessons that may come from our not-so-rewarding moments. Most of all, it's important to recognize that we may not always be able to sustain success in every moment, but that we have the tools available to us to remind us to reconnect with our success.

Wright

So, how can you still be successful even when you feel things are crumbling around you?

DiGiovanna

The biggest thing I've learned, when things don't go my way or it feels like things are crumbling around me, is to stop resisting. I can't say I'm an expert at it, and I don't always recognize it right away, but I can say, when I do recognize I'm resisting, inevitably it loses its power and no longer has a strong hold on me.

When things feel like they're crumbling around you, and you find yourself fighting it and resisting it, stop and acknowledge the resistance. Remind yourself that you're human and it's okay to resist. Feel what you feel and get it out in whatever way works for you. It's so important to release anger, frustration, regret, or whatever feelings come up, because when you don't, it will eventually show up in your bodies as dis-ease. Releasing it will also enable you to move through it faster.

Another powerful technique is to begin to get curious about the resistance without judgment. Allow yourself to wonder what the frustration might be helping you to learn. As soon as you relate to it differently, things will begin to shift around the issue. When two forces are pushing against each other and one suddenly backs away, what happens to the other? It doesn't actually back away, it falls forward. So, when you're challenged, ease up on the resistance and watch it begin to fall forward so you can move through it.

One of the other things that helps me through is to remind myself that this too shall pass. So often, when we are in the eye of the storm, it feels like there's no hope; but it is the remembering and trusting that it will all work out that keeps us going. It is then that we grow more rapidly, we become stronger, and we peel back another layer and leave it behind, feeling lighter and freer. In those times, I remind myself that one day I will look back at this and know what place it had in my life.

Wright

How did you come to realize this definition of success?

DiGiovanna

I'd like to say it was an easy and fast road, but it took some time and some bumps along the way. Since I was young, I've always had a strong desire to exceed and stand out, so I became good at many things. I noticed, though, once I mastered something, I would get bored and move on to the next thing. I came to discover that it was actually the journey that I loved, and once I achieved the goal, it was not fun anymore. What I also noticed was, no matter how many skills I mastered, I was never ultimately fulfilled. I had moments of excitement and joy for the achievement, but they quickly vanished.

When I became burnt out as a management consultant in the corporate world, I hired a coach to help me discover my life's purpose. As many endeavors into growth and change, I got a lot more out of it than I ever imagined. Through the combination of intense growth and development courses and working with my coach, I began my internal work. I began to peel away the layers and truly reveal my genuine self and practice fully accepting the good, the bad, and the ugly. I began to understand what made me tick, what patterns I was repeating, and what ultimately was empowering and disempowering in my life.

Over time, I began to recognize and appreciate my gifts and talents and stand in my personal power in such a way that no matter what happened around me, it didn't tip me over. No matter who told me what I should do or be, I had an inner compass that was stronger than anyone else's outer compass. I was able to stay open to others' opinions, determine what fits for me, and disregard the rest. I began to uncover the person I truly am and enjoy all of me.

So often, many of us walk around hating aspects of ourselves, and those are the very same aspects we often dislike in others. What we dislike or resist persists, so what I've learned to do is recognize all the aspects of who I am and who I am not, and accept that I may resist some elements, and that's okay too. (Some of us are so hard on ourselves, more so than we would ever dare to be on others.)

With the help of mentors and coaches throughout my life, I'm happy to have discovered my life's purpose and utilize my gifts and talents to make a profound difference in individuals and organizations. And I love what I do, so when I experienced the impact that had on me and how rewarding it was, I began to realize that success is not about what I have or what I do—it's about who I am in the world.

While I'd like to say I'm done with my growth and development, the journey continues. Having a commitment to continued growth requires discipline and patience. Seeking support from others is extremely critical. People are surprised that as a coach myself, I continue to have my own coach. It's no different than professional athletes who have one or more coaches. A coach is like a mirror that helps you to see what is working, what's not working, and helps you discover the answers within yourself. I coach extremely successful people who want even more out of their lives, and what enables their change—like my own—is a commitment to grow and be open and willing to change.

Wright

So, are you ready for the million-dollar question: is it truly possible to have it all?

DiGiovanna

I've always believed that happiness and success is all about perspective. We have the incredible ability to shift our perspective in every moment, if we choose. Happiness and success is a choice. We can choose to have it all or not.

Sadly, many of us don't believe we deserve to have it all, so these feelings of being undeserving will halt our ability to attract all that we want in our life. Sometimes it's difficult for us to imagine a life where we could have it all, so either consciously or unconsciously we push the possibility away.

Having it all requires first a shift in our thinking and beliefs, and second, it requires a shift in our ability to imagine it is possible for us. Lastly—and this is the most challenging stage—is to *allow* it to come to us. It is often in this last stage of allowing that we fall short. We can set very clear intentions of all that we want, and we may even begin to visualize and imagine it coming to us. Then, as time passes if we don't get it all, we start to get impatient. We forget that it may not all come to us at the time we want it to, so we stop allowing the process to take its course, halting our ability to manifest it.

Unfortunately, we don't always have control over when things come to us. We may think we do, but that is an illusion. Allowing all that we want to come into our life requires a deep level of trust and letting go, and that can often feel like losing control. But, if control is really an illusion, in reality we're not actually losing anything at all. Allowing also requires having patience and faith that all will come in due time. These are traits that don't always come easy, but with practice and persistence, it absolutely is possible to have all that you want in your life.

Wright

You mentioned earlier that part of what success means to you is making a difference, so what can our readers do to help make a difference at work and at home?

DiGiovanna

In the last decade, there has been such a decline in human connection, in business, in our communities, in our faiths, and in our families. Yet, we're considered more global and technologically able to connect to anyone, anywhere, in an instant. The current generation is texting instead of talking, and calling or e-mailing each other while sitting in the next cubicle over. We've become so isolated that the desire to help one another and reach out has diminished. Then, when we disagree, we avoid each other or we resort to arguing.

When I work with organizations to help create a learning environment, I ask them to take on a new perspective, and that new perspective is, "How can I make you successful?"

In other words, for each employee, I ask him or her to come from the perspective, "How can I make my boss successful, my direct reports successful, or my peers successful?" And then, listen for the answer and follow through with it. Taking on that question shifts the way you think, work, and communicate at work.

Can you imagine what your office environment would be like if everyone were genuinely wanting everyone else to succeed? Can you imagine what businesses and organizations would be able to achieve?

At home, take on the same perspective, "How can I make my spouse or significant other successful, my child, my mother, my father, sibling? How can I make my neighbor or my community successful?" When you take on that perspective, you step out of your shoes and instantly the attention is directed outside of yourself and on someone else. If we all did that, everyone and everything would be taken care of.

That is how you can make a difference. Just ask one simple question, "How can I make you successful?" Do this every morning before you go to work and every evening you come home to your family and see what shifts in your life.

Wright

So, in closing, what have been your greatest lessons for success that you would share with our readers?

DiGiovanna

There are many lessons learned that I'm happy to share in hopes that even one will make a difference in your life. I call them *The 17 Lessons Learned* and I will share them here:

Lesson 1: Don't pretend to be someone else because in the end, your self will always catch up with you.

Lesson 2: You have to move through the tough times, not over them, otherwise they just come back in other forms.

Lesson 3: Don't jump to conclusions. You never really know where the other person is coming from or what he or she is thinking unless you ask.

Lesson 4: Remember, others are just as scared as you are. After all, we all come from the same core of being human.

Lesson 5: Patience is not only a virtue—it is a necessity in life.

Lesson 6: Go beyond yourself, your things, and your world because there is so much more to experience. You are not your home, you are not your car, and you are not the income you generate.

Lesson 7: Life is too short to feel drained. Do what lights you up and surround yourself with people who support and energize you.

Lesson 8: When you're at a crossroad choosing between options, instead of asking what you most want, for each option ask yourself, "If I didn't take this option, could I still do it at a future time?" Making your choice will inevitably feel more effortless.

Lesson 9: Take the time to discover work you enjoy. It truly is possible to have fun every day in what you do. You deserve to do what you love.

Lesson 10: If you don't know where you're going, any road will not take you there. Set clear intentions, a vision for what you want your life to look like, feel like, and be like. Visualize that intention coming true until you feel it in your bones—as if you've already achieved it. If you're not sure of what you want, set an intention to get clearer. Just set intentions.

Lesson 11: When you've been stuck in the same issue or challenge, it usually means you have to either let something go or fully accept something. Look to see what there is to let go of or fully accept. Tell the truth about it and it will inevitably help you move through it.

Lesson 12: Choose your friends and business partners carefully.

Lesson 13: When you feel stuck, go outside, take a walk, get fresh air, and be in nature. Your mind will clear and you will feel more alive.

Lesson 14: Put your body and your health first, no matter what. You only have one body and without that body, you really can't do or enjoy anything you have or will achieve. So, care for it as you would for a prize possession.

Lesson 15: Don't go it alone. Life is about connection, not separateness. Seek support from friends, mentors, and loved ones. Provide support as well.

Lesson 16: When you find yourself thinking too much, or too inwardly focused, simply ask the question, "How can I serve?" It will always take you outside yourself to a place bigger than you. Life will begin to flow again.

And last but not least, *Lesson 17:* Most of all have fun, laugh, and see the humor and joy in everyday life. Life is a journey, not a destination, so have a blast on your trip!

Wright

Well, what a great conversation. It was worth talking to you just to get your seventeen lessons. I really do appreciate the time you've taken to talk with me today and answering all these questions. I really learned a lot, I'm thinking about a lot more and I appreciate your starting that process.

DiGiovanna

It was my pleasure.

Wright

Today we've have been speaking with Jean DiGiovanna. She is a personal and executive coach, speaker, and trainer. She coaches executives and their teams to achieve their highest potential by delivering comprehensive training courses on communication, coaching skills, and leadership. As we have found out today, she is a personal coach who works with individuals helping them pinpoint their deepest desires and achieve accomplishments beyond what they thought was actually possible.

Jean, thank you so much for being with us today on *Success is a State of Mind.*

DiGiovanna

You're very welcome.

ABOUT THE AUTHOR

Jean M. DiGiovanna is President and Founder of ThinkPeople®, a Consulting and Coaching firm specializing in authentic leadership, effective teamwork, and professional and personal growth. Jean is a Certified Professional Coach, speaker, facilitator, and trainer with over seventeen years of experience. She delivers workshops, seminars, and training courses in the areas of communication, coaching, and leadership to Fortune 500 companies, non-profits, and academia. Jean has a unique gift for shifting people's perspective of what's possible, empowering them to break through their greatest challenges to achieve what matters most.

As an executive coach, team specialist, and facilitator, Jean guides executives and their teams to achieve professional excellence transforming challenges into immediate bottom line results. After working with Jean, leaders and their teams experience renewed trust, more open communication, and increased effectiveness. As a personal coach, Jean works with individuals from the inside out helping them pinpoint their deepest desires and accomplish beyond what they thought was possible. Jean launched Workshop University, a division of ThinkPeople, to help Entrepreneurs package their expertise into workshops and seminars enabling them to reach a larger audience and get their message out. She has spoken both nationally and internationally on life and business strategies, and her work has been described as life changing. Jean is a member of the National Speakers Association (NSA), a member of the International Coaches Federation (ICF), and was recently named one of the top ten coaches of Boston by *Women's Business Boston*.

Jean M. DiGiovanna

ThinkPeople®

P.O. Box 79112

Belmont, MA 02479

Phone: 617.489.7494

E-mail: jdigi@thinkpeople.com

www.thinkpeople.com

www.workshopuniversity.com

SUCCESS IS A STATE OF MIND 11

An interview with…
Judy Ellison

David Wright (Wright)

Today we're talking with Dr. Judy Ellison. She is a psychologist, research scientist, success coach, published author, and motivational speaker. She is the inventor of AlphaKardia™ a life transformation system that combines leading edge heart and brain science and spirituality. This system is designed to make effective changes in physical, spiritual, and emotional well-being in order to live a more relaxed and happier life.

Dr. Ellison is the director of research at Sequel Institute, Inc., overseeing leading edge brain and heart research for the purpose of contributing to the development of spiritual scientific processes of change. In addition, merging her experience from twenty-five years of personal counseling and success coaching along with her education, Dr. Ellison is passionate to lead individuals into personal growth and life transformation. Applied with wisdom, intuition, and decisive clarity, she guides individuals through programs that provide proven results and inspires audiences around the world in her keynote presentations.

Dr. Ellison, welcome to *Success is a State of Mind.* May I call you Judy?

Judy Ellison (Ellison)

Thank you, David. I would love to have you call me Judy. I have been Judy for a lot longer than Dr. Ellison so I am very comfortable with it and pleased that you asked.

Wright

Judy, from your years of experience as a therapist, research scientist in human behavior, and in more recent years as a success coach, do you truly think that success is a state of mind?

Ellison

I'll jump right into that question by sharing a story. Recently I was having a conversation with a new client who was describing how he continually lived with a knot in the pit of his stomach as he fought and struggled to fulfill his life goals. In the course of the conversation he described that a few years earlier he had experienced an *"a-ha! moment"* when he ran across an interview article with Dan Rather in *Esquire* magazine. That article made a tremendous impact on his state of mind, creating dramatic changes in his business and personal life. Rather was quoted as saying: "It comes down to TR: time remaining. When you're in your thirties or forties or even your fifties, time remaining can seem like infinity. TR hits different people at different stages. But you get to your seventies and you're thinking about TR. Exactly how do I want to spend my remaining days?"

My client was in his early fifties and resonated so deeply with this article by Rather and its question about how you would want to spend your remaining days that he quit his job, got a divorce, and committed the rest of his life to pursuing the success he had always hoped he would achieve. He had been living with the tyranny of the urgent for many years to become a success in his chosen field, but now with this new thought of TR he went into complete overdrive to make it happen. The thought of *time remaining* had him running scared.

Given that it had been a few years since my client had read that article, I asked him if he felt that he was any closer to achieving the success he thought he would accomplish after making all of the changes in his life. He went silent for a moment and then quietly answered, "No."

I went away from this conversation thinking about it for some time, wondering what held my client back. He was tremendously talented, so talent wasn't enough. He desperately wanted to achieve success, but desperately wanting success obviously wasn't enough either.

Then I had *my own a-ha! moment.* I had inadvertently answered my own question. He *desperately wanted* success! He was panic-stricken and was actually driving away the success he so desperately wanted. His state of mind was paralyzed by fear. Whatever is not of faith is fear. Desperation is a success repellant! My client was actually repelling success from coming to him. And by the way, panic is a very unhealthy state of mind, for your physical health and well-being, as well.

There is an old saying that rings true on this subject, *"Fear knocked at the door. Faith answered. No one was there."* That's about as simple as it gets. If we apply our faith and trust to a situation, more often than not we find out there is nothing to fear but fear itself.

Wright

So you are saying then that the state of his mind was hindering his success, even though he had tremendous talent and he really desired to be successful?

Ellison

Absolutely! He is just like so many other people who are making a mad dash for success, desperately trying to accomplish their goals. Their desperation pushes success further away. This desperation creates something like mental madness as the ego drives them harder and harder out of fear—fear of not succeeding! The ego is needy! The immature ego has a need to accumulate material things and chalk up accomplishments in order to feel successful. If we don't see this mental tally board filling up the way we have planned, then panic sets in and the desperate clawing to make something happen overtakes our sanity and our peace of mind. As time passes and we realize we are getting older, there is an increasing desperate drive within that tells us that the time remaining is quickly slipping away and if we are going to make it to the finish line with enough stuff and accomplishments, we are going to have to sacrifice the joy and peace of the journey to make it happen. Wrong! It just isn't so.

As most people know, the ego is not our True Self but is the earliest stage of our developing personality. We come into the world self-focused. The attention of our mother or primary caregiver is on our individual needs and making sure those needs are met. We are fed, burped, diapered, and changed by others. Someone is always watching out for our needs. It's all about us! Through maturation and growth we are able to develop our ego from self-absorption into an awareness of our higher purpose and an expanded world-view. This maturation process happens when the ego and the True Self merge into a unified field through a conscious connection to the Spirit within.

So, the concept of TR for the underdeveloped ego is like living with a noose around your neck. If you let go for a moment you are afraid that you will hang yourself by failing to accomplish the goals you set out to accomplish in life. But that feeling is out of the immature ego's competitive pressure to perform. It is a fear-driven competitive aspect of our personality and not the consciously connected spirit of the heart. It is a little like a rat running on a wheel in a cage, never reaching a final destination, always running faster and faster trying to keep up, but never really getting anywhere. Gandhi said, *"There is more to life than increasing its speed."* The rat race for success is never satisfying for more than just a moment, then it is on to the next desperate attempt at finding happiness in other things and with other people.

Henry David Thoreau wrote, *"The mass of men lead lives of quiet desperation."* This driving desperation pushes us to achieve, succeed, acquire, and to be loved by someone, but still leaves us dissatisfied because there is always something bigger and better than what we have already. Driven by the ego, this person finds him or herself constantly tiring of all accomplishments and acquisitions. The treadmill never stops. These goals are all fine and good to have, but the ego will never be satisfied because it is focused on externals.

I believe success isn't just about amassing things in life (although I like fine things) or just having a meaningful relationship (something I find very important as well). Success is a by-product of fulfilling the purposes for which we were born. It is consciously connecting to the internal power within us that removes the pressure of performance and allows us to fulfill our highest purposes and calling in the most relaxed way. True success is the fulfillment of our passionate purposes and the added benefits of wealth in body, health, relationships, finances, and spirituality.

Wright

You speak about purposes for our lives. Do you think there is a specific purpose for each individual that we are here on earth to fulfill?

Ellison

I believe that each person is put on this earth for a reason. I believe everyone is special. I know that the topic of our discussion is about success but it is about a lot more. It's about purpose and calling and the power to fulfill our calling successfully. Each one of us is created for a purpose.

Look around you and see the various objects in the room where you are sitting right now. Can you find one thing that does not have a purpose? The chair or sofa you are sitting on holds you at a certain level, in relative comfort, and removes the strain from your legs and feet. The book you are reading at this moment contains information that you can accept or reject. Perhaps you are drinking a beverage while you are reading. The cup or glass was created for the purpose of containing a small amount of beverage. There is a purpose for everything under the sun.

You are no different. I don't think there is a singular purpose. When you were created there were distinct purposes for which you were born. You are a divine spark—an ember of God waiting to ignite into passionate purposes that wake you up early in the morning and won't let you go to sleep at night. No one else can fulfill them because there is no one just like you. You are the only *you* that will ever be. It is important to know why you are on earth! Your success and wealth will come spontaneously out of your intense passion and desire to fulfill these life purposes. Do what you love and the money and success will follow.

After studying the lives of the wealthy for twenty years, Napoleon Hill wrote in his book, *Think and Grow Rich*, "Desire is the starting point of all achievement." I am not so sure that desire is the starting point at all. As I see it, you have to know the purposes of your life in order to develop the desire to fulfill them.

It's not difficult to get in touch with your inner purpose because you have always known that there is purpose within you—purposes essential to who you are. As you give thought and attention to your purposes, desire grows into a powerful source of energy to make these purposes come alive. Purpose precedes passion.

There is a children's song that describes what I am suggesting about relaxing into your success: "Row, Row, Row your boat gently down the stream." If you push up-stream against the current you are going to struggle and strain without making much progress. That is not to say that you will not make some progress but you will do it with a lot of blood, sweat, and tears. The underdeveloped ego thinks it has to drive you into working harder at what you are doing in order to be successful. When you relax into the flow of the river or stream of life you will make significant progress floating down river. Although, there is a catch—you can't float willy-nilly down stream without giving the boat direction. Direction comes from the oars. Without direction you might find yourself upside down from crashing into the rocks. Direction in fulfilling your life purposes and calling comes from within, out of the conscious connection to the life-stream of your heart. By listening to the intuitive guidance within, you will be directed into overflowing success and fulfillment.

In every religious tradition there is reference made to a source of all there is. This source may be called, God, Spirit, Allah, or Jehovah. Every great teacher, sage, and scientist will agree that this source is energy and that it is the basic component of every physical entity in existence. We are not the physical being that we appear to be, but an eternal energy called Spirit. You are a spiritual being having a physical experience. As I've already stated, your ego is not the true you, it is just a personality made up of experiences and memory. Let your Spirit guide you; don't let the ego drive you.

Living from the heart and spirit allows you to live knowing there is enough time remaining to do all that you want to do, be all you want to be, have all you want to have, and enjoy love, peace, and happiness along the journey. When you look inside and realize the power that is resident within, all things become possible. Life becomes a game to be played with joy using all the tools the creator placed inside of you in order for you to fulfill your purposes with passion.

Wright

Could this approach to success be considered an attitude adjustment?

Ellison

When we connect to the heart and remember the purposes for which we came to this earth, we can relax into our success. There will be more than enough passion and desire to fuel the purposes and bring them into existence. By finding our purposes we can move into them with a relaxed state of mind. This is definitely an attitude adjustment for most people. It takes all the strain and pressure off when we realize that the *time remaining is enough time* to fulfill our life's purposes successfully.

It is important not to be discouraged by setbacks. It is said that all setbacks are really setups for something better. All things are done in divine order. Just keep your attitude positive, your faith unwavering, do all that you can do, and then relax, knowing that everything will work out with order and ease in the right time. The competitive mind of the ego can't relax. It has to fight and strain and try to force something to happen. The consciously connected mind follows the intuitive information flow and does not panic. It is composed, at peace, and at rest, knowing that success in business, health, wealth, and relationships is already determined and is just a matter of time before it happens.

Wright

Judy, I notice that you talk a lot about the heart—living from the heart and consciously connecting to the heart. How did you get interested in the role that the heart plays in our lives?

Ellison

Early in my life, I began noticing as I read the Bible that there were many scriptures that made mention of the heart. "The heart of the wise instructs his mouth" (Proverbs 16:23), and "out of the abundance of the heart the mouth speaks" (Luke 6:45). This intelligence of the heart fascinated me. I spent over a decade studying the heart and its role in personal empowerment and self-development and came to the conclusion that the heart was the intelligent seat of the soul.

When I went to graduate school I wanted in some way to study the heart's intelligent role in our lives. I began my studies by looking at cellular memory of the heart and found riveting true stories during my research. There were cases where heart transplant recipients would experience a total lifestyle change after receiving a new heart. Claire Sylvia's book, *A Change of Heart,* came out describing her experiences after undergoing a heart and lung transplant. Soon after the transplant, Claire noticed that her attitudes, habits, and tastes changed. She suddenly had an urge to eat chicken nuggets from Kentucky Fried

Chicken for no apparent reason. This was highly unlike her as she had always eaten healthy food and didn't like fast food. She later learned that the donor of her new heart, an eighteen-year-old young man, had literally lived on chicken nuggets. These and other stories were of great interest to me.

However, after reading so many wonderful stories about these fascinating individuals, when it came time to write my dissertation, I couldn't find enough empirical studies to validate the hypothesis that cellular memory could outlive physical death. Cellular memory was an embryonic field of study at that time. So, eventually I turned my attention to the research studies being conducted on treatment modalities that used a heart-focused meditation practice to facilitate change. I had been using a heart-focused relaxation system that I had created with my clients for many years.

What spiritual traditions have taught down through the centuries, science has recently corroborated through rigorous scientific studies. Within each individual, there beats both a physical heart—a biological pump that circulates blood throughout the body—and a metaphorical heart allegedly considered to be the seat of emotions. For centuries, philosophers, writers, and poets, have referred to the metaphorical heart as a source of "self-realization" and divine inspiration. I would like to take it one step further and state that the heart is the power plant that connects us to the source of all that is, all that was, and with all that is to come. It's the intelligence that directs my intuition and guides me continually when I am tuned into the flow of divine information.

Let's consider some of the facts that we know about the heart. Statistics show us that in America the heart generally functions for seventy or eighty years without maintenance or replacement. (Of course, your genetics help to make this statement accurate.) During this time, the heart beats approximately one hundred thousand times a day—roughly forty million times a year, and almost three billion beats in a lifetime. The heart pumps two gallons of blood per minute, adding up to more than a hundred gallons in an hour. Wow! Now this is where it gets even more interesting. *This blood is moving through a vascular system that is long enough to wrap around the earth two and one-half times—over sixty thousand miles—and it is all inside of you.* Isn't that amazing? It doesn't stop there. The heart is like a nuclear power plant. It generates five thousand times more electromagnetic energy than the brain, and that powerful organ sits inside each and every one of us sending out magnetic frequencies attracting like energies back to us.

I discovered something mind-boggling in my research that explains why we should live from the guidance of our heart. The heart has a mind of its own and it is not taking direction from the cognitive brain! On the twenty-first day of life after conception, even before a woman knows she is pregnant, the embryonic heart has formed and has started to beat. Inside the heart, the sinoatrial node—a tiny mass of cells—comes to life and starts beating, activated by a non-local energy we cannot as yet measure. The brain doesn't tell the heart to start beating. It isn't even formed as yet. And by the way, at the end of life it doesn't tell the heart to stop beating. It is believed that the intelligence of the heart lives outside of the body but flows into the body through the energy system of the heart. You can be brain-dead but the heart will keep on beating with life force. This conscious connection to the universal intelligence allows us to live intuitively guided to our highest and fullest potential and purpose through this flow of energy and information.

Dr. Jonas Salk (1984) wrote in *The Anatomy of Reality: The Merging of Intuition and Reason* that when intuition and reason come together to become a system, what emerges is greater than either alone. When the brain, as a machine of cognitive events, and the heart as a mere pump, relax into an alpha state of entrainment they form a new relationship for which science still lacks an adequate language (Ellison, 2005). When heart and brain frequencies entrain, they enter a synchronous, resonate, or coherent wave pattern. It is a frequency of creative conception. The miracle of creation takes place in this joining scientifically and spiritually. It may be said from a transpersonal point of view that the mere pumping heart is transformed into an instrument of higher consciousness (Taylor, 1999). The intelligence and dynamic energy of the heart moves matter out of the immaterial world and congeals it into physical manifestation. Years ago, Karl Pribram, a neuroscientist, proposed that the brain draws its materials for constructing our world experience from a "frequency realm that is not in time space" (1991). Imagine this heart frequency as a conveyance of information just like a radio band such as 1500 or 1620 on the AM dial that can convey a great deal of immeasurable information when the right connection is made.

Wright

That is some very interesting material about the heart. I know that you started Sequel Institute out of your years of research. What was the purpose of starting the institute?

Ellison

In 2002, I took the research that I had accumulated and started Sequel Institute, Inc. The purpose of this research was to evaluate through empirical measures (scientifically) the descriptive claims of individuals participating in the heart-focused relaxation program that I developed and was using in my private practice. This in and of itself is a story that I would love to share with our readers. This will illustrate how the power of intentional connection to the heart during alpha state relaxation can create in the immaterial world those things desired to manifest in the material. I literally relaxed into my success. Here's how it happened.

I made a clear intention that I would be fully funded to conduct empirical research on the AlphaKardia System when it was time for it to birth and come to life. I held that intention in my mind and heart for many years. I was incubating the idea! I used this process twice every day to relax and connect to my heart. I knew intuitively that the research was a key aspect of the purposes of my life. This desire was like a fire inside of me. I had passionate purpose that woke me up early in the morning and kept me up at night. Creative energy flowed as my purpose carried me in the path of its flow and fulfillment.

During the time I was making my intention for full funding of my research, I was barely making ends meet, living from paycheck to paycheck. The money to do research wasn't going to come from my bank account. However, one day, after five long years of making my intention, I got a call from a gentleman. He invited me into his office and we began to discuss the purposes of my life and the desire that I had to do research on AlphaKardia. He became so excited about seeing me fulfill my destiny that he made a commitment to provide start-up capital for Sequel Institute. He was not aware of my intention! He did not know that I had stayed plugged into the power of my intelligent heart every day for five years! But here he was offering to seed the money to get the research project going.

It was time for my passionate purpose to give birth. That was an exciting day for me as I left with enough funds to rent an office, hire employees, and get the research study started. I didn't have any clue on where to begin looking for an office so I made my intention for the perfect office to come to me, and then let go. I stayed consciously connected to the guidance from my heart's energy field.

I received an e-mail blast from a woman I didn't even know who needed to sublease her office. The moment I saw the e-mail I intuitively knew that this was my office. Sight unseen, I agreed to lease the space. When I met with the leasing agent at the office to sign the lease agreement, I found out the office was absolutely perfect— exactly what I needed.

Success flows from a relaxed state of mind and everything falls in place when you follow your passion and purpose. Over the next three years, I received over a half million dollars to fund the research on AlphaKardia. We moved three times in the same office complex due to outgrowing our space as word spread about our exciting research project. It was before the book, *The Secret,* had been published but was based on the power of intention and the law of attraction, and people were magnetically drawn to the positive energy in our program,

Thankfully, the results from the three-year study conclusively corroborated the effectiveness of the AlphaKardia System in making significant transformative changes in people's lives (Ellison, 2005). When we started I was somewhat reticent in doing scientific research on AlphaKardia. What if the descriptive claims of my clients couldn't be validated by empirical measures? I had a team of collaborators working with me from major universities around the country who would tease me and say that maybe the success I was having with my clients was coming from something as simple as the perfume I was wearing when I worked with the research participants and it wouldn't have lasting results. Follow-up measures were taken at six months and then at the year mark after the clients had gone through their original program. In every case the client continued to improve their scores on all the measures used in the original study.

These were very exciting days for me as I watched my clients develop personal empowerment skills using the AlphaKardia System to successfully create transformative changes in their lives. They literally were relaxing into the fulfillment of their life purposes and intentional goals in their business, health, and personal life.

Wright

You mentioned earlier that success in business, health, wealth, and relationships is already determined and is just a matter of time before it happens. Will you share a little more on that subject?

Ellison

As I have already stated, there is a time of incubation for ideas to germinate and grow in order for them to become successful. You have to learn to relax into the success and allow the idea to mature and come to life. If we become impatient and try to force something to develop we are actually forcing it away from us. Success comes from a natural flow of energy, not forced energy by our will. Willpower is good and every one has it, but relaxing into success and enjoying the journey will not happen by self-willing it to happen. Force does not equate to success. Beethoven understood the importance of incubation. He is quoted, as he started his workday, as saying, "Nothing comes to me today; we shall try another time." He relaxed into his creativity knowing that in time music would emerge from his soul. He knew his purpose and calling.

Another composer who was commissioned to create a symphony ran into a creative block and tried to force something to happen. He tried harder and harder to create the composition, losing night after night of sleep. Friends and family urged him to take a break and get away. His health and even his sanity became jeopardized. Finally, he went to his doctor with failing health and his doctor ordered him to take a vacation. He went away to a remote village in Italy. On the first morning that he was there, he awoke to the chime of church bells ringing in the distance and in an instant the pieces he had been working on all fell together to create a masterful composition. If he had only understood incubation he could have relaxed into his success just as Beethoven was able to do without jeopardizing his health and well-being.

Often, when we are struggling with business or personal issues and are trying to make something happen, we try to force the solution to come. When the answers are not forthcoming, the pressure mounts and our desperation increases.

Wright

Judy, in your opinion, what are the steps that can be taken to take the stress out and stop the desperate drive to success?

Ellison

Take Time Out! The following three steps will provide the break you need to put you into a state of relaxation and creativity:

1.) You have to take the time to relax and connect. My clients use the AlphaKardia System but you can gain this relaxed state by other practices such as the Relaxation Response, TM, or Mindfulness Meditation. Use whatever means of relaxation you want to use and meditate, knowing that the answers are within.

2.) Then get away from the situation. Invariably, my clients are disgusted at themselves for having the urge to get away and so they suffer with guilt and self-loathing for not buckling down and making something happen—anything happen! Many people just want movement whether it is right or wrong. But instead of doing what is necessary they tend to persevere by going over the same line of reasoning that they have gone over a hundred times before expecting a different outcome. It is time to let go. Take time out to relax and let go of the problem. Do something you love to do. If you are a golfer, hit the greens and golf. If you love to shop for antiques, go to a new antique store and stimulate some new brain synapses by what you see. Let the intuitive creativity inside of you incubate your idea until it has matured into a solid solution or answer. Typical signs that indicate you are in a competitive egoic state of mind instead of a connected state of mind and need to step back are: fatigue, mental dullness, irritability, despair, impaired memory, and physical signs of stress such as shortness of breath, tightness in the chest, or muscle tension.

3.) Another way to allow your creative ideas to incubate is to sleep on them. The injunction to "sleep on it" is not just a metaphor, but it is a time to allow the mind to rearrange and order the mental content gleaned from the conscious and unconscious mind. Sleep is the playground of spirit that leads to intuitive discoveries either in dreams or upon awakening. Winston Churchill and Thomas Edison took catnaps during the day and claimed their greatest creativity came from these seemingly useless time-outs during the day. My father, Richard Ellison, was a pastor and would claim, when I found him napping in the afternoon, that his best sermons came from his catnaps.

I personally like the idea of sleeping on it and use it regularly. I often give instructions to my mind just before going to sleep to provide me with an answer to a question, a solution to a problem, or guidance in making a decision. Just drop the idea into your mind and then let it go. Sleep on it! You will be amazed by the flashes of inspiration and intuitive solutions that will come to you. Be sure and keep a pen and pad of paper on the nightstand so you can write down any information that comes to you in the night. If you go back to sleep, invariably you will forget it by morning. These flashes of insight may not happen during the night or upon awakening but they may come *when you least expect them.*

Wright

In closing, do you have any other thoughts that you would like to leave with our readers on the subject of *Success is a State of Mind*?

Ellison

I'm so glad you asked. Not long ago, I was going through a particularly difficult time in my life. My husband of over thirty years filed for a divorce. I was devastated and carried a deep wound in my heart and soul that wouldn't heal. For many months, I couldn't seem to lift myself out of the abyss of sorrow. I kept focusing on my losses—especially the loss of the family system that I loved and valued above all else in my life. A mental state of inertia overpowered my normal vibrant, positive attitude. This was not like me as I have always looked at a glass half full instead of half empty; but going through divorce, all I could see was the empty half of the glass. I was mentally stuck. I picked up Joel Osteen's book *Your Best Life Now* and began to read his thoughts on refocusing your thoughts on things that are good.

His concept on how to make an attitude adjustment is not new. It's as old as the Bible. It was recorded in the scriptures in Philippians 4:8, *"Fix your thoughts on what is true and good and right. Think about things that are pure and lovely, and dwell on the fine, good things in others. Think about all you can praise God for and be glad about."*

If you get into a mental state of inertia and it seems like things are not moving forward in your life, there is a very powerful technique you can use to shift the energy out of your head into your heart. You can make a simple but profound attitude adjustment that will without doubt change the state of your mind and the results of your efforts.

Make a gratitude list! The easiest way to get focused on things that are good is by making this list! I programmed my gratitude list into my Blackberry (BB) so that it would be close at hand (and my friends will attest to this fact, the BB is always nearby). It would be with me everywhere I would go. As soon as I would start thinking about my losses and feeling sorry for myself, I would pull out my BB and open the file with my gratitude list to help me focus my attention on the things in my life that were good. It was the turning point in my recovery and I began to see my positive state of mind returning. Some days I would have to live moment-by-moment in an attitude of gratitude to be able to keep moving forward. But on those days when I needed an attitude adjustment the most, I just kept going over the list.

Gratitude of the heart changes the frequency of your thoughts and places you back into the flow of a positive state of mind—the state from which we are meant to live our lives. It is creative, inspired, energized, generous, magnetic, clear, insightful, and filled with joy and peace. Connecting to the inner power of your heart while in a relaxed state will create a magnetic state of mind to help you successfully fulfill your life's passionate purposes and bring you all the success you desire in wealth, health, relationships, and spirituality.

Wright

Today we have been talking with Dr. Judy Ellison. Judy, thank you for sharing your thoughts on success.

Ellison

It has been a pleasure David. Thank you for this opportunity.

ABOUT THE AUTHOR

Dr. Judy Ellison is a psychologist, research scientist, success coach, published author, and motivational speaker who earned a bachelor's degree in Counseling Psychology from Prescott College in Prescott, Arizona, a master's degree and doctoral degree in Psychology from Saybrook Institute in San Francisco, California.

She is the inventor of AlphaKardia,™ a life transformation system that combines leading edge heart and brain science and spirituality. This system is designed to make effective changes in physical and emotional well-being, identify internal purpose, improve mental clarity, enhance spiritual connection, reverse the affects of aging, develop intuition, increase problem-solving capabilities, increase productivity, and reduce anxiety and stress in order to live a more relaxed and happier life. It combines the following interventions in a clinically proven integrated transformative system: biofeedback, diaphragmatic breathing, alpha relaxation, heart-focused connection, visual imagery, therapeutic suggestion, intentionality, and cognitive restructuring.

Dr. Ellison is the director of research at Sequel Institute, Inc., overseeing leading edge brain and heart research for the purpose of contributing to the development of spiritual scientific processes of change. In addition, merging her experience from twenty-five years of personal counseling and success coaching along with her education, Dr. Ellison is passionate to lead individuals into personal growth and life transformation. Applied with wisdom, intuition, and decisive clarity, she guides individuals through programs that provide proven results and inspires audiences around the world in her keynote presentations.

Dr. Judy Ellison
AlphaKardia LLC
P.O. Box 5264
Scottsdale, Arizona 85261
Phone: 480.735.9741
Phone: 877.293.0767
Fax: 480.699.1674
E-mail: DrJudy@AlphaKardia.com
www.AlphaKardia.com

SUCCESS IS A STATE OF MIND

12

An interview with…

Ligia Houben

David Wright (Wright)

Ligia M. Houben is a professional speaker and author and is the founder of My Meaningful Life. She is a life transitions consultant and has specialized in helping people transform their losses and hardships into a personal growing experience. Ligia has combined different areas of expertise to provide the best care in a holistic manner. Her studies have concentrated on psychology, spirituality, aging, and loss and healing. Ligia holds a master's degree in Religious Studies and Gerontology complimented with a graduate certificate on Loss and Healing. She is certified in grief counseling, thanatology, addiction, holistic hypnosis, theta healing, and Neuro-linguistic programming. She embodies a whole-hearted approach to coaching with her care, enthusiasm, and passion for life.

Ligia, welcome to *Success is a State of Mind*.

Ligia M. Houben (Houben)

Thank you, David.

Wright

How did you come up with putting together a specialty in life transitions?

Houben

Well, actually it was not planned when I started on this path. I started out studying psychology and then I got interested in the spiritual dimension of people because I realized that to deal with life and transitions you do not only need the emotional tools and psychological tools. There is another dimension that is equally important—the spiritual one. Because I got very interested in exploring this area, I did a double major in psychology and religious studies at the University of Miami. Then I earned my master's degree in religious studies at Florida International University with a specialization in gerontology, the study of aging. I chose these two courses of study because I realized that as people grow older, the spiritual dimension takes on a new meaning. The element of hope is vital to continue living with meaning.

To compliment these studies I entered a graduate program focused on loss and healing at the University of St. Thomas in Miami, Florida. I thought this was a great compliment because spirituality and psychology are also great tools to deal with the different losses we face in life. We are not only talking about the death of a loved one, but other losses or transitions we face in life like the loss of a job, loss of health, divorce, or loss of a country. All these different losses may involve a grieving process. This is the reason why I wanted to put this program together—to offer a more comprehensive approach to life transitions.

Wright

Why did you feel attracted to grief and loss? Is this only related to death?

Houben

No, it is not because we go through stages or transitions and generally, "transition" means a change. Some of these changes may not involve a loss, but some of them do, especially those related to death and dying.

The first step is to accept the loss, go through it, and then be able to transform it. If we do not process something that is hurting us, it stays within our heart and soul and it can manifest in a negative way later on.

Wright

Regarding Dr. Kubler-Ross, author of the popular book, *On Death and Dying*, and the studies she conducted several years ago, was her work only related to death or did she go beyond that subject, as you're doing?

Houben

When Elizabeth Kubler-Ross came on the scene with her stages of grief—*denial, anger, bargaining, depression,* and *acceptance*—she based them on a study she did with dying patients. She recognized the stages that dying patients went through. Eventually these stages were taken and applied to death and different losses.

It is important to notice that these stages do not have to be linear but may be circular. Grieving people may go through the stage of denial, then to anger, and then back to denial. People going through grief become very rigid in the sequence of these stages; it is vital we understand this concept.

Today, new theories have been developed that propose a more active perspective. These stages were more passive, but now because we understand the concept better, we have to take action and be responsible in our own manner.

There are now some other perspectives like tasks in grief—you have to be active in order to grow, in order to process your grief, and to keep on living.

Wright

Do you work with any kind of population?

Houben

I work with any kind, including middle age and older adults. Among the people I work with there is a beautiful lady who is one hundred and two. She is incredible. She is totally functional—physically and mentally. I have a great passion for older adults because they have so much to offer, starting with wisdom.

I also work with young adults. I teach at the university and I develop a close relationship with my students. In one university I teach world religions and in the other university I teach death and dying.

I also teach a virtual course on Ethics. Some of these students go through their own transitions. For example, once they graduate and they have their diploma, some of them face the transition of being in school to facing the "real world." Some of them wonder, *"Now* what do I do?" It's interesting because this situation may involve a kind a kind of a grief—"Okay, now I'm not a student anymore, now I'm an adult"—and some of them even wonder that if they had to study, what they would study. So it is interesting because it can apply to different dimensions or perspective.

Wright

Do you believe spirituality is a powerful tool in the lives of human beings? Is this the same as religion?

Houben

I do believe that the spiritual dimension is a powerful tool, not only at a personal level, but as a professional. I've seen its manifestation in many people. It gives us the element of hope and when we go through a transition, a hardship, or a loss, if we do not have that ray of light—hope—at the end of the tunnel, it's difficult sometimes to face our new reality. That hope is brought from religion/spirituality. Sometimes people get turned off by the word "religion," based on denominations and various sects, but being spiritual is a great source of bringing comfort to people.

Wright

Is this the reason why you wrote the book, *The Devotion to the Virgin Mary?*

Houben

Oh yes, it is. The book is titled *La Virgen María y la Mujer Nicaragüense: Historia y Tradición,* and it's written in Spanish. It was actually my thesis. It is the thesis I wrote to earn my master's in religious studies. This study was done with one hundred and twenty-five women, between fifty-five and eighty-five years of age. It was a qualitative and quantitative study. It was beautiful, David, because when I did the study and I interviewed these women, I participated in rituals with them, like praying the rosary, going to see their houses, and seeing the altars they have. I was able to witness their devotion.

I understood how present the icon of the Virgin Mary is in their lives. The presence of Mary—the Virgin Mary—is very strong in my country, but at the same time, it can be any icon that gives spirituality. I could see how much their faith in the Virgin helped them to overcome obstacles related to illnesses, loss of a job, or loss of a child. It was very, very interesting. That is why I wanted to publish it as a book in Spanish. The thesis was written in English because I did it here in Miami, but I translated it into Spanish to make it into a book and I edited it. I made it more devotional—totally focused on Mariology and on the devotion people have to her in Nicaragua, including rituals and traditions.

On the other hand, I wrote it because I wanted the world to see how important the Virgin is for Nicaraguans. We know about the beautiful faith Mexican people have for The Virgin of Guadalupe, but I wanted to show the devotion of the Nicaraguan people. My book appeals to any woman or man who is devoted to Mary. You don't have to be from Nicaragua. Devotion to Mary is universal.

Wright

What does hypnosis have to do with spirituality? Is this why you call it "holistic hypnosis"?

Houben

That is correct. I decided to complement my services with hypnosis because I believe a lot in the power of believing in yourself and in being able to overcome limiting beliefs. Sometimes, let's say in grief, we think that we cannot make it, that we cannot go on, that we won't be able to be happy again. In the area of achieving goals, our thinking is sometimes sabotaged by what we believe about our ability to reach them. I highly believe that we have the power to achieve what we really desire in our lives. That's why I felt so attracted to contributing to this book, *Success is a State of Mind*. I do believe that our thoughts are so powerful that we can really achieve success if we put our heart and our minds into it.

In reference to hypnosis, there's a lot of myth about hypnosis, David. People think that you have to be sleeping or that you don't know what is happening to you, when in reality, it is based on suggestions given to your subconscious mind. Furthermore, it is even said that what actually happens is self-hypnosis. The person is the one who does the hypnosis because it is based on suggestions given to yourself—to your subconscious mind. If the client desires, I integrate the spiritual dimension and that is why I call it holistic. What is beautiful about hypnosis is to see the results in the lives of people as they achieve things they thought they wouldn't be able to achieve; but their achievements are based on their own resources. Hypnosis gives them the tools and makes them aware in their subconscious mind that they have the resources and they can really achieve what they desire.

Generally I complement hypnosis with what I call *transition coaching* and the results are so powerful.

Wright

Do you plan to have another radio show? I saw you had a segment called "The Meaning of Life."

Houben

Yes! I am planning to have a program on loss and transformation. I have the demo in Spanish and in English. The program would be called in Spanish *Transforma tu perdida*; in English it is, *Transform Your Loss*. I am trying to have it first in Spanish because it is the name of my second book that is being published just now, actually by

Insight Publishing. It is called *Transforma tu Perdida: Una antologia de fortaleza y esperanza*. The translation in English is *Transform Your Loss: An Anthology of Strength and Hope*. It is a self-help book that has to do with what we have been talking about—losses, which are part of our lives, but we have the power to transform them and change our lives.

The book consists of three parts. The first section talks about losses and grief. The second part consists of an anthology of sixty personal stories that were either sent to me via e-mail or direct interviews I conducted with people. Each one of these stories has a message of strength and hope.

The third section of the book is the transformative part. There I provide *The Eleven Principles to Transform your Loss*. These principles are based on my personal and professional experience. As I say in the book, I don't intend to have the answers—I can only speak through my own experience. I lost my dad when I was twelve years of age and the book is dedicated to his memory. I have gone through different losses in my life—many, many losses—and I have realized that my attitude and the desire to transform those losses into something meaningful helped me to grow spiritually and personally.

The radio program would have a sensitive and transformative format. The ideal would be to take calls from people who want to share their losses and to give them hope with the necessary resources. I would also allow others to share, contribute, and inspire.

David, we do not talk too much about losses in this society. We're always focused on, "I'm okay, you're okay;" but sometimes we need to share what is going on in our lives, that way we can really feel released—just by the action of letting go.

Wright

Are you planning to translate your book into English? Would you do seminars with this book?

Houben

Oh yes, I would. That is my desire because now I offer the seminar titled, "The Eleven Principles to Transform your Loss," in English as well. The ideal would be to have the book in English; that is my next step.

Wright

So, do you think one has the power to change or in this case transform any area of one's life?

Houben

I do believe that people have the power to change/transform any area of their lives. I know that sometimes at the beginning it can be difficult and painful.

For example, the first principle I mention in the book, is "Accept the Loss." And the second is, "Live your grief." We have to go through that process if we really want to move on, but it is a process. Therefore I could never suggest to a person the tenth principle if he or she hasn't gone through previous ones.

One has to go through different steps of principles. After one goes through all the different principles I then tell them, "Visualize the life you want." This could be, for example, in the case of losing a loved one, establishing a foundation, or mentoring a child. The most important element is having a meaningful purpose and to have the faith that one can do it.

For example, parents who lost a child might set up a foundation. If the child died of leukemia, they could establish the foundation for the benefit of leukemia research. We have the example of MADD, Mother's Against Drunk Drivers. They've transformed their loss because they put together this incredible foundation. They're helping others in their fight against drunk drivers.

There are many ways to transform loss, but it takes time and it is a process.

Again, I believe that what matters is to find the meaning of what you are doing—to have a clear purpose and a meaningful intention behind the action.

Wright

What do you think is more important, purpose or faith?

Houben

I believe that purpose, is vital. But, at the same time, if you can't combine purpose with faith (not only in God, which I find is also vital, but also in yourself), it is very difficult. We need to have the conviction that we are able to make wonderful things and to see in these things in our world every single day. People come up with ideas, and because they believe in their ideas and they have faith that these ideas will work, it happens. Moreover, the best idea cannot have real meaning to us if we don't have a clear and fulfilling purpose behind it.

Wright

Who has been your greatest inspiration?

Houben

My greatest inspiration has been my dad, Julio C. Martinez. As I told you, he died when I was twelve years old, but as a child I saw his example. He was a self-made man in Nicaragua and he touched many lives. Besides being an entrepreneur, he was a motivating speaker. He had so much faith in God, himself, and people that it was really inspiring. He motivated people to achieve their goals and to have an ethical and meaningful life. I heard his message since I was a little girl and I grew up with that example implanted in my mind and in my heart. Even though thirty-six years have passed since his death, his message has stayed with me.

I have the blessing to possess some cassettes of him talking. We all need a coach from time to time and when I need to hear his motivating message I to one of his cassettes and it is amazing—I feel that he's talking to me. So it's beautiful because he has really been the force behind my desire to help people and bring my message of inspiration, of hope, purpose, and success. So yes, I would say my dad is still my greatest inspiration.

Wright

Death and loss affect us all, regardless of age. You have talked about eleven different stages of going through loss. Do children handle loss the same as adults?

Houben

They handle it differently because of their developmental stage. For example, small children of five or six don't see death the same as ten- or eleven-year-olds, but they do know something has happened. Even younger children perceive a change in the environment and they need to be taken into consideration. Sometimes we don't realize the capacity of understanding and perception children have. It is vital for parents to explain to children at their own level what has happened and never lie to them.

With children, there are other things that play a role, for example, magical thinking or the messages they see in cartoons. Let's take the example of the duck that dies in a cartoon and then it springs back to life. The message this sends can be contradictory and confusing. For that reason we need to be able to tell children what has happened. They may not have a clear understanding of what death is, therefore it is important to be willing to give answers, to listen, and to be patient.

Children may not understand death the way we do, but they perceive more than we think they do.

Wright

Well, what a great conversation. I really appreciate the time you've spent with me today answering all these questions. The issues of death and loss really affect us all, don't they?

Houben

Thank you so much, David. I appreciate as well the time you have given me and to be able to talk about these issues because they touch our hearts and our souls.

As I said, I am very excited with the idea of being part of this wonderful book, *Success is a State of Mind*. How we deal with our transitions depends on the state of our mind. It is based on our attitude, our faith, and our desire to make a real difference in the world.

Wright

Today we have been talking with Ligia M. Houben. She is a professional speaker and author. She is founder of My Meaningful Life, where she works as a Life Transitions Consultant. She has combined different areas of expertise to provide the best care in a holistic manner. She embodies a wholehearted approach to coaching with her care, enthusiasm, and, as we have found here today, passion for life.

Ligia, thank you so much for taking all this time and being with us today on *Success is a State of Mind*.

Houben

Thank you, David.

ABOUT THE AUTHOR

Ligia M. Houben is the founder of My Meaningful Life. She is an author, life transitions consultant, and professional speaker. She obtained her B.A. from the University of Miami in psychology and Religious Studies and a Masters Degree in religious studies and gerontology from Florida International University. Ligia also has a Graduate Certificate in Loss and Healing from St. Thomas University and is a Certified Grief Counselor and a Certified Thanatologist: death, dying and bereavement. Ligia is a Certified NLP™ coach and has specialized in transition and transformation coaching.

Ligia M. Houben
My Meaningful Life
7800 SW 57th Ave., Suite 215B
South Miami, Fl 33143
Phone: 305.663.8118 and 305.299.5370
info@meaningfullife.com
www.mymeaningfullife.com

13

An interview with…

Les Brown

David Wright (Wright)

Today we're talking with Les Brown, internationally recognized speaker and CEO of Les Brown Enterprises, Inc. He is also author of the highly acclaimed and successful books, *Live Your Dreams* and *It's Not Over Until You Win*. Les is former host of the *Les Brown Show,* a nationally syndicated daily television talk show that focused on solutions rather than on problems. Les Brown is one of the nation's leading authorities on understanding and stimulating human potential. Utilizing powerful delivery and newly emerging insights, Les's customized presentations will teach, inspire, and channel any audience to new levels of achievement.

Les Brown, welcome to *Success is a State of Mind.*

Les Brown (Brown)

Thank you very much. It's a pleasure to be here.

Wright

Les, you've been a role model for thousands of people down through the years because of your triumph over adversity. Tell our readers a little bit about your early life and who was responsible for your upbringing.

Brown

Well, I was born in a poor section of Miami, Florida, called Liberty City. I was born on the floor of an abandoned building along with a twin brother. When we were six weeks of age, we were adopted. When I was in the fifth grade I was identified as EMR (Educable Mentally Retarded) and put back into the fourth grade. I failed again when I was in the eighth grade.

I attribute everything that I've accomplished to my mother. Whenever I give a presentation I always quote Abraham Lincoln by saying, "All that I am and all that I ever hope to be, I owe to my mother." I saw a sign once that said, "God took me out of my biological mother's womb and placed me in the heart of my adopted mother." I love my adopted mother's faith, her character, her drive, her dedication, and her willingness to do whatever it took to raise seven children by herself. She only had a third grade education but she had a Ph.D. in mothering.

Wright

If I remember correctly, you were diagnosed at the age of thirty-six with dyslexia. How did that happen?

Brown

No, I was never diagnosed with dyslexia; but I was in special education from fourth grade all the way through my senior year in high school. My formal education ended at that time; but I became very much interested in personal development tapes and books because of a high school teacher who challenged me to do something in a class. I told him I couldn't do it and he insisted that I could.

Finally, I said, "I can't because I'm Educable Mentally Retarded."

He said, "Don't ever say that again. Someone's opinion of you does not have to become your reality."

This teacher's name was Mr. Leroy Washington and he's still around today. One of the things he emphasized to all of his students was that you don't get in life what you *want*—you get in life what you *are*. What you achieve—what you produce in life—is a reflection of your growth and development as a person. So you must invest in yourself.

He often quoted scripture by saying, "Be ye not conformed to this world: but be ye transformed by the renewing of your mind . . ." (Romans 12:2). He said most people fail in life because "they don't know that they don't know and they think they know"—they suffer from mental malnutrition. He said take the time each day to develop your mind, read ten to fifteen pages of something positive every day, and find some goals that are beyond your comfort zone that can challenge you to reinvent yourself. He told his students that in order to do something you've never done, you've got to be someone you've never been. He told us the possibilities of what you could achieve by developing your mind and developing your communication skills (because once you open your mouth you tell the world who you are). You can really begin to climb the ladder of success and do things that will literally amaze you.

Wright

So your education is self-education.

Brown

Yes.

Wright

Listening to tapes and reading books and that sort of thing?

Brown

Yes. Going to seminars and then testing and experimenting. I think it's very important that people experiment with their lives and find out what it is that works for them—what gives their lives a sense of joy and meaning. What is it that brings music to your life? That way you're able to discover some talents, abilities, and skills you don't even realize you have.

Wright

I remember reading your first book, *Live Your Dreams*. This bestseller is helping people even today. Can you tell us what you're trying to say in this book and why it is important?

Brown

What I'm doing in *Live Your Dreams* is challenging people to look at their situation and ask themselves some crucial questions. Is life working for me? Is it really giving me what I want?

When most people get out of high school, they end up doing things that other people want them to do. Albert Schweitzer was asked a question, "What's wrong with humankind today?" He replied, "Men simply don't think." He meant that statement in a generic sense. Men *and* women simply don't challenge themselves to think about what it is that really makes them happy and gives their lives a sense of meaning, purpose, power, and value.

I want to challenge people to think about what it is that really gives their lives a sense of meaning and power. Once you determine that, assess yourself. What are your strengths? What are your weaknesses? What is it you bring to the table of life? What help? What assistance? What training? What education? What resources? What do you have to tap into that will help you to become the kind of person that can produce those results?

Then next is to commit yourself. Don't ask yourself, "How am I going to do it?" The "how" is none of your business—what is most important is to get started—the how will come. The way will come. Everything you need to attract—the people, the resources, and the assistance—will come to be available at your disposal.

Wright

What do you think about goal-setting? There has been so much written about it lately.

Brown

I think it's very important that people set goals because what that does is allow you to focus your energy. It helps you to put together a game plan and a strategy and an agenda for your life. If you don't have an agenda for your life, then you're going to be a part of somebody else's agenda; therefore, you want to set some goals. There's a quote I love very much that says, "People who aim at nothing in life usually hit nothing dead on the head."

Wright

Oh, my.

Brown

Yes, so you want to have some goals you are setting in each area of your life. You want to monitor those goals after you put together a plan of action to achieve those goals. Break those goals down into manageable increments: long-range and short-range goals, three-month goals, thirty-day goals, and weekly goals. You should have daily tasks and activities you engage in that will move you in the direction of your goals. Dr. Robert H. Schuller said something that is true, "By the yard it's hard, but inch by inch anything is a cinch."

As you begin to look at the big picture and come back to where you are right now, looking at the completed big picture of where you want to go, then you can begin to put together a strategy of things and activities you need to do each day to move you in the direction of those goals. As you get closer to those goals you have set for yourself in the various areas of your life—your physical life, your emotional life, your spiritual life, your financial life—then you can begin to push the goals back. Continue to stretch—continue to push yourself—and reach farther.

Wright

A few years ago you had a nationally syndicated television talk show. It's next to impossible to get a show of that nature on the air. Tell us the circumstances that helped to get your show on the air.

Brown

I believe I'm coming back, I don't think it's impossible to get back on again. I wanted to go in a different direction. During the time I ventured into it, television was based upon a formula the executives were accustomed to which they'd always implemented—the show must be based upon conflict and controversy. So you had Phil Donahue, Oprah Winfrey, Sally Jesse Raphael, and Geraldo. My show was based upon solutions. I believed you could have a show that was not based upon conflict and controversy—you could have a show where you would look at what challenges people are facing and who has gone through a challenge and come out on the other side? Talk to that person and find out how he or she got there. Interview a guest who is in the middle of a challenge and find one who's just approaching that challenge. Have an expert work the person through that process during the hour of the show, asking what is it that brought you here? There's an old saying that goes, "Wherever you find yourself, at some point and time, you made an appointment to get there."

The other thing is that success leaves clues. What we must do is talk to someone who's had the same problem you've had and find out from his or her experience what is it you can do to implement a game plan. What help and support will you need to work through this problem?

The *Les Brown Show* was very successful. It was the highest rated and fastest cancelled talk show in the history of television. It was cancelled because, even though it had successful ratings, the producers of the show wanted me to do a show based upon conflict and controversy and sensationalism—fathers who sleep with their fourteen-year-old daughter's boyfriends—and subjects like that. I decided to be true to my concept and not venture off into those other areas to do those Jerry Springer type shows, so they cancelled the show and brought someone else in who was willing to cooperate with what they wanted.

Wright

Did you learn any lessons from your highly competitive talk show?

Brown

Yes I did. The lesson I learned was I should have been the executive producer. I was hired talent and "the hand that pays the piper calls the tune." Had I been the executive producer of my show like Oprah Winfrey, then I could have done what Oprah did after she saw the success of my show—she changed direction and used the formula I'd come up with and the rest is history.

If I had it to do over again I would've put my own production company together, continued to do the show I was doing, and would've found someone else to syndicate the show nationally. If I couldn't find someone to syndicate the show nationally I would've set it up to do it locally and then rolled it back out nationally myself.

Wright

I bet you still get stopped on the street by people who saw your commercials on the PBS station for many years. Those were some of the best produced I've ever seen.

Brown

Well, thank you. We've gotten a lot of response from PBS. We just did one show four months ago called, *It's in Your Hands*. In fact, I end the show with my children because five of my seven children are speakers as well; they're also trainers. What we're doing is teaching people how to become responsible for their careers, their health, and for their family life. The response has been very, very successful on PBS.

Wright

So you're growing your own speakers, then.

Brown

Yes, and I'm training speakers—I'm more of a speech coach. I've developed a reputation as a speaker, but I have a gift of helping people tell their story and to position it so it has value for an audience. I have people's stories create special, magical moments within the context of their presentation so that those stories can create a committed listening audience and move them to new heights within themselves.

Wright

Yes, you don't have to tell me you're a sought after speaker. Some time ago we were planning a speaking engagement in Ohio and the two people who were requested more than any others were Stephen Covey and Les Brown. They really came after you, so you do have quite a reputation for helping people.

Brown

Thank you.

Wright

A lot of our readers have read many books that advocate focus in their career. I know you've done several things and you've done them well. Do you advocate going in one direction and not diversifying in your career?

Brown

I think that you have to find one area you want to focus on and as you develop momentum in that area and reach a certain measure of success, then you can branch off into other areas.

Wright

Les, you had a serious bout with cancer several years ago, right?

Brown

Yes.

Wright

How did this catastrophic disease affect your life?

Brown

What cancer did for me was help me live life with a sense of urgency that tomorrow is not guaranteed. It helped me reprioritize my life and find out what's really important. When something major like cancer happens in your life you spend more time focusing on those things. So, even though I always practiced and advocated that people live each day as if it were their last, my cancer battle helped me to focus even more so on priorities. That's what I began to be about the business of doing—thinking about my legacy, spending more time with my children, my grandchildren, friends I cared about, and working on the purpose I've embraced for my life.

Wright

My wife was going through cancer at the same time you were, I remember. I heard her say recently that even though she doesn't want cancer again, she wouldn't give anything for the lessons she learned going through it.

Brown

Yes. It helps; it gives new meaning to life, and you value things you used to take for granted.

Wright

So, you gained a lot of insight into what's important?

Brown

Oh, without any question I did.

Wright

Your book, *It's Not Over Until You Win*, was long awaited, of course. Would you tell our readers what it's about and what you're trying to say?

Brown

I think what people must do is challenge themselves to overcome the inner conversation that has been placed in them through their conditioning, through their environment, and their circumstances. We live in a world where we're told more about our limitations rather than our potential. We need to overcome and defeat that conversation.

If you ask most people if they have ever been told they can't achieve a goal they envision for their life will say, "Yes." My whole goal is to help people learn how to become unstoppable. Yes, it's going to be difficult—it's going to be hard. You're going to have obstacles thrown in your path. You will have setbacks and disappointments. But you must develop the mind-set of a winner. You must come back again and again and again. You must be creative and flexible, versatile and adaptable, and never stop until you reach your goals.

Wright

I read many years ago that 98 percent of all failure comes from quitting. Would you agree with that?

Brown

Yes, I agree with that without any question. Most people become discouraged and they see delay as a denial. I encourage people to go back to the drawing board in their minds, regroup, and get some fresh thinking. Einstein said, "The thinking that has brought me this far has created some problems that this thinking can't solve."

Sometimes we have to allow other people to be a part of the process—to look at the situation we're battling with new eyes that can help us overcome the challenges we're facing.

Wright

As I have said before, you have been a role model for thousands of adults as well as young people. Do you have any advice to give our readers that would help them to grow in body, mind, and spirit and live a better, fuller life?

Brown

Yes. I think it's important for people to raise the bar on themselves every day. Look at your life and understand and know you are greater than you give yourself credit for being; you have talents and abilities you haven't even begun to reach for yet.

Jim Rohn has a quote I love, "When the end comes for you, let it find you conquering a new mountain, not sliding down an old one." So, therefore, we have to raise the bar on ourselves constantly and assess ourselves.

The other thing is I believe it's important we ask for help, not because we're weak but because we want to remain strong. Many people don't ask for help because of pride. "Pride cometh before a fall" because of ego. E-G-O means edging God out.

I think that you also have to ask yourself, what is your plan for being here? Most people take their health for granted; but living a long, healthy life is not a given—pain is a given—you have to fight to stay here. You have to have a plan of action to stay here. So what is your plan for being here? Put yourself on your to-do list. Develop a plan of action on how you're going to take better care of yourself and spend more time with people you care about. Focus on living the goals and dreams you've envisioned for yourself that are the calling on your life.

Wright

Down through the years, as you've made your decisions, has faith played an important role in your life?

Brown

Yes, faith is very important. I think you have to believe in yourself, believe in your abilities, believe in your dreams, and believe in a power greater than yourself. There's a quote I love which says, "Faith is the oil that takes the friction out of living." Do the best you can and leave the rest to a power greater than yourself.

Wright

Les, you don't know how much I appreciate you being with us today on *The Power of Motivation*.

Brown

Oh, thank you so much.

Wright

Today we've been talking with Les Brown, an internationally recognized speaker and CEO of Les Brown Enterprises. He's the author of *Live Your Dreams* and *It's Not Over Until You Win*. I suggest you run down to the bookstore and look for both of them. Les has been a successful talk show host and as we have heard today, he is now coaching speakers.

Thank you so much for being with us, Les.

Brown

Thank you, I appreciate you very much.

ABOUT THE AUTHOR

Les Brown is an internationally recognized speaker and CEO of Les Brown Enterprises, Inc. He is also author of the highly acclaimed and successful books, *Live Your Dreams* and *It's Not Over Until You Win*. Les Brown is one of the nation's leading authorities in understanding and stimulating human potential.

Les Brown Enterprises
PO Box 27380
Detroit, Michigan 48227
Phone: 800.733.4226
E-mail: speak@lesbrown.com
Web site: www.lesbrown.com

An interview with…

Max Bolka

David Wright (Wright)

Today we're talking with Max Bolka. For over twenty-five years, Max has been associated with the financial services industry. After working with an investment banker, he started his own independent financial advising firm and developed a nationwide financial planning and investment clientele. Simultaneously, he became a twenty-five-year student and practitioner of Vedic Science and Ayurveda, the five-thousand-year-old science of life and consciousness from India. Today, Max unites these two diverse areas into a coherent, consciousness-based business and personal development practice, providing professional speaking, writing, retreats and one-on-one coaching, teaching individuals, entrepreneurs, and business owners how to grow themselves and their businesses.

Max, welcome to *Success is a State of Mind.*

Max Bolka (Bolka)

Thank you David, it's a pleasure to be here.

Wright

Your chapter is titled "Consciousness and Success," so let's start with definitions. How do you define consciousness?

Bolka

Consciousness is simply awareness. Pure consciousness is pure awareness. Most people live life on the surface level, not really becoming aware of the subtleties of life; but that's where all of the power, success, and fun are. Consciousness is a state of being as opposed to a state of doing, having, thinking, or talking. It lies underneath all of those—underneath everything there is. Science is now starting to verify the existence of a Unified Field, which is consciousness or existence itself.

We live in a scientific age and science is rapidly demystifying the concept of consciousness. Scientists can now objectively measure what ancient sages have experienced directly and have explained to us since the beginning of time. The Greeks said, "Know thyself," and at our deepest core, we're all made of the same substance called consciousness, which then gets projected out into the world.

Wright

And how do you define success?

Bolka

True success means living 200 percent of life—100 percent outer achievement along with 100 percent inner fulfillment. It's the inner fulfillment part that's been absent for the majority of people today. I call living both parts of life 200 Percent Success™.

We live in the most prosperous country in the world in its most prosperous time in history. We throw away and waste more food and junk than many other countries ever use, and yet many of us are not happy. We're materially rich and spiritually poor, even bankrupt. So to me, true success means being happy, evolving to a state of eternal liberation, accomplishing and enjoying the maximum in life, and achieving the greatest good for one's self and for others.

This generation has discovered that more stuff is just not going to cut it. If we're unhappy, we've missed the very essence of life. If our power, creativity, intelligence, peace, love, joy, and happiness are not constantly developing, then we have lost our direction.

A person of limited mind and heart, who's busy in the world, is often unable to appreciate the very purpose of life. Their mind is so occupied with small things that they can only create in small, limited ways. The conscious capacity of many people is so limited that they're not even able to enjoy life.

It's difficult to get the big picture if you have a small screen!

Wright

So, how is consciousness related to success?

Bolka

All lack of fulfillment, all suffering—even if we achieve some degree of outer success—is due to the inability of a way to unfold the unlimited, creative intelligence that is present within each and every one of us. Consciousness is not only what's been missing as the basis of our fulfillment, but it's also the foundation of our success. Our thoughts, attitudes, and beliefs literally craft our own reality. The inner precedes the outer, and raising one's consciousness—awareness—turns out to be the very basis for achievement.

Wright

Is what you are talking about similar to "The Secret"?

Bolka

It's similar, but it runs deeper. This knowledge of how success is a state of mind, how our thoughts produce our reality, and the mechanics of how like attracts like, is being rediscovered in this age through the entire human potential movement. Having worked for twenty-five years in finance and business, I tend to use a lot of direct, concrete questions that focus on the material, practical aspects of life. For example:

Do you *believe* it's possible for you to double your income?

How about triple or quadruple?

How hard do you think one has to work for that kind of money?

Do you feel you don't have enough time—always rushing around?

If you feel this way now, how can you possibly triple your income?

Wouldn't you have to give up your family, health, free time, or fun?

More than just positive thinking, your answers to these types of questions start to reveal your core beliefs and subsequent behavior, which then determines your results.

Perception is key here because the world is as we are. If we're tired, nothing is any good. If we feel great, then we get into the zone. We're faced with the same problem, but we perceive it differently. If we're wearing green glasses, then everything we see will be tinted green. If we're wearing dark colored glasses then everything is filtered through that darkness. What I'm suggesting is that if we don't like what we're seeing, maybe it's time to change our perception. So let's keep digging.

Do you *deserve* to double, triple, or quadruple what you earn?

Do you really deliver that much value to the marketplace?

Do you charge enough, according to the value you provide?

Why do you charge what you do?

What's your underlying reasoning?

These types of questions reveal one's core beliefs around money and work.

Wright

Isn't this simply a case of improving one's self-esteem?

Bolka

Well, that's definitely one element of it because we all have core beliefs about our self-worth, but its more profound than that. For example, *you earn what you do because that's how much you've allowed yourself to earn right now*. Our self-limiting, internal core beliefs hold us back from earning a higher income far more than anything "out there" such as education, experience, or even ability.

Emerson once said, "Who you are shouts so loudly in my ears, I cannot hear what you say." Success depends primarily upon who you *are*. In fact, success depends first upon the purity of one's heart and only second upon talent, skills, and ambition. Who you are ultimately is reflected in your business and in life. Your income can only grow to the extent that you do. So investing in yourself, expanding yourself, your awareness, or consciousness—your mind as well as your heart—is of utmost importance.

Wright

You talk about the secret behind "The Secret." What is that?

Bolka

Well, it's simply this. *Most of our core beliefs are subconscious.* We're constantly forming our own reality, but most of us do this unconsciously. We're unaware of the connections between cause (our thoughts) and effect (our life).

Wright

What types of self-limiting core beliefs are you talking about?

Bolka

Many of these negative, self-limiting core beliefs usually fall into three categories: fear, lack, and struggle.

Fear—Examine any negative belief you hold and ask yourself what are you really afraid of? The answer may astound you. For example, we may have a fear of failure, but most people have a far greater fear of success. And while fear of failure can motivate you to a minimum level of safety and security (usually associated with the comfort of mediocrity), fear of success is bound to imprison you there!

We're afraid of everything! We're afraid of failure, afraid of success, afraid people won't love us, or afraid they *will*, and the list goes on. Getting real about the fears underneath your beliefs is a good place to begin. Admittedly, it takes courage just to ask the right questions and start becoming honest about these issues.

Lack—Another origin of many self-limiting beliefs is the concept of lack. You either believe the universe is unlimited or you don't.

There's no in between. For many people, their world consists entirely of lack; lack of time, lack of money, lack of energy, lack of health, lack of relationships, lack of security, and so forth down the line.

Is there enough to go around or isn't there? You tell me, because either way, you're right and your world will reflect your beliefs. Look at *why* you feel you don't have enough time, money, et cetera. Become aware of your intentions, beliefs, and subsequent actions and try to make those connections between cause and effect.

Struggle—A third area that trips up many people is the core belief that life is a struggle. After all, we're supposed to be serious, especially in business, right? The harder you work, the more responsible you are and the more you deserve a higher income, right? Says who? Where did this belief come from and is it really true?

Most people love to demonstrate how hard they work and how they've overcome obstacles to prove they deserve the good life. *Some people even create their own obstacles to overcome.* We love to sacrifice and use struggle as an excuse to show what good, deserving people we are. Movies are famous for this. We get eighty-nine minutes of struggle with one minute of happy ending. We love the drama, don't we? Living 200 Percent Success™ does not require one to struggle.

Wright

When talking about the outer 100 percent of success, we have to talk about attaining goals. Goal setting has really been studied and reviewed for the last decade. What's your approach to goal setting?

Bolka

Well, in my speeches, workshops, and consulting regarding goal setting, I start with two rules: Number one is to think big. You have no idea what power lies within you and how much you could achieve—if you really wanted to. All that's needed is to become clear on your vision and perhaps get a little guidance or encouragement. Helen Keller was once reportedly asked, "Is there anything worse than being blind?" She replied, "Yes, a person with sight and no vision."

In over twenty-five years of working with clients, I have found that a lack of vision is the major reason why many people never reach their full potential. People who think big tend to achieve big things both in business and in life.

Many people in their teens and early twenties start out feeling invincible. But by the time they reach their forties they may feel fortunate just to get out of bed in the morning without too many aches and pains, perhaps barely able to pay their bills. So what happened? While we all start out thinking big, several factors tend to constrict our vision over time. First, we slowly become socialized through reward and punishment until we conform to society— thinking and acting like everybody else, which is smaller.

Sir John Templeton, one of the greatest money managers of all time, taught me that everybody can't beat the market because everybody *is* the market. You must be willing to do something different than everyone else if you want superior results. Now admittedly, thinking big is going to put you in "The Two Percent Club," so you must be inner directed as opposed to outer directed.

Second, we often become so engrossed in the necessary details of living that we lose sight of the big picture. Thinking big is really an exercise in emotional detachment, in gaining perspective, and taking time out from the incessant activity of life that can impede our long-term growth. Taking time out to think—to develop our state of mind—is not always an easy thing to do in the fast-paced world in which we live, but it's an essential requirement. Even when we take vacations, many people are so busy doing that they never get any true down time just to *be*, to truly rest, and to have alone time with their thoughts and feelings.

A third obstacle to thinking big is fear. As we discussed above, fear comes in many forms. We're afraid to think big, we're afraid to ask, we're afraid of failure, success, and rejection. But successful people act in spite of their fears. They realize that one should never act (or not act) out of fear—they always come from a position of strength.

Wright

After thinking big, what is your second rule for goal setting?

Bolka

Be specific! Everybody wants to work less, make more, lose weight and be spiritually fulfilled. The problem with these goals is that they're not specific. If you want to make more money, ask: how much are you making now and how much would you like to make? Write down where the money is going to go because money flows more easily when you have a specific purpose for it.

Similarly, if you want to work less, specifically how many hours are you working now, and how many would you like to work? If you can't measure it, it's not a good goal. So make a list of what you would do with all that free time. These activities now become your new goals.

Most people are unwilling to write down really big, specific goals. They're afraid to ask for what they really want. But you need to give yourself permission to think big. As Les Brown says, "Dare to live your dreams!"

Wright

Along those lines, you have some unusual advice for those who are stuck on their goals. What about people who have the vision, they think big, and do all the right things? They write everything down, they're clear and specific about their goals and take action, as you recommend, and they're still not seeing the results they would like. What would you say to those people?

Bolka

Double it—double your goal. I know this one always takes people by surprise and often it's a stretch. It even ruffles a few feathers, but that's okay. I find that, in these cases, a few feathers need to be ruffled. Some belief systems need to be shaken up a little.

From my days of running a nationwide financial planning and investment business, I learned how to become a true contrarian, and it turned out to be a very successful strategy when addressing most other areas of life. In investing, you buy when everyone else is panicking because that's when prices are the lowest. Then you sell when everyone else is running around, wildly elated that things are going so well, because that's when prices are the highest. Admittedly, this takes the greatest emotional fortitude, but pays the greatest rewards. We can transfer this concept of being a contrarian to the process of goal setting. What do most people do when they get stuck?

Wright

They just stop.

Bolka

That's right. They either keep knocking their heads against the wall, give up, or compromise their goals. But each of those options violates the first rule of goal setting, which is to think big. It doesn't say think big *unless* things get really difficult or frustrating and then it's okay to think small, shrink from your dreams, or give up altogether.

This backward way of thinking has lead to an entire system of goal setting that says you should set "reasonable" or "attainable" goals. What those people are really saying is, "Let's not even try for anything too big or difficult because we don't want any chance of failing. We want guarantees." I don't really even call that goal setting.

In almost every case I've seen, when individuals, business owners, or entrepreneurs have the courage to overcome obstacles by thinking outrageously big, they far surpass their original goal. It's almost as if the universe is saying, "Think bigger!" It does you no good to play small and settle for something less than what you truly want. You are destined for greatness, but you are going to have to step up to the plate and not settle for anything less.

You see David, it's impossible for us to take in the billions of pieces of information that we're bombarded with every day, so we carve out our own little slices of reality. We all have selective perception. Dogs hear high pitch sounds that we can't. Bats detect objects through sonar—a method beyond our capability. What we choose to perceive comes down to the power of our attention.

For example, let's say you go out to purchase a new car and you end up buying a Toyota Camry because you really like the car and the blue color that you picked out. And to top it all off, you got a bargain because it was on sale. Now, for the next few weeks, what do you notice on the highway? A lot of Toyota Camrys—especially the blue ones. The interesting part is that they were *always* right there on the road driving along beside you and they were always on sale! You just didn't notice them because you didn't have a reason to—it wasn't part of your world. Perception is everything—it's a state of mind.

When you walk into a room, if you don't smoke you're probably not looking for an ashtray. It's not part of your awareness. It's not part of your consciousness. Just like radio waves that proliferate throughout the place where you're sitting right now. There are a multitude of stations broadcasting, but you can only hear the one you're tuned into . . . and your radio must be in proper working order.

When we come up against obstacles, very often we can't see the solutions because we aren't looking in the right places. We aren't searching high enough. Our attention is stuck on the lower levels. Einstein said we cannot solve problems using the same level of thinking that created them.

Opening up your mind to seemingly impossible goals allows the filters of your perception to pick up on the ideas, meet the people, go places, and do things you would not have otherwise done, leading to previously unimaginable success. But to succeed beyond your wildest expectations, you've got to begin with some pretty wild expectations.

Wright

And your third rule for obtaining goals?

Bolka

Take action! Take action and the universe will react, I promise you. It doesn't always react the way your ego likes, but it reacts. The truth is you have the freedom to be anyone, do anything, and go anywhere you want. If you want to be successful, you can start right now because your only true failure lies in the failure to start. The reason why so little is ever accomplished is usually because so little is ever attempted. You get out of life what you put into it. It's just that simple, based on physics—action and reaction, cause and effect. If you don't act, you won't get the results. So if your ship doesn't come in, swim out to it! You don't need all the answers to get started, just some really good questions. Pay attention, go inside, and feel what's right.

I call this The Corridor Principal™. Imagine you're standing at the end of a long corridor and at the other end is an exit sign, which is your ultimate goal—your vision. As you start to take each step toward your vision, you come across many different doors on both sides of the hallway. The trick is, *you'll never see any of these doors unless you start walking.*

For example, if your goal is to get an exquisite new car, it doesn't necessarily mean that you go into debt, but it might mean going out and test-driving one. If you want a more lavish home, get out and walk the neighborhood where you'd like to live. *Envision* what it would be like for you to live there. *Feel* what it would be like for you to live there. It costs you nothing. It's very advantageous to open each door a crack, take a peek, and see if what's behind it appeals to you. Lean into what seems to be the right action at the time and see what happens. Check the feeling you get inside. *Most people know the right answers, they only have to get quiet, listen, and honor what they hear.*

Wright

And, if you make a mistake?

Bolka

Well, that's what everyone's afraid of isn't it? So what? We all make mistakes from time to time. But you can't let the fear of making a mistake paralyze you. As James King says, "Don't be so hard on yourself. Go ahead and mess up in style. If you're going to make a mistake, do it with flair!" I'm not saying to blindly take unnecessary risks, but if you just start right from where you are, and just take the next step, it's usually not that risky. If you do make a mistake, make it once, learn from it, and move on. Learn from other people's mistakes too because you'll never live long enough to make them all yourself.

The universe is constantly sending us signals, but many times we're not listening. First, it whispers gently, in the form of intuition or a gut level feeling. Then it sends people and things into our life to try and communicate with us. Next, it flicks us in the eyebrows to try to catch our attention. If that doesn't work, sometimes we just have to get hit over the head with what's called The Universal Two-by-Four. While that may sound a little funny, it usually manifests in our life with some kind of tragedy. So just tune in and be with the experience. Don't resist it—feel what the situation is trying to tell you. Don't superimpose your will—what you think *should* be happening.

The formula for success is as follows: Have the desire, take action, and let go. Rinse and repeat. That's all there is to it. You don't need to worry because the results will absolutely be according to the action. Newton's third law of motion says that for every action there is an equal and opposite reaction. You can restate this law using many other perspectives. In computers it's GIGO: Garbage In, Garbage Out. In Eastern philosophy it's called karma. Western religion states that, "As you sow, so shall ye reap." And down South, they have a saying, "What goes around comes around."

Just take the action and get out of the way. The thing is to begin. See the opportunity and pursue it, even though in the beginning you're not totally sure of all the answers. Don't wait to overcome all possible objections before you start. Take the first step down that corridor. Peek behind each door and see if it holds something of value for you. To paraphrase Oliver Wendell Holmes, it's not so much where we stand, but what direction we're moving in that counts.

The only prudent way to start down the road to success is to move your feet one step at a time. Once you take the action, you'll find the entire universe conspiring with synchronicity to support your intentions which are life-supporting and right for you at the time. Pretty soon you'll find yourself having to run just to keep up. Then the question will become, "How much success can you stand?"

Wright

You keep saying it's a matter of being, as opposed to doing. Will you explain that to our readers?

Bolka

Sure. Most people believe in *do, have,* and *be.* They're thinking, "First I'll work really hard and struggle to obtain the goals I've set. Then, if I get what I want, I can be happy, and if I don't, I'll be miserable." But they've got it all backward. The way things really work is *be, do,* and then *have.* (I told you I was a contrarian.)

First get established on that level of awareness or consciousness that reflects the kind of person you want to *be.* Then plunge into action. Let go of your emotional attachment to the outcome. As a result you'll be far more apt to achieve your desires. You'll end up doing less but accomplishing more. As Gandhi said, "*Be* the change you wish to see in the world."

I've never seen so many people as I do today working so hard just to be happy. They are taught that if they don't get what they want, they need to exert their willpower and work even harder. But most people just end up getting stressed out. In his classic book, *As a Man Thinketh,* James Allen states, "Circumstances do not make the man; but rather, they reveal the man to himself." How true! Everything we see in our world is a reflection of what's going on inside us—it's a mirror image of our state of mind.

The obstacles we face are real, our circumstances are real; it's just that most people fail to recognize the role they play in generating those obstacles. The root of any problem is in your mind and is just another opportunity to recreate yourself. Ask yourself the following:

Why am I doing what I do? What is my true intention here?
How might I be participating in creating this situation?

How do I consciously want to act or react in the world?

How am I presenting myself in this particular circumstance?

Is my being this kind of person serving me well?

If we take responsibility for our condition, sincerely ask these types of questions, get quiet, and listen carefully for the answers, we will always find what we're looking for, and the solutions for overcoming any obstacle are revealed. Then it is wise to honor those solutions.

Wright

What does a higher, expanded level of consciousness look like? Can you tell what a person's state of consciousness is just by looking at him or her? What are the practical implications of higher consciousness? How does it manifest itself in business and in life?

Bolka

I don't think you can judge anyone's level of consciousness simply from outward appearances. But when the ultimate expansion of pure consciousness is stabilized in one's everyday activity, that state of mind is what's known as the state of enlightenment. *Because consciousness is the basis of success, raising one's level of consciousness improves every area of life.* There are innumerable qualities we can point to in people who have grown in this higher state of awareness.

Joy—First, enlightened people are "lighter" by their very nature. They don't exhibit the heaviness that pervades so many people in situations today. Instead, they exude joyfulness, no matter what activity they're engaged in. From high level negotiating to writing a book to taking out the kitty litter, they tend to have fun and express a certain joyfulness in whatever action they are involved in.

Generosity—People with an expanded state of consciousness tend to enter into relationships with an attitude of giving. They understand the Law of Action and Reaction—of cause and effect. Enlightened people give with pure intentions, with no strings attached. As a result, they receive back many times over.

This attitude of giving is especially useful in business today where tradition has held that the sole purpose of business was to make money. Recently, it seems that the purpose of business is simply to make the most money possible, as quickly as possible, even at the expense of relationships, long-term profits, or ethics. However, those times are rapidly coming to an end, with some very enlightened businesspeople leading the way.

Unity—Enlightened people also understand the Principle of Unity. Physics tells us that everything is made up of waves of vibrations. The fascinating part regarding this principal is that everything we *don't* see is also made up of waves. It turns out that this field of pure awareness (we can't see it, but we can experience it directly with our mind) is the same field for all of us. Quantum Physics calls it The Unified Field. It's home to all the laws of nature—the very place where these vibrations come from. In other words, we're all made of the same stuff and we're all using the same playbook!

This has tremendous implications for science, religion, and philosophy, all of which are rapidly converging into one paradigm of human nature, human potential, and of our understanding of how the world works.

Process Oriented—Another quality demonstrated by those with higher levels of consciousness is that they emphasize process as much as results. They stay centered no matter what outer circumstances seem to be because they know they are constructing those circumstances and just playing out a role like an actor on a stage. Therefore, they stay in the process, stick to the script, and play their part without all the drama. There's an inner stability—an inner silent witness—who is emotionally detached throughout the entire process.

You know, life can sometimes seem like a test. But if we accomplish something in the world at the expense of the feeling level, nothing of real value has been achieved. Anyone who's been married can verify this. Even if you're right or get the project completed, if you've crushed the feelings or damaged the heart of the one you love, what good has come of it? Preserving the relationship comes first. The ironic part is that because success is a state of mind, once this attitude of staying in the process and preserving the feeling level is adhered to, more success starts to happen automatically with much less effort. So again, we end up doing less but accomplishing more. Our job is simply to see the work, do the work, and then stay out of the misery.

Abundance—People with an expanded awareness also have an abundance mentality. They don't feel a lack anywhere in their life. They feel they have all the time they need to accomplish what's important to them. They feel they have all the money they need to accomplish what's important to them. Notice, I didn't say *will* have, but actually have *now*. And guess what? They always do! Money is such a funny, uniquely manmade tool. Perhaps someday we can talk more about cultivating an abundant mentality versus a poverty mentality.

Love—Enlightened individuals also live in love. They love who they are, what they do, and who they're doing it with. It's a palpable feeling that you get from them. Whether their goal in life is to make a million dollars or be the very best grandparent they can be, you can just feel their enthusiasm, joy, and love. As a result, they have a sense of peace, confidence, and optimism. And because they are comfortable with themselves, they allow others to feel comfortable in their presence as well.

Gratefulness—While there are many other practical qualities of higher levels of consciousness, the last one I will mention here is gratefulness. Enlightened individuals are grateful. And while everyone knows what gratefulness is, very few people stop to consider how it actually works.

Gratefulness operates on the principal that what you put your attention on grows stronger in your life precisely because your attention helps to produce it. In the financial world, for example, we say something appreciates when it grows in value. Similarly, when we appreciate something non-financial in our life, it too grows in value. This principal works both in the positive and negative sense. However, most people constantly complain about those things they don't have instead of being grateful for those things they do have, so what grows stronger in their life? Those things they didn't want in the first place! They do this mainly out of habit, but that's just another way of saying they do it unconsciously. They wake up in the morning and the mind starts going automatically.

An easy way to get spectacular improvements in your life is to affirm your gratefulness all day long—from the minute you get up until the minute you go to bed. Write it down if you have to. Start a gratitude journal. You'll be astonished at the difference it makes in your life. Remember, everything is energy, including your thoughts. Positive thoughts carry positive energy, negative thoughts carry negative energy. *If you want to have unlimited energy, the place to start is with your thoughts.*

Try this for thirty days: Don't gossip, don't criticize, and don't complain. And don't be surprised if there's nothing to talk about in the beginning! It's not an easy thing to do. All we're doing here is changing a habit, but it's a habit that has infinite implications for your health, wealth, and well-being—all areas of life. And you'll have unlimited energy too.

Scientists can now measure the biochemical changes we produce in our bodies when we feel grateful—the physiological reasons why we feel so good when we appreciate someone or something. So instead of expending negative energy avoiding situations and conflict, expand your energy and sphere of influence by staying centered. Find a way to love it or leave it, but don't be attached and don't complain. Commit to this for thirty days—commit yourself to establishing your new habit and tell me if it doesn't significantly change your entire life.

Wright

So how can people actually increase their consciousness?

Bolka

We can go right to the source of thought through meditation. Meditating tunes up the nervous system and the brain functioning that actually does the thinking. You expand the capacity of the container into which the data flows, increasing the ability to think more powerful thoughts, leading to 200 Percent Success™.

Wright

How does the meditation you're talking about work?

Bolka

Meditation is like diving deep within this vast ocean we call our consciousness. Most psychologists tell us that we use perhaps 10 to 15 percent of our brain. Meditation enlivens that subconscious part of the mind, allowing it to become conscious, which enables you to fulfill your potential and achieve more success with less effort. You become more aware of who you are and what your true nature is, which is pure consciousness.

Wright

What are some of the benefits of meditation?

Bolka

Increasing one's awareness through meditation affects all areas of life. Everyone knows the stress-reducing benefits of meditation, which have been scientifically documented over the past forty years. However, as soon as one starts to meditate, it becomes very obvious that something more is happening. One *does* feel lighter, more joyful, more giving, more generous, more abundant, more connected to others, and more sensitive to staying in the process, doing less while accomplishing more.

Meditation also very naturally enables us to remain present. Most of us are already experts in time travel and we don't even know it. We live in our head. As Deepak Chopra has said, the average person has about sixty thousand thoughts a day. The interesting part is that about 95 percent of those are the same thoughts we had yesterday—we just replay the old tapes automatically, unconsciously. Meditation teaches us how to be present and not live in the past or the future. We become fully conscious of what we're doing, focusing our attention 100 percent in the present. These thoughts are more powerful, resulting in more success.

Another benefit of meditation is that we become less attached to the results we want to achieve, making it easier to let things go and accept what is. The ironic part is that we can enjoy the fruits of the world even more, just like a child who outgrows toys when he or she sees there are greater joys in life. We don't live in fear that these joys are going to be taken away because that's simply called change. But we no longer get upset about it and just accept what is. Acceptance plays a big role in being enlightened.

Wright

Doesn't over-acceptance of everything just lead to passiveness and *lack* of success?

Bolka

The nature of life is to grow, to change, and progress. Sometimes our only choice is either to let something go or be dragged along behind it. *Acceptance leads to lack of struggle, not lack of success.* Success is our natural state. Happiness is our natural state. Life was never meant to be a struggle. Everyone reading this book now knows that there is no more excuse for suffering, lack of success, or lack of fulfillment. Achieving 200 Percent Success™ can easily become our living reality.

I always recommend that everyone meditate and spend some time away from constant activity at least once a day, and preferably twice a day. Do it morning and evening for about twenty minutes, giving the mind enough time to settle down. There's an article you can access on my Web site called "Meditate Your Way to More Money." It lists more benefits as well as providing a simple meditation technique for all our readers. This will get them started. It also has a list of more resources about meditation—and it's all free.

So we can see that living 200 Percent Success™ is far more than even a state of mind, it's a state of being.

Wright

What a great conservation! I've learned a lot here today, and you've opened some doors that I'd like to know a little bit more about. I really appreciate all the time you've taken with me this morning to answer these questions.

Bolka

Well, thank you, David. You know, there are no accidents. It was our destiny to meet and create this book together at this particular point in time, and I am honored to be a part of it. I've genuinely enjoyed the entire process. I hope you've had as much fun as I did, and I hope the book is a huge success!

Wright

Today, we've been talking with Max Bolka, who has integrated two very different aspects of life. Max has twenty-five years' experience both as a financial advisor and business consultant along with Ayurveda, the five-thousand-year-old science of life from India. Today he has united these two areas into a successful business and personal consulting practice. He provides professional speaking, writing, retreats, and one-on-one coaching, teaching individuals, business owners, and entrepreneurs how to grow themselves and grow their businesses.

Max, thank you so much for being with us today on *Success is a State of Mind.*

ABOUT THE AUTHOR

For over twenty-five years, Max Bolka has been associated with the financial services industry. After working with an investment banker, he started his own independent financial advising firm and developed a nationwide financial planning and investment clientele. Simultaneously, he became a twenty-five-year student and practitioner of Vedic Science and Ayurveda, the five-thousand-year-old science of life and consciousness from India. Today Max unites these two diverse areas into a coherent, consciousness-based business consulting practice, providing professional speaking, writing, retreats, and one-on-one coaching, teaching entrepreneurs how to grow themselves and their businesses.

Max Bolka
Comprehensive Business Consulting
134-E Charlotte Highway
Asheville, NC 28803

Mailing:
P.O. Box 15765
Asheville, NC 28813
Nationwide: 800.472.3288
www.maxbolka.com

SUCCESS IS A STATE OF MIND 15

An interview with…

Katrina Mikiah

David Wright (Wright)

Today we're talking with Katrina Mikiah who is a professional life and wellness coach. Her practice, called Alchymia: Resources for Personal Transformation and Soulful Living, supports people in transforming the everyday experiences of life into treasures for self-knowledge and fulfillment. Katrina believes that success is achieved naturally when we witness life situations and ourselves with awareness and an attitude of acceptance, enabling apparent obstacles in our lives to dissolve without force. This thoughtful and gentle way of approaching life frees us to live soulfully, bringing deep and unconditional happiness. Her background includes group facilitation, teaching, coaching, and social service. She also enjoys art, singing, and improvisational dance and theater. She is a graduate of Coach for Life, an ICF accredited school. Her own personal journey, spiritual studies, and private practice have been nourished by the teachings of Sri

Nisargadatta Maharaj and Eckhart Tolle. In 2007 she published two books, one of her writings titled, *Already Who We Want to Be,* and another of her artwork called *Visionary Collage.* Her private practice includes her popular seminar titled "Becoming an Alchemist: Practicing the Art of Personal Transformation."

Katrina, welcome to *Success is a State of Mind.*

Katrina Mikiah (Mikiah)

Thank you, David.

Wright

So what is success?

Mikiah

That's a very good question and one that perhaps doesn't get asked often enough. The drive for success is behind so much of what people in this culture do, yet many people have never really investigated what success means or what they actually expect from the achievement of their dreams.

As a coach, I think about the topic of success fairly routinely. I recently looked up the definition of success in the dictionary and found two definitions: "the achievement of something desired, planned, or attempted," and "the gaining of fame or prosperity." It struck me that there is no mention in either definition of contentment (which is defined as "happiness with one's situation in life"), and yet I think the hope for contentment or happiness underlies anyone's drive for success, regardless of his or her specific ambitions. Likewise, my personal experience has shown me that contentment and happiness are not so much the results of accomplishing a goal as they are an attitude—a way of approaching our day-to-day lives, a way of being in our world just as it is right now.

In my twenties I had a sense that I had to hurry up and figure out what my life purpose was. I knew I was here for a reason and I wanted to know what it was so I could get on with my life and be fulfilled—be successful.

Then, in my early thirties, I kept hearing an inner voice saying, "Just . . . sit . . . down," and what that meant to me was, "Stop fighting so hard to find success." Essentially, I was running a race. I was afraid life was going to pass me by before I figured out what my purpose was. The message I was getting was, "You're not going to find that fulfillment or that purpose in any kind of race—it's right here. Learn to be with yourself; learn to stay put; learn to see what the present has to offer, and trust that the gem is right here."

Wright

Will you tell our readers how we balance the drive for success with being content with things as they are now?

Mikiah

I think that question reflects a widespread belief that the drive for success and contentment with things as they are now are at odds with each other, when in truth, real success is born in contentment.

In recent years, the subject of *being in the now* has become quite popular. Many books, seminars, movies, and talk shows have caused people to think more about what it means to *be* present—to live from the awareness that all we have is *the now*. However, while that message can be refreshing and inspiring, it can also stimulate concerns and questions: "If I allow myself to be okay with things as they are now, what's going to drive me on? Won't I become complacent? How can I make sure the parts of my life that I don't like will change? How will I accomplish my goals for the future if I live only in the now?"

Analogies are often very useful in understanding difficult concepts and in integrating them with our own unique lives. One that is particularly resonant for me is that of boating down a river. Whether we're enjoying our lives and ourselves or not, we're each floating down this river of life. Though it's the same river, our journeys are each different depending on the kinds of boats we have, the kinds of people we are, the particular part of the river we're on, the weather and season, our unique ways of viewing and responding to the river, our own strengths and limitations, and the resources we each have available. There are endless variations among the boaters and many different ways of approaching the river, but to learn from this analogy, I ask myself, "How would any masterful boater approach the river?"

A skilled boater is always very grounded in the present—very aware and accepting of any immediate conditions—in order to see and respond to both obstacles and opportunities when they come. However, even while primarily focused in the present, the boater also keeps an eye out for what lies ahead. This expanded awareness permits clarity of and attention to any immediate circumstances, as well as the ability to navigate in harmony with the course the river seems to be taking ahead.

For me, that imagery helps bring the future and the present together; it shows that we can be fully present and still have a vision for the future—we can still see up the river a little ways, and we have an idea of what may be coming and can plan for that. However, if we're not primarily focused on the here and now, and if our plans don't arise from a state of presence, we are likely to miss the beauty and opportunities right before our eyes and, in our lack of attention to the present, we might actually compromise our highest intentions.

Wright

I once heard a man say many years ago that there is no pot of gold at the end of the rainbow, but that people who walk along rainbows pick up the gold as they go along.

Mikiah

That's right. The instant we focus our vision on an imagined pot of gold that is *out there* somewhere at a future destination, we miss the mark. It is so tempting to seek elsewhere and to think that something better lies ahead, but nothing is ever offered to us outside of the present moment and we have to be present to receive what comes. The treasures are always right here, amid the nuts and bolts of our lives.

Wright

How can we be sure that our ambitions will be fulfilling?

Mikiah

Most importantly, if the motive behind an ambition is to bring about a sense of contentment or happiness that you can't find in the present, once achieved, the ambition will certainly be disappointing. Ultimately, all of our ambitions are motivated by desires to experience particular qualities—security, peace, enjoyment, appreciation, competence, etc. Since those qualities are not dependent on any particular achievement, but are, rather, related to our state of *being*, it is quite possible to *experience* them in the here and now—as long as we are open to releasing the idea that we need something we don't have in order to experience them.

Lack of awareness about what the qualities that motivate our desires are can lead to much struggle and ultimate disappointment when we finally get what we thought we wanted and find that we are not happy. Rather than looking to future achievements for the qualities that are meaningful to us and hence, for the feeling of being successful, we can nurture and recognize those qualities in our lives right now.

There's a tool I use in my coaching practice to help clients clarify what they really want and as a result, to take more effective and rewarding action.

On a piece of paper, draw a chart with four columns. In the first column, list the things you desire to have. For example, improved health, a new car, career advancement, more money, or more time.

In the next column, name the essence of each object of desire— the quality you expect to gain or experience by having each of those things. Here, we're looking for words like freedom, stimulation, purposeful activity, security, ease, autonomy, etc.

The next step is to ask, "Who or how would I have to *be* in order to experience that quality right now?" For example: "How can I express freedom right now? How can I meet my need for stimulation right now? How can my present action be more purposeful? What would it take for me to feel secure right now? How can I create more ease right now? How can I express autonomy right now?" Your responses may include changes in attitude or specific actions. Write them in the third column.

Then, in the final column, write down how or where that quality is already expressing itself in your life. You might write: "I'm walking to work every day; I have flex time at work; I just received an award for the program I implemented; I have an income that more than meets my basic expenses; I enjoy spending weekends in my backyard garden." This step bridges the gap between the future and the now. We discover that the qualities we have associated with objects of desire that we don't yet have can be expressed, and are in fact *already* being expressed, in our current circumstances.

As we investigate the essence of our desires and make our focus *living* those qualities or values in the midst of our current circumstances, we create a magnet for more of those same qualities packaged in the forms that are most aligned with who we really are. We may also find that the list of things we thought we wanted becomes simpler and more cohesively oriented around what really matters to us.

This way of living eliminates the struggle to get someplace or to accomplish things. Those things truly in alignment with our souls' yearnings will tend to unfold naturally because we're embodying the essence of what we want. It isn't that we won't have to exert any effort, but that our efforts will feel supported by clarity and energy.

Another way to determine whether an ambition is in alignment with what we really want is to notice if it's accompanied by an energy of anxiety or by an energy of inspiration or at least acceptance. Typically, when we are not accepting the present—when we don't like what *is* and are trying to distance ourselves from it—we set goals motivated by fear or anxiety. These goals are often at cross-purposes with our deepest, truest desires and, when pursued, can cause more anxiety. On the other hand, when we are willing to accept and experience the present just as it is, even if it's uncomfortable, clarity and conviction arise, which move us toward action that feels inspired and is efficiently directed toward our highest intentions.

When unsure whether a plan of action is likely to bring happiness, you can ask, "Am I primarily focused in the here and now with a vision for the future or am I primarily focused on the future out of resistance to the present?" Make it your intention to be the masterful boater and trust that you will get to the places most fulfilling to you when you are willing to be with your life exactly as it is now. Clarity and happiness are both born in the now.

Wright

There's currently a lot of emphasis on self-improvement. As we accept our lives and ourselves in the present, is there a place for self-improvement?

Mikiah

Yes, but we hurt ourselves when we interpret the presence of aspects of ourselves that seem yet imperfect as an indication or proof that we are not good enough now. When our desires to improve ourselves are colored by lack of acceptance for who we are now, our actions toward improvement are actually more wounding than helpful. When we truly embrace ourselves as we are now, ironically, the actions needed to create change for the better come naturally. Change is a natural, effortless process reflected in the ways of nature all around us. The ape did not try to change into the modern human. The tadpole does not try to become a frog. No forced effort is needed for us to be the best people we can be. If there is a feeling of unwelcome effort, it may be helpful to reevaluate what you're trying to do and the energy of motivation behind it.

Beneath much of what we do with our time and energy is a deep-seated belief that we are not good enough. Because this belief is so ingrained, it is often an unconscious motivation for the actions we take as well as for the goals we set for ourselves. When we are acting in order to feel good enough, our actions are coming out of resistance to who we think we are now. The only way that we will ever truly feel happy is when we love ourselves and enjoy our own company. Yes, we might meet any number of goals set with the purpose of attaining success, but that success leaves us with an empty feeling if it is not matched by a deep and abiding acceptance of and appreciation for who we are with or without having met that goal.

Wright

I've read that Michelangelo believed the statue of David already existed in its entirety in the block of stone and he only chipped away what wasn't David. Could this be a metaphor for what you're talking about?

Mikiah

Exactly. The nature of self-discovery is really more of a clearing process than a search. We are *already* who we are. We are already perfect and in no need of refinement or improvement. We miss the mark and begin to feel lacking when we identify ourselves with the thoughts and experiences we have and with the feelings that pass over us. These identifications preclude awareness of who we really are—of the wonderful, miraculous beings that we *already* are. Unaware of the wholeness that already exists, we set out to achieve something that we think is in the future that will be better than the life or self we have now—something that will make us better people. In fact, the perfect self is inside, just like the statue of David was already inside the stone. All we have to do is chip off what *isn't* us. In other words, recognize the self-judgments when they come up, consciously speak the truth, and let them go. "Oh, that judgment that I'm inadequate—that's not me. That judgment that I'm depressed—that's not me. I may be *feeling* inadequate or *experiencing* depression but they are not *me*." So instead of running away from the unfriendly ideas of who we are, we chip them away with the conviction of the truth that's inside of us. Michelangelo had a conviction that there was a beautiful statue already in existence in that stone. In the same way, with growing awareness, we develop the conviction that we are truly only beauty, only perfection, only fullness, and that the only reason we think otherwise is because we've not fully chipped away what isn't true.

Wright

How do we deal with, or "chip away," the things we notice about ourselves that just don't seem acceptable—the traits or behaviors we label as "negative"?

Mikiah

The reason "negative" thoughts, feelings, and experiences are so troubling to us is that we equate them with who we are. In order to deal with these perceived negative aspects of ourselves, we need to understand that we *are not* them. We need to shift our perception of ourselves away from what we perceive to that which is doing the perceiving. This creates an expanded field of awareness that allows us to be simultaneously more fully present with what's happening in our lives, and yet more free because we do not define and limit ourselves according to what's happening.

Looking again at the river, we see that many things influence the flow and direction of the river—logs, rocks, rapids, and waterfalls, for example. The river is not just a smooth, clear channel to a destination; it is alive, ever changing, unpredictable, and sometimes chaotic. Our lives are like that too, and it's this diversity—including challenges and obstacles—that makes life rich and fulfilling. As a boater on the river of your life, you are likely to bump up against things that feel uncomfortable to you—things you don't like and wish were not there: perhaps a log representing a thought that you are inadequate or a rock representing a feeling of depression.

When you bump up against those obstacles—those thoughts and feelings you'd rather not experience—you have two choices. You can assume that because they're in your path they must be *yours*, in which case you put them in the boat with you. Or you can bump up against them and realize, "Oh, there's a log of inadequacy" or "There's a rock of depression," and instead of putting them in the boat with you and making them a part of your identity, you just notice them, feel them, and then use your paddle to steer yourself back into the current of life. Once you attach your identity to every negative thought, emotion, and experience that comes your way, you begin to feel pretty stuck. You're so bogged down with logs and rocks and debris that you can't flow anymore—you're stuck in a logjam with a sinking boat.

The tendency, when we're feeling stuck, is to want something to come along and rescue us. Now, you can't wait for the next jet boat to come along so you can hop aboard and leave your inadequacy and depression behind. If, however, you hadn't put the log and the rock in the boat with you, and had instead let yourself experience them and keep on going, you wouldn't need those quick fixes. You wouldn't need the jet boat to come and save you from your life.

Wright

What would be analogous to the jet boat in our lives?

Mikiah

The jet boat could be anything that we look toward to free us from having to fully accept and navigate through whatever feels difficult in our lives. It is that thing that promises to bring us a happiness that we're not currently experiencing. It could be a new hairstyle, a drug, food, a movie, an educational program, a new lover, a diet, or even a self-help seminar. None of these things are necessarily meaningless and are certainly not "wrong," but if we find ourselves moving toward these out of resistance to what *is*, we will ultimately be disappointed. "Jet boat rides" can provide temporary rewards as well as respite and inspiration, but enduring contentment and true happiness always come from the willingness to lovingly be with ourselves, to accept opportunities to see and apply our own strengths, and to be guided by our own innate wisdom.

Wright

Will you give our readers an example of how knowing what we are not can transform a painful or uncomfortable situation?

Mikiah

I had a profound experience a few years ago during the weekend of Hurricane Katrina. It was particularly meaningful because my name is Katrina and the situation involved a person who was living in the South. The incident that happened in my personal life was tumultuous and emotionally devastating, giving rise to many feelings of anguish and confusion. However, while in the midst of those very difficult feelings, I realized that they weren't *me*. It was as if I myself was a hurricane, simultaneously experiencing all the tumult in the realms of emotion and thought, yet connected to a very calm center inside myself—a peacefulness that remained steady and still and which I knew to be my *self*. This calm reassurance enabled me to let all the pain and heartache wash through me until it naturally dissipated.

This imagery of the hurricane is very powerful for me and has been for a lot of the people with whom I've worked. From it, we learn that while our lives typically consist of a lot of activity—in terms of the experiences we have, our emotions, and the thoughts running through our minds—there is always an ever calm center of stillness at the core of our being. We don't need to *create* it or go *get* it. We just need to remember that we *are* it.

When we find ourselves feeling caught up in stressful circumstances or being pulled off balance by negative thoughts and emotions, we can recognize this chaotic motion as the outer part of the hurricane and remember that we are, in reality, the "eye of the storm." With this awareness, a sense of peace begins to permeate our lives, regardless of what's swirling around on the outside.

Wright

How do you apply this learning to your practice as a life coach?

Mikiah

As a life coach, my primary intent is to help my clients back up, see their lives from a broader perspective, and develop their capacity to accept themselves and their lives as they are now. In doing so, they are free to float down the river of life with greater trust, greater ease, and the ability to find joy in the here and now, freed of entangling and wounding self-judgments. Just like the master boater who both surrenders to the river while using his or her resources and intelligence to navigate around the logs and rocks, my clients grow in their ability to trust life and themselves. They see more clearly where they're going and how they want to get there, yet they know the importance of being present and the importance of cultivating an attitude of acceptance toward themselves and an energy of openness to life.

This attitude of openness is essential to success. Imagine you are looking at a person who is communicating "no" with their whole being. They're likely to be in a constricted posture, looking down or away. On the other hand, someone who is communicating an energy of "yes" is standing with arms open, eyes alert, and receptive. It is nearly impossible for someone to move back and forth between these energies according to circumstances. Life happens with too much unpredictability and spontaneity for any of us to shift into an energy of "yes" or "no" at will. What tends to happen is that we choose one or the other.

If we choose an energy of "no," we're in a state of resistance like a boater stuck in a logjam, unable to enjoy the bounty of life when it presents itself. If we choose an energy of "yes," we are receptive and can embrace opportunities, support, and blessings when they come.

The better choice might seem obvious, but saying "yes" means saying yes to everything, including the things we think we don't want, and that's the hitch. That's why it is so important to develop the ability to distinguish the false ideas of who we are from the truth. From an energy of "yes," the false can be explored and revealed as the imposter. From an energy of "no," we take the imposter for the real and in doing so we run from the gem of our true selves that remains sure and steady right here.

We often need a little bit of help and encouragement saying "yes." This does not mean we give up all hope for things to be different or that we stand passively by in situations that call for action, but that we are willing to accept that the present circumstances *are* the path right now. What would it be like to accept this path, to trust this path, and step right into whatever presents itself, whether it's uncomfortable or exciting? What would it be like to move forward knowing that the only way you're ever going to get to where you want to go is by surrendering to the step that's right in front of you?

Wright

So when we surrender are we giving up on our dreams?

Mikiah

No. Surrendering is really letting the river take us where it naturally wants to go. This doesn't mean that the masterful boater throws away the paddle and lets the river do all the work. There is a time to put in the oar and a need to use it in cooperation with the river. Nevertheless, the boater knows that the river is the greater force—that he or she is not primarily in control and cannot ensure any particular outcome. Surrendering to the river of life is difficult for us because our minds are so strong. We hang so desperately onto the idea that we can control circumstances if we just try hard enough or know enough, but I have learned that the mind doesn't always know how to assess things correctly, and that the wiser guide is the unknown—life itself. I have a sense that, like the ocean calls the water back to itself, the ambitions that are really right for us, that are truest and most aligned with our souls' yearnings, are pulling us toward them. We don't have to fight and work hard to get there; we can let our yearnings draw us toward them. Then, just like the river flows finding the course of least resistance until it gets back to the source, we can allow our lives to unfold with ease and trust.

Wright

How does this relate to the law of attraction?

Mikiah

The law of attraction describes a phenomenon that has always been a force of nature. It has recently been brought into the public eye with the advent of books, movies, and seminars describing how the law of attraction directly influences our lives and how we can utilize it more fully to bring about the attainment of our desires. It's a particularly popular concept in the field of coaching.

Essentially, it explains how thoughts generate feelings that, in turn, emit an energy or magnetic field attracting things of like vibration and repelling things of incompatible vibration. So, for example, if I'm entertaining negative thoughts and I let negative feelings generate out of those thoughts, I may attract negative experiences into my life. If, however, I focus on positive thoughts, which engender positive feelings, I attract what I want into my life.

Awareness of this relationship is very good. It allows us to begin to make the associations between what we're thinking, how we're feeling, and what's showing up in our lives so that we can more consciously participate in how our lives unfold. However, the law of attraction can be misunderstood to be a tool that we can pick up and use with effort to try and get what we think we want. If we pick up this tool without first exploring the essence of our desires, it is quite possible to expend a lot of mental and emotional energy acquiring things that, when it comes right down to it, fail to bring fulfillment.

The clarification of our real desires requires *being*, not *doing*. It requires quiet, calm reflection—stillness. Being in a place of stillness brings our perception of self toward the eye of the hurricane. From that stillness, clarity arises on its own. Out of that clarity our lives begin to unfold with relative ease according to our deepest desires. This is a piece that seems missing in the popular teachings on the law of attraction.

I watched this natural expression of the law of attraction in my own life a year and a half ago. As I was sitting in meditation, I noticed the return of a life-long desire to go paragliding. While this was something I had thought I wanted to do ever since I was about eighteen, I had never really believed I would do it because I was afraid of heights. However, on this particular morning, I noticed the thought that I *did* want to fly pop up out of nowhere. I didn't force the thought; I wasn't even thinking about paragliding—the recognition and clarity were just there.

About a month and a half later, I was in the sporting goods store downtown and I heard a shopper mention the word "paragliding." The thought occurred to me to ask him whether there was anyone in the area who taught it. When I did, he pointed me to the owner of the store, who was himself a paraglider and who volunteered to take me out. A month or so later, I was soaring off a butte near my home. All I did to allow this experience to happen was to quiet my mind in meditation, notice the clear desire arise, and accept the opportunities that came to me.

So I would offer to those who are interested in applying the law of attraction to enhance their lives the possibility that it's not a tool to use with effort; but rather, a natural force to notice and allow. The manifestation of what we want happens on its own when we're clear about and embodying the essence of our desires, and when there are no longer any limiting thoughts or fears standing in the way.

Wright

You've talked a lot about fear and anxiety. How can we make sure that our fears don't stand in the way or motivate actions that aren't rewarding?

Mikiah

The most important thing to remember is that you are *not* whatever thought, feeling, or experience you are having. This recognition allows you to refrain from running away from or suppressing the discomfort and to go ahead and feel it, just as the boater can bump up against the log or rock in the river, feel it, get to know it, and then navigate around it. Whatever discomfort you're experiencing is *not* who you are. It's part of your life experience, like the outer swirling of the hurricane, but it's not your core—your essence. Knowing that allows you to get curious about what it is, whether it's a fear, a pain, or something bad that just happened in your life. You can lean into it a little bit and perhaps even recognize that this uncomfortable thing could contain a treasure if you're willing to accept it and walk through it. It just might be the magical gateway.

When you're feeling uncomfortable about something, you can also notice what kind of story you are telling yourself about what happened. What meaning are you giving to what's going on in your life right now? Let's say you applied for a job and you weren't asked for an interview. You can write all kinds of stories about what happened—"I'm not good enough; my resume was not good enough; they don't know how valuable I am; I should have gotten this job"— any number of interpretations that can set into motion all kinds of reactions that are not necessarily helpful to you in the end.

Once you've acknowledged the meaning you're assigning to what happened, you can ask, "Is that story true? Do I honestly know without a doubt that my interpretation is true?" Almost always (perhaps *always*), we don't have the verification to say with absolute conviction that our stories are true and we have to admit that we don't know.

Once you can admit that you don't know, you can let go of the meaning and all the reactions that ensue. At least you can begin to consider what it would be like if you didn't hang on to your particular interpretation, and even further, what it would be like if you knew that this situation or circumstance is the perfect path to where you want to go. There is likely something beyond the ability of your mind to understand that makes your current life situation the perfect situation. How would your life be different if you could just step out and trust it?

Wright

Do you think there is something—a universal desire— underlying all our different ambitions?

Mikiah

Well, as I mentioned regarding the dictionary definition of success, I think what we really want is contentment; we want happiness; we want fulfillment. We want to feel good. The problem for most of us is that we don't know specifically what that would mean for us—what it would take to feel good. We tend to equate happiness with the attainment of certain things we want or the elimination of other things we don't want. These changes in the circumstances or appearance of our lives can be meaningful, but fundamentally, what we truly want is to live lives that are full of the qualities or values that are most important to us. The more those qualities show up in our lives—the more that we express them in whatever we do and appreciate them in the world around us—the more fulfilled we feel.

Our challenge happens when we see and experience qualities that don't feel good and begin to think that the presence of these unpleasant qualities means there's something *wrong*—that this isn't the right place to be. At this point, we start trying to move away from what's present in order to go somewhere that feels better. When we're aware of what it is we really want, we can begin to cultivate and acknowledge it right here with things just as they are.

Wright

In closing, what is the most important guidance that you can give us?

Mikiah

You *are* the treasure you have been seeking. However, as long as you don't recognize this, you will keep seeking and that search will take you away from yourself. It takes courage to stand in the presence of the mind's judgments and life's uncomfortable experiences, notice them, and yet not *be* them. But when we do, we begin to notice deep peace, ease, and contentment flowing into our lives and through us into the world.

We are all in a process of self-discovery, but it's important that we not lose perspective and become consumed with trying to arrive at a future self or destination we perceive to be preferable and neglect to fully appreciate what beckons our attention right now. What is showing itself right now if you bring your focus in? *Here* is the key to your happiness.

Life is like a mountain hike. We may or may not begin the hike with a destination clearly in mind, but we have a sense that we're going somewhere. As we walk along, we may get a glimpse of a place in the distance at which we'd like to arrive—a place that can fill us with a sense of accomplishment. This glimpse is an inspiration and it can contribute to our moving forward with enthusiasm. There is, however, a danger in getting so focused on that destination and on wondering how the path will unfold that we lose site of where we are here and now and of the fact that our attentive presence exactly where we are now is essential to arriving at the destinations that inspire us.

The present circumstances of our lives *are* the path to where we hope to go. There is no other path. It is ironic that we so often try to sidestep the present because it seems too tedious or uncomfortable. But then we become like a hiker with eyes set on the peak across the valley, unable to get there because his or her eyes aren't free to see the next step.

What is the step right in front of you? It may seem small; it may appear to have nothing to do with your goal; it may even seem to take you away from your goal. But what if you knew that whatever is before you is the magical gateway? What if you were to stride confidently ahead, trusting that your life path, though winding and at times unclear, is taking you safely and in perfect time to exactly where your soul wishes to go?

Wright

What a great conversation. I really appreciate the time you've spent with me today. I've learned so much and you've given me a lot more to think about. I appreciate that.

Mikiah

Thank you for the opportunity to speak with you today. It's been a pleasure.

Wright

Today we've been talking with Katrina Mikiah. She is a professional life and wellness coach who helps people transform the everyday experiences of life into treasures of self-knowledge and fulfillment. As we've learned here today, she believes that success is achieved naturally when we witness life's situations with awareness and an attitude of acceptance, enabling obstacles in our lives to dissolve without force.

Katrina, thank you so much for being with us today on *Success is a State of Mind.*

Mikiah

Thank you, David.

ABOUT THE AUTHOR

As a coach and writer, Katrina Mikiah invites us to an easier and gentler way based on learning to trust ourselves and on being open to our current life circumstances as the magical gateway to unconditional happiness.

Katrina lives with her son in northern Idaho.

Katrina Mikiah
P.O. Box 9512
Moscow, ID 83843
Phone: 208.882.1198
katrina@alchymia.us
kmikiah@verizon.net
www.alchymia.us

An interview with…

Noorah Hansen

David Wright (Wright)

Today we're talking with Noorah Hansen. Born to travel the world, Noorah is an international seminar and retreat leader who focuses on clear, consistent, and cross-cultural communication skills. Her seminars include Mastering Authentic Communication, Conscious Creating, Igniting Passion for Your Life Purpose, and Awakening your Heart. Noorah circumnavigated Australia by vehicle, sailed in the French Polynesian Islands, and created a walk-about in New Zealand to expand her global awareness and develop her intuition and expertise. Aliveness and passion vibrate from Noorah to her clients as they resonate to a deep and powerful place in their own hearts, and from there access their unique vision and purpose in life.

As a wilderness guide for over twenty years, Noorah leads annual wilderness retreats for women. She also brings meditative experiences from Machu Picchu in Peru and the Egyptian pyramids into her deep exploratory gatherings. Her favorite sites are Mount Shasta, California, and the Grand Tetons in Wyoming. Hundreds of clients have been assisted successfully in her coaching program to become concise and truthful in their daily communications. She currently lives in Mount Shasta and is the owner of EarthSpirit Services.

Noorah, welcome to *Success is a State of Mind*.

Noorah Hansen (Hansen)

Thank you very much. I'm grateful to be here.

Wright

So what led you to choose this business?

Hansen

David, I was born to travel, as you mentioned. From the time I was a child, I have had a passion for understanding people; I've been curious about why they think the way they do. I've wondered what kind of experiences people have had to form their way of thinking.

The first time I traveled I was only four months old. My family and I went to visit relatives in Minnesota in the summer. By the time I was five we were visiting the National Parks in the Western states. One time we were in Yosemite and I asked a ranger how old he was and if he liked his job. He laughed, yet for me it was completely natural to ask him those questions.

I started loving nature and I felt so happy there. As I became older, I would come home from school and tell my mom everything that happened that day. Looking back on those younger years I saw how much I loved communicating.

After working in the corporate world, from the ages of nineteen to twenty-nine, I left my job and went sailing to French Polynesia, which included the islands of Moorea, and Bora Bora. We were at sea for twenty-seven days, an experience that brought me closer to the nature of oceans. We then sailed to Hawaii, and from there I flew to Australia and I met my older brother. We drove around the continent in three months, logging 30,000 miles. Then he was off to Bali and I flew to New Zealand. For months I participated in a walk-about on the North and South Islands. It was quite an experience. During that time my confidence became stronger and I could talk to just about anybody. I really loved traveling and my experiences added to my comfort in communicating. Strangers would pour out their stories to me and I loved listening. My heart yearned to start teaching what seemed to come so naturally to me.

After New Zealand, I still had wanderlust and drove across the Southern states to Miami. I sailed to the Caribbean and enjoyed many islands there. After returning to Miami I drove up the East coast and into Canada. Once again I noticed the ease with which I made friends and communicated with people. People would tell me how inspirational I was and how much fun I was to have around. I loved meeting different people from all walks of life.

I started to bring women together to talk about their similarities and to discover how they were different. I enjoyed helping them practice speaking authentically. My mind opened to a new creation of how the world might be, and I fell more in love with life. My passion was ignited.

After staying home for a few years to develop better communication with my parents, I was off exploring the world again. Egypt was a place to remember my soul's wisdom and I loved being there. I then traveled to Machu Picchu, Peru. My deep awakening in both places laid the foundation for my spiritual retreats in Mount Shasta and the Grand Tetons. In these retreats women develop their ability to receive their inner wisdom and to feel their divine feminine; they meditate and hike in nature to gain a deeper sense of their being.

Women come to these retreats to clear concerns they are having at work or with their family or with their health. They come to meditate and feel spiritually connected before going home. New friendships, nature, and meditation heal their hearts, and the deeper knowing of who they are emerges.

Wright

With all your traveling, were there one or two people who inspired you the most to begin teaching the way you do today?

Hansen

Actually, my parents were my *greatest* gift for learning to speak truthfully. As they got older, and I got older, I realized I desired to have a deeper connection with them. I *intentionally* chose communicating first about what did not work in our relationship. When I would visit, we would sit around the kitchen table and talk. At first this activity was more challenging than I expected and even though my communication skills were highly developed, the conditions of the patterns set in my past would show up rather quickly. I'd blame them for what was not working in my life. I judged them for their lack of communication between themselves. My focus was on what wasn't working and how they were at fault for the shortcomings I saw in myself.

My first *positive* step was to ask their forgiveness for how I treated them when I was a teenager. They gave their forgiveness, and I felt an opening in my heart. I learned to speak from "I" rather than blaming in the form of "you did." I practiced stating clearly what was true for me, and I found my heartfelt authentic communication with them. I felt so much joy as Mom and Dad and I became closer. We deepened our connection and love for each other every time we were together.

In one of my authentic communication seminars, there was a student who had brought her parents to the class. I told my story about being forgiven and as I did so the student started crying. I looked at her and said, "Is now the time?" She stood in front of her parents and asked for forgiveness. It was a powerful moment for everyone and a life-changing experience for the parents and their daughter. Teaching through my experience of my past has helped others to go deeper within. I feel so *blessed* to be able to share my life in this way and to support women to clear their past.

The other day I was telling a friend about the commitment I made to myself twenty years ago to have deeper communication with my parents before they passed. I feel grateful to have reached my goal. As my mom became more forgetful, I experienced compassion for her, patiently answering the same questions over and over. My commitment really paid off when I was with her the night she passed. I whispered in her ear, "It's okay to go to the light; we are all ready." Her breathing changed and she passed a few hours later. Had I not *consciously* and continuously shifted my state of mind for all those years prior, I would never have been able to say that to her. I feel fortunate to have been with my father also on the day he passed. During my conversation, my friend tearfully said she wished that my story could have been her story.

I know there are many women who do not have good relationships with their parents, I understand that sometimes it is not appropriate to pursue deep communication with them in the way I did; and I knew this was the right path for me. If other women feel this is their path, I will support them in opening to what is true for them.

I have been coaching two college students who are having conversations with their fathers to heal the past. These young women are learning to communicate what did not work, and, without blame or judgment, they feel their feelings in order to find clear communication.

One client said to her father, "Dad, I say this to you because I love you, not because I think you did something wrong." My heart is filled with love by the healing between fathers and daughters, and I also know from my own experience, the healing between mothers and daughters is really beautiful. I thank God every day that I'm guided to assist in these life-changing sessions. I know helping families heal is my path. I believe that when families heal, our communities become better places to live and our world begins to change.

Wright

What influenced your choice to become a communications coach?

Hansen

As a fourteen-year-old, I had a difficult time communicating with my mom. I felt angry whenever she tried to talk with me. I did not know what skillful communication was and neither did my mom, so she started to write me letters. Writing gave us a way to feel connected, and I was grateful for her initiating this form of communication.

As I moved out of my teenage years I started hearing my little voice inside. One day I decided to listen to that small voice—my internal dialogue—to hear what I was saying. Here were some of the phrases I was saying to myself: "You can't do that, what's the matter with you?" "You're stupid." "I can't get anything right." "I'm sad." "I'll never get to do what I want." "I don't even know what I want." I discovered that listening to my inner dialogue all day was exhausting me, and at the same time I realized that my negative thoughts were dragging me down. That's when I asked myself, "*How do I change to speaking kindly to myself and how do I change my negative thoughts?"* That was when I experienced my "ah ha" moment, and I started on the path of understanding how the mind works.

From then on I studied how our language affects our thinking and how the subconscious stores memories of all our experiences. I began to realize the past conditioning and patterns that were keeping me from being successful. I *changed* my language, I *allowed* myself to feel those painful emotions of past traumas, and I *became* clear.

I studied how what we eat affects how we think, and how we think affects our emotions. These experiences helped me to decide to be of service to others. I was changing quickly and I wanted to support others to do the same. I felt more joy and love, I saw that having *fun* is part of the balance in life, and my purpose emerged. I chose to work with women to support their opening to themselves in ways they had not imagined before. My *passion* became clear.

Wright

You said the subconscious mind stores memories. How do you help your clients work with stored memories?

Hansen

Every past experience, whether it is a trauma or something fun, is programmed into your subconscious mind. You learn from your parents, grandparents, siblings, teachers, and friends. Every *word*, *feeling*, and *experience* has been stored in your cellular memory. All of those experiences affect your life today. For example, let's say a teacher shamed or embarrassed you in front of other students. This memory may still be held in your subconscious and now as an adult you have a fear of speaking up and saying what is true for you. The experience may have closed you off to your feelings, and now as an adult, you stay closed and may feel unloved.

I assist clients to open by helping them to feel the past hurt and to recall what they told themselves. I encourage them to identify the belief they began forming at that time. Since the subconscious mind *responds* to feelings, it is through the feeling of their emotion they then hear the unhealthy belief. Once they know the language of the old belief, they can rewrite it to a new healthy belief that will be more productive for them. The new healthy belief is written with specificity and stated with repetition. Clients add a new heartfelt emotion and *imagine* the new way of being. Since the subconscious mind does not know the difference between reality and the new imagined outcome, the new outcome is programmed into the subconscious. Now their *state of mind* has shifted and *success* can enter into any area of their life.

For example, a client was feeling disconnected from her son. She felt a separation and did not know what to do. I helped her feel the emotion of being disconnected and as her sadness was expressed, she heard her inner voice say, "He doesn't really feel my love. He thinks I'm being critical." After she released her sadness fully, I had her rewrite her old thinking. Her new statement was this: *"I am a loving mother, and I communicate easily and know exactly what to say to my son."* She repeated this phrase for a few days feeling her love and because of her statement she was able to open her communication with her son in a new way. He felt very supported and loved, and now they have a new connection.

Having worked with hundreds of clients I can say that to make the changes you intend to make, be *willing* to keep repeating your new belief, and *feeling* the new emotion with *imagining* your outcome until you *receive* what you are asking for. If you choose to transform your belief and the new belief does not come to you in a reasonable amount of time, you may need to rewrite it and feel more deeply. Having your whole body feel what it is you are choosing to have, and sustaining that feeling for a long enough period of time will assure your success.

Wright

Success enters into areas of our life we choose and our internal dialogue influences the process, so how does this work?

Hansen

Whatever you tell yourself comes into manifestation quickly. Words are powerful and you need support to take action. Success is how you *choose* to think in every moment. Success is a *state of mind*. If you have thoughts of lack or low self-esteem or negativity, you will stay in that state of mind. When you shift and rewrite what your inner dialogue is telling you, you open to new opportunities for personal growth and success. You can shift from wanting something to choosing to have something. No matter what you are choosing to have in your life, your internal dialogue will bring you closer to your goal or take you away from your goal. Your mind takes you away from your goals by stating, "I can't; I'm not good enough; I don't do the right things; I'm just a phony," to name a few examples. Being aware of how you speak to yourself, *inside*, will help you to rewrite your internal dialogue with *powerful* thoughts that will support you to succeed in the outer world.

Let's say your goal is to build a million dollar company within one year. All your internal dialogue would be focused toward your goal. The unique vibration of every powerful word you speak internally will help you take the right action steps toward your goal. Choosing a dialogue for your business goal such as, "*I am so excited to be of service*," and "*My marketing plan is working every day*," instead of, "I'll never be able to do this," supports you in imagining how you would feel to have a million dollar company. If you feel joy and enthusiasm or any other emotion, bring this feeling into your entire body. Your body will then vibrate at the level of already achieving your goal. As you focus on your new vibration every day, your actions will be accomplished with greater ease, and if during your day another disempowering thought comes in, rewrite it immediately and keep feeling your imagined outcome. Your *specific* words, in addition to your *heartfelt* feelings of success work together to *create* your success.

In one of my seminars a woman shared that for years she wanted to go to a special training in the summer for her work. The training was at the time of her two sons' birthdays. She had assumptions that her family did not want her to go or that she couldn't go because she had to be there for the birthdays. In the seminar she opened her thinking and decided to talk to her family about her desire to go. She realized she had been telling herself, "My family won't want me to go," and, "I just can't be away at that time." Once she changed her thinking and opened her heart to speak truthfully, her family completely supported her. This example demonstrates that her assumptions were incorrect and once she changed her thinking she gained confidence to speak to her family. She created a statement in the seminar to support her *heart's* desire, and then she repeated the statement, feeling love for her sons.

After she shared her feelings with her sons, they both said, "Mom, we want you to go to the training. We can celebrate our birthdays at a different time." Her focus of *love*, with her *transformed thoughts*, created a *new reality* for her life, and she was off to the training the next summer. I was so happy for her.

In my two-day course we have an exercise saying words and feeling their vibration in our body. Need has a different vibration from want, and want feels different from choose. Happy feels different from sad. Love feels different from anger.

Here is what you can do to experience the difference in the way each word feels. Make a list of words that feel disempowering on the left side of a sheet of paper. Notice how your body feels. Now write words that feel empowering on the right side of the paper. Notice again how your body feels. The practice is to keep feeling the words on the right side to stay empowered.

Wright

I understand that now you work mainly with women. Why only women?

Hansen

I am working with women because women are *ready* to speak up and say what is *true* for them. Women are opening up to know who they are deep inside and they are looking to be free of the old paradigm. They are choosing to stand up for what they believe in and they are ready to take action. I feel that it is time to gather women of all ages and from all walks of life.

I provide a place where women heal their past wounds, forgive, and express their joy and compassion—a place where they feel safe to speak what is true with empowering communication. I provide a place where they learn to be in deep caring relationships with their husbands, children, friends, family, and colleagues. I also provide a place where they feel connected to themselves in a new way, and they recognize their uniqueness—a place where they find their next step.

It is time for a *balance* of the feminine and masculine and time to create balance in our world. To come into balance will a take a commitment to listen to each other, say what is dear to our hearts, and honor and respect each other. My part of the divine plan is to teach the communication that will bring *freedom* to women. Freedom comes from within and transcends social injustices. Bringing women together, I believe, is a beautiful starting place for peace.

Wright

How have you helped women find their authentic voice?

Hansen

Because of the layering of our educational system, our societies, and our cultures, we have different voices inside our head. It is easy to forget the sound of our own authentic voice. In my work I help women *remember* by taking them deeper into the place of their truth where their own voice can be heard. By finding and hearing their *authentic* voice they leave the seminar or coaching session with a sense of how to use their voice in current relationships.

Here's an example. I was working with a Japanese woman who felt unloved by her mother. We found that she had several different voices that all wanted to be heard. She had emotional pain to release in order to come to clarity about how to communicate and what to communicate. In the last session, I had her imagine her mother loving her. At first this was a challenge because all she was seeing was how the past was. As she continued to imagine, she suddenly felt her mother's love. She was amazed and filled with joy. I then felt the presence of the Divine and asked her what that was for her. She said it was the Creator. We both felt the energy of the Creator all around us. At the end of the session she looked beautiful, she had light shining in her eyes, and her aura was very bright. We then found the right words she would say to her mother upon returning to Japan.

Another client was having difficulty speaking her truth to her boss. After an experience at the age of four, when her mother said, "I just don't understand you," she thought others did not understand her too. She started holding on to her emotions and became very shy. I taught her a set of skills she could use to say what was true to her boss. As she started to practice saying her truth, she recognized that she needed to release her sadness first, so her confidence would be strong and she could speak up. She felt her sadness until she was calmer, and through my guidance she was then able to find the right words to speak to her boss and be able to say what was true for her.

When a client *first* starts to open to her authentic voice, *practice* is her key to finding confidence. Yet if she has held on to her emotions for years, the truth won't come out right away. I assist her in practicing with people who will give her loving *support,* *listen* to her, and *encourage* her to stay open to her truth.

Wright

What do your clients learn in your Conscious Creating and Mastering Authentic Communication seminars?

Hansen

I teach clients to notice the thought they are thinking that created the emotion they are feeling. I have them locate where the emotion is residing in their body. Next they express the emotion, releasing sadness or fear or anger. Every emotion has a voice and wants to be heard. Once that part of them has been heard, and the energy of the emotion released, the client is ready to rewrite the original thought into *new,* powerful language.

In my seminars I show women how to be comfortable in their bodies, to feel centered to speak what is true. One practice is to have them make eye contact with another person. I teach them to keep their own energy with themselves, and not project their energy to the other person. Next they stand in front of the group and I ask them to bring their attention to their feet and stay present in their body. While the audience is looking at the person in front, they are to hold a soft gaze and a feeling of love and appreciation for the person. When the person standing begins to relax, staying present with the audience becomes easier. She can speak truthfully while holding eye contact. The practice is for the speaker to be aware of her body while speaking.

Through different exercises during the day, all the women in the seminar become very *present* with each other. Their communication shifts from speaking from their mind to speaking from their heart. They also learn to be *conscious* of what they are choosing to say in every moment because they have learned to hear what they are thinking *before* they start to speak. They have felt that they have been heard by the audience, and their childhood experiences of not being heard or listened to starts to heal. As their bodies relax, they quiet their mind and start to bring the energy of their soul through themselves. They speak now from the higher consciousness and the wisdom of their soul is heard.

Some women have a spiritual awakening during class as they feel the difference between their mind speaking and their soul speaking. The soulful experience is profound and life changing. Their Presence creates love and compassion and understanding for themselves and others. Then the practice is to sit and access their Presence whenever a challenge arises.

Wright

In your opinion, how can people become successful and stay that way? Will you recommend some key points?

Hansen

Yes, I have eleven key points I practice and I'd like to share them:

1. *Trust yourself and have faith.* Trust comes from faith in the plan of action that is for you. Your trust will be calming and will help you settle into your body and be connected to your inner self. Trust is all knowing, and your knowing creates a day of an even flow of energy for whatever you choose to do.

2. *Have perseverance and courage.* Perseverance is keeping a steadfast pursuit of your goal. Having courage, which is the opposite of fear, will help you to keep going. Fear constricts

your body, especially your heart center, and can immobilize you from further action. What I do is take two action steps whenever I am fearful: *First,* I write down all my fears as fast as I can. I'm usually very upset, so I scribble the words. When I feel the fear has moved out of my body, I shred my pages and throw them away. *Second,* I take one small action step to get me in motion again and by now my courage has returned.

3. *Stay in integrity at all times.* Integrity is being honest and doing what you say you are going to do. If you are to start a meeting at 9 AM, start right on time. Keep your agreements with yourself and others, and feel good all day.

4. *Be a good listener and communicate clearly.* Being present while listening takes mindfulness to stay focused on what is being said. Drifting off into thinking of what you will say next will take you away from the connection you have with the person. Relax and know you will be able to communicate what is on your mind in the right timing. To communicate clearly will require you to be present with yourself and hear what you are saying.

5. *Be your unique self.* Comparing your uniqueness to someone else can be absolutely disempowering for your whole being. Accepting your uniqueness and knowing you are part of the whole will bring joy in the present moment.

6. *Accept yourself.* How many times have you heard your critic say you weren't good enough or pretty enough or slim enough or whatever enough? The critic is only one of the voices that have been developed from your childhood. When the critic is relentless in saying hurtful words, know these words are just *not true.* Send love and kindness and be gentle with your critic, giving the critic different words to say to you.

Accept yourself for learning new ways and for exactly who you are.

7. *Appreciate and love yourself.* By keeping your state of mind in appreciation for what you do and for who you are, you can shift to feeling *any* experience as a gift. Loving yourself even when you think you have made a mistake can be part of your spiritual practice. Practice loving yourself for an entire day and *notice* what happens.

8. *Express gratitude.* Being grateful for your creation of your life is an uplifting experience. If you are not feeling grateful, take a few moments to write down one or two things. Are you grateful for flowers or children or poetry or electricity or friends and family or chocolate? The focus on gratitude will bring peace of mind and open your heart.

9. *Have fun and laugh.* A couple of times a day take time to have a mini play session. Find something to laugh about or do a celebration dance and then get back to work. Start your day by laughing or feel the inside of you smiling even before getting out of bed.

10. *Be in the Now.* The mind can resist being in the Now. Since there is no time in the Now, the mind gets scared it will not be able to function or be in control and perceives this as a threat. Take a deep breath and put your attention on your breathing. The mind will quiet for a few moments. As you keep practicing staying in the present you will notice a shift in your awareness. Eckhart Tolle says, *"The moment your attention turns to the Now, you feel a presence, a stillness, a peace."*

11. *Open to Spirit.* Opening your consciousness beyond your mind will bring you the Presence of your Spirit. When you

are relaxed and trusting the Presence, you are comforted that *All is Well*. Focus on *All is Well* and find internal peace.

Wright

Do you believe that humanity is going through an awakening?

Hansen

Yes I do believe we are going through a spiritual awakening and it is time for us to create a new future. Our state of mind influences how we receive our *wake-up* call and whether we keep a focus on what we are truly choosing to have. For instance, if you choose peace on this planet, then peace starts first inside. Every thought creates an energy that our bodies feel. You can shift from one feeling state to another by putting your focus on your breath and your heart center. It is our *state of mind* and our *open hearts* that create our awakening with grace.

Wright

So what questions would you like people to think about in building a foundation for their future?

Hansen

With all the challenges we face I am wondering, when you wake up in the morning, are you excited to start your day? Do you think about creating a life exactly the way you would like it to be? Do you imagine your life in a new way? What *is* the new way for you and how do you envision the new way for all of humanity?

Think about the qualities of a new life. Write them down and keep adding to your list every day. If you are not sure what this new way is, find time for silence and open to the wisdom of your soul's knowing. Will you envision a place to live where we all honor and respect each other and will this be a place of loving, caring attention to each other's needs? Will it be a place of devotion to your spiritual practice and honoring everyone's practice? Will we stop fighting and end war? Is it possible for you to imagine the feeling of peace? Are you willing to feel a deeper connection to others? Will your heart center open and express love? Will you care enough about the planet that you take action? Will you raise your vibration and say *yes* to your calling? What will *you choose?*

Wright

What a great conversation. I really appreciate all the time you've taken with me this afternoon to answer these questions. It's been very interesting. I've got a lot to think about.

Hansen

Thank you very much for having me be part of *Success is a State of Mind.* I appreciate the opportunity.

Wright

Today we've been talking with Noorah Hansen who is an international seminar and retreat leader. Her seminars include Mastering Authentic Communication, Conscious Creating, Igniting Passion for Your Life Purpose, and Awakening your Heart. After listening to her views, I think that she knows what she's talking about.

Noorah, thank you so much for being with us today on *Success is a State of Mind.*

Hansen

You are very welcome.

ABOUT THE AUTHOR

Born to travel the world, Noorah is an international seminar and retreat leader who focuses on clear, consistent, and cross-cultural communication skills. Her seminars include Mastering Authentic Communication, Conscious Creating, Igniting Passion for Your Life Purpose, and Awakening Your Heart. Noorah circumnavigated Australia by vehicle, sailed in the French Polynesian Islands, and created a walk-about in New Zealand to expand her global awareness and develop her intuition and expertise. Aliveness and passion vibrate from Noorah to her clients as they resonate to a deep and powerful place in their own hearts, and from there source their unique vision and purpose in life.

As a wilderness guide for over twenty years, Noorah leads annual wilderness retreats for women. She also brings meditative experiences from Machu Picchu in Peru and the Egyptian pyramids into her deep exploratory gatherings. Her favorite sites are Mount Shasta, California, and the Grand Tetons in Wyoming. Hundreds of clients have been assisted successfully in her coaching program to become concise and truthful in their daily communications

Noorah Hansen
EarthSpirit Services
P.O. Box 680
Mount Shasta, CA 96067
800.927.2527, ext. 4692
earthspirit@snowcrest.net
www.earthspiritservices.com

SUCCESS IS A STATE OF MIND

17

An interview with...

Patrina Clark

David Wright (Wright)

Today we're talking with Patrina Clark, Founder and President of Pivotal Practices Consulting. Her company offers professional consulting services in change management, leadership, and organizational development. She has been an effective change agent in multiple organizations, including the United States Department of Defense, where she received a medal for notorious civilian service, and the Department of the Treasury where her performance was rated as outstanding for fifteen consecutive years. Patrina is a Certified Senior Professional in Human Resource Management and serves on the Board of Directors for the Anne Arundel Chapter of the Society of Human Resource Management. She is an active participant in numerous professional organizations and holds a top-secret security clearance.

Patrina, welcome to *Success is a State of Mind.*

Patrina Clark (Clark)

Thank you, David.

Wright

So tell us, how do you define success?

Clark

Well, before providing my own personal definition for success, I think it's important at the outset to say that success is a very personal thing. I believe that it's critical for people to determine for themselves what success means. There are sure to be many definitions with which an individual can identify, and it can be very helpful to consider these varying perspectives while developing your own personal definition. But until you actually take the time to develop your own personal definition, you might not ever feel completely comfortable responding to the question, "Am I a success?"

We all have different aspirations—different goals that motivate and inspire us—and different hopes and dreams. The one thing I believe we all have in common though is a desire to be happy and satisfied with who we are and what we're doing with our lives. The recent surge in books on living with purpose and living a meaningful life are testaments to this. By defining success on our own terms, our feelings about how successful we are is much less dependent on what others think.

Now, for my own personal definition: Success means being at peace with every aspect of my life and fully present in the here and now while continuing to move confidently, even boldly, toward tomorrow. It is more about how I handle the journey than arriving at any specific destination. And, it is definitely not defined in terms of material wealth; but rather, in terms of how I will feel about myself and my life at critical junctures along the way.

Wright

I understand that you believe there is a difference between being happy and being at peace. Would you tell our readers more about that?

Clark

Sure. I think there really is an important distinction. When you're at peace, it is more difficult for the things that are going on around you to derail you or create these big mood swings. Happiness actually tends to be conditional and much more dependent upon present circumstances. In other words, when things are going really well, we tend to be very happy—when they aren't, we tend not to be. On the other hand, when you are really at peace, you can face those times when things aren't going so great with a sense of calm assurance. Let's face it—our actions are usually very closely aligned with how we're feeling. By learning to be more at peace, we are better able to respond to the inevitable challenges we face and then transition more swiftly to a better place.

The one thing that peacefulness and happiness have in common is that both states of mind are tied to our beliefs about our present circumstance, which gets us back to success as a state of mind. But peacefulness examines the present state much more holistically and less emotionally.

For example, let's say you're having a very difficult time at work that could result in your losing your job. It would be very natural to focus on the potential negative consequences of that happening, and the more negative your thoughts, the more unhappy you become. But if we truly believe that we are more than capable of handling whatever comes our way and work to make the best of the present situation, we limit our negative thinking and have a better overall attitude about the experience. Life is going to have its challenges, and the key is developing a positive focus for dealing with those challenges.

Wright

It sounds as though you truly believe that success is a state of mind.

Clark

Absolutely! In fact, I believe that everything is directly connected to our state of mind. Because I strongly believe this, I was really excited about the opportunity to contribute to this particular book project. It is especially rewarding to be featured with other dynamic individuals like Les Brown and Deepak Chopra who have been helping others achieve greater success by motivating them to think differently about themselves and their lives.

Wright

So how does this belief factor into your consulting practice?

Clark

It actually provides the foundation for the practice. In my twenty-two years as either an organizational leader or change agent, I observed repeatedly that lasting and meaningful change was only achieved when limiting beliefs were *minimized*. I emphasize the word "minimize" because even small changes in limiting beliefs often result in significant positive changes.

One might think that limiting beliefs have to be eliminated before change can occur, but that is simply not the case. Dealing with limiting beliefs is a process—often a lifelong process—but progress can be seen and measured with small shifts in limiting beliefs.

I once worked with a client who called me to facilitate team development exercises for a group that simply was not delivering even though the team was composed of very bright and capable individuals. After my initial meeting with the group, it was clear that one person seemed to be sabotaging meetings by being very critical of other members' ideas during group discussions. It would have been simple—and ineffective—to focus on the behavior rather than the underlying beliefs contributing to the behavior. By focusing on the underlying beliefs, I was able to help the individual confront some of the beliefs that were interfering with his effectiveness. I used a partner versus police officer analogy and saw fairly quick and dramatic changes to the group dynamic.

The key in these situations is to recognize that behavior is a symptom. Lasting change will only occur if we address root causes rather than symptoms.

Wright

You use the phrase "limiting belief," would you tell us what you mean by that?

Clark

A limiting belief is anything that gets in the way of our living our best life. It can be something as simple as, "I'm too short," "I'm not as smart as she is" or "I could never do anything like that." In the workplace, limiting beliefs can really slow down or completely derail change initiatives. A couple of the more familiar limiting beliefs in the workplace are "It will never work" and "It won't matter anyway."

It is important to acknowledge that each and every one of us has limiting beliefs. If we're going to effectively address barriers to change, whether personal or organizational, we have to identify the limiting beliefs that are interfering with our getting where we want to go. By being more conscious of the barriers, we can develop more effective strategies for achieving our goals and objectives.

An interesting characteristic of limiting beliefs is that while the beliefs are often not obvious to the believer, they are almost always obvious to observers. Think about how many times, usually during a time when we are not at our best, a friend or colleague tells us that we're not seeing things clearly. Then, the friend or colleague shares a different perspective that frees us to act more positively in the situation. Some people are naturally more introspective and can begin working on their own limiting beliefs. However, most can benefit from working with a professional, such as a coach or mentor or someone they can trust to be honest with them about their opportunities for improvement.

Wright

What do you think are some of the more significant obstacles people face in trying to become successful?

Clark

Without question, David, I think the biggest obstacles people face are their own internal beliefs about their success.

I remember vividly a time fairly early in my career when my personal beliefs about myself were challenged and I was given an opportunity to examine how I really saw myself. Even more significant, I had the chance to see how others saw me at the time and how they would come to see me in the future. I was experiencing a very difficult time at work, caught in the middle of a leadership battle, and began to really feel badly about my career options and myself.

In the midst of the storm, so to speak, I met someone who later became a very close friend. He was able to actually help me address the limiting beliefs that I had and see myself in a much more positive light, which probably was more consistent with how other people outside of the situation were actually seeing me. I developed a more positive personal outlook and renewed confidence that I believe resulted in my very quickly moving up the leadership ranks.

All too often our beliefs about ourselves become self-fulfilling prophesies, whether those beliefs are good or bad. In speaking with so many would-be high-performers who seem to be stuck, the consistent elements are limiting beliefs about what they can accomplish and the degree to which others actually control their fates.

When I think back to that time in 1998, or more recently to a professional challenge that was perhaps even more difficult than the 1998 event, I was plagued by limiting beliefs and focused on all the things that could go wrong and had gone wrong. These beliefs and negative focus, more than anything else that was happening around me, were the greatest contributors to my unhappiness and perceived inability to change my present circumstances.

Once I began to change my beliefs and focus on the possibilities rather than what I believed to be the probabilities, I truly began to soar—literally and figuratively. And, when I look back at those difficult times, I wonder how it was that I could have allowed myself to be so upset. Holding onto this recognition, as well as having a very solid support group, is what allows me to be more peaceful when the challenges come and to continue to be an active participant in my life, shaping my own future, and creating my own wonderful, new opportunities.

Wright

Will you share with us some of the people, other than personal role models, who have had the greatest impact on your views of what it means to be successful?

Clark

Wow, David, that is a very long list! Each person with whom I have been fortunate enough to interact has in some way influenced my views about what it means to be a success. Some interactions were easier or more pleasant than others, and interestingly, the interactions that proved to be the most challenging often provided the greater insights for my own personal growth.

From the easier interactions and relationships, I gained tremendous insight and perspective on positive behaviors and perspectives that I wanted to adopt as I evolved. And from the more challenging interactions, I gained invaluable insight into personal beliefs or behaviors that I wanted to change, as well as lessons in patience, tolerance, and understanding.

Wright

I was interested to learn that one of your more requested client engagements is about organization inclusion. Will you tell me how inclusion differs from diversity?

Clark

As our society grows increasingly more diverse, organizations are devoting significant resources to all sorts of diversity initiatives. At their best, the thing that most of these initiatives seem to have in common is a focus on individual differences and how to work around or in spite of those differences. At their worst, some initiatives actually place an emphasis on numbers. For example, Company A may decide it needs ten more women or a specific number of other types of individuals and then it will know that its diversity efforts are successful. In my opinion, that is absolutely the wrong way to implement and measure a diversity initiative. In fact, experience shows that these efforts can actually have negative, unintended consequences and make individuals from different cultural backgrounds feel singled out for special attention.

Inclusion, on the other hand, offers a more holistic approach based on an organization's culture and values. Inclusion efforts build mutual accountability throughout the organization to ensure that policies and practices are consistent with organizational values, that they are applied consistently throughout the organization, and that all similarly situated members of the organization are treated equitably. "Similarly situated" is a human resources term that just means employees in similar occupations in the same geographic area because it may be appropriate to have different rules for different employee groups.

What I often tell my clients is that diversity done poorly is divisive and inclusion done even poorly is still inclusive.

Wright

Speaking of inclusive versus divisive, I understand you're working on a book that addresses some of the division in government agencies. Will you tell us a little bit more about this project and why you decided to undertake it?

Clark

The title of the book is *Political Sensibility: Bridging the Gap between Careerists and Politicals.* One of the things that is painfully clear to me is that we need tools to bridge the divide between public or government career employees and those individuals who receive political appointments to government agencies. There are so many misperceptions about public service, particularly in the federal government, that do a disservice to so many, including long-time government employees, would-be government employees graduating from college, congressional representatives who make policy decisions affecting government workers, and political appointees who move in and out of various government agencies. I want to be able to share my observations and experiences as a way of bridging the cultural divide that I believe limits our nation's greatness.

Wright

In preparing for our interview, I saw that one part of your practice focuses on coaching individuals who are transitioning from the private sector into government jobs. Have you identified any themes or common limiting beliefs in this area of your practice?

Clark

That's an easy one. The most common theme relates to the perceived lack of professionalism or intelligence of government employees despite research documenting the fallacy of these misperceptions. Individuals who harbor these misperceptions while transitioning into government positions are at risk of limiting their success in these new positions and adversely impacting the career employees with whom they work. Unfortunately, these views are all too prevalent among political appointees who come into organizations believing that they alone will be the one to "straighten things out." While there are certainly limitless opportunities to achieve improved efficiency and effectiveness, it is unlikely that it will happen without effective collaboration.

One of my more satisfying professional experiences is when I can work with a new government executive in developing a genuine appreciation for the men and women who are long-time public servants and show them how to integrate their views and objectives into those held by their career colleagues. When this happens, it results in a truly great experience, both for the new executive and the individuals he or she is charged with leading.

Wright

Have you seen someone you believe who was very successful at making the transition?

Clark

I have had the opportunity to work with some truly phenomenal and dynamic organizational leaders. But the one who really stands out for me in this area is Charles Rosotti, who I met while working at the IRS. Mr. Rosotti was appointed as Commissioner of the Internal Revenue Service at a time when the agency's reputation was suffering horribly.

While it would have been easy for him to do, based on all he had achieved in the private sector and the very negative media coverage about the agency, Mr. Rosotti did not storm the agency with a disdain or disregard for long-time employees. Instead, he surrounded himself with the brightest and the best and made every single employee of the organization—even at the lowest levels—feel as though they had an important role to play in the historical changes the IRS was to undergo. I emphasize "lower levels" because there were some senior leaders who were extremely resistant to the changes, and eventually decided to leave the organization.

I had never been more invigorated or inspired in my fifteen years with the agency as I was under his leadership. I was only fortunate to observe him at work in a few meetings, but his ability to connect with the key players and quickly reach a sound decision was amazing to see, and he truly had an impact at every level of the organization.

While his change management strategy was classic textbook, it was his confidence, passion, graciousness, enthusiasm, and ability to engage rather than alienate that made it a tremendous success in my opinion.

Wright

I'm guessing you probably have a list of individuals you don't think were as successful as Rosotti, right?

Clark

I think that most of us operate from a place of doing what we believe to be best and go through our days doing the things that make the most sense to us. So, rather than focusing on the negatives, I like to focus on positives and possibilities. What I try to do with each of my clients is to establish the practice of viewing actions through the eyes of those impacted the most. Obviously, you can't strive to make everyone happy or to be liked by everyone, but I do think it's important, particularly for individuals in management and leadership positions, to have a very good understanding of how their actions impact those they lead and manage. In that way, they become active managers and leaders, taking responsibility for the things they say and do. Accountability is all too often a novel concept among leaders, and I believe it should be the law of the land.

Wright

By the way, do you work with people who are transitioning in the opposite direction—those who are coming out of the government service and going into the private sector?

Clark

Yes, I do. So many of the principles involved in transitioning are exactly the same and the skill sets and tools are nearly identical. What differs is the organizational focus. Corporations tend to be very bottom-line profitability focused, while the government focus is more mission-driven and goal-directed. Most of my clients are transitioning into rather than out of the government because it often does represent the opportunity to achieve greater work-life balance while at the same time serving their country.

I have a passion for public service excellence that I believe makes my coaching of individuals transitioning into government especially meaningful and constructive. However, there are certainly a number of individuals who retire and transition into the private sector, and I am always happy to work with them.

Wright

So what thought would you like to leave with our readers to summarize what we've talked about here today?

Clark

I do not believe our individual successes are accidental or coincidental. All of our experiences—positive and not so positive—are preparing us for the next great opportunity or adventure. And, if we are active participants in our lives rather than casual observers and if we maintain the right frame of mind, we will be successful, however we define success.

Wright

Well, what a great conversation. I've learned a lot. I think I'm going to throw away the word "diversity" and just use the word "inclusion" if you don't mind.

Clark

I don't mind at all and I appreciate your advancing the cause. It may lead to more constructive conversations around what I believe to be an organizational imperative as organizations strive to remain competitive in an increasingly global economy.

Wright

You know, I've never thought of it that way—seriously.

Clark

So many people have not, and we just have to keep an open dialog to improve awareness and understanding. Diversity can have such a negative connotation that the minute you say the word, it gets in the way of whatever positive action it is that you're trying to accomplish.

Wright

Well, I appreciate all the time you've taken to talk with me today and answer all these questions. As I stated, I've learned a lot and you have given me a lot to think about.

Clark

I appreciate the time this afternoon.

Wright

Today we've been talking with Patrina Clark, founder and President of Pivotal Practices Consulting. She's been an affective change agent in multiple organizations, including the United States Department of Defense and the Department of the Treasury.

Patrina, thank you so much for being with us today on *Success is a State of Mind.*

Clark

Thank you, David.

ABOUT THE AUTHOR

Patrina Clark, Founder and President of Pivotal Practices Consulting, has more than twenty-two years of executive and organizational leadership experience. She has been an effective leader and change agent in multiple organizations and the recipient of numerous awards and commendations. Patrina holds a master's degree in Human Resource Management, is a certified Senior Professional in Human Resource Management (SPHR), and is an active participant in numerous professional organizations. She holds a top-secret security clearance.

Patrina Clark, MSM, SPHR
Pivotal Practices Consulting
"practice really does make perfect" ™
202.360.5121 (Metro Washington, D.C. area)
1.888.360.5121 toll-free and fax
president@pivotalpractices.com
www.pivotalpractices.com

SUCCESS IS A
STATE OF MIND 18

An interview with…
Miles Richmond

David Wright (Wright)

Today we're talking with Miles Richmond, MA. Miles helps radical right brainer artists, entrepreneurs and small business owners install a marketing system, and offers personal coaching for those seeking life balance, accountability, and support.

Miles, welcome to *Success is a State of Mind.*

Miles Richmond (Richmond)

Thank you.

Wright

So just to start off with, what is your definition of success?

Richmond

That's a very Socratic question. My current personal definition of success is that it's something you don't acquire—it's something you already possess right now. It's tapping into the state of mind of success. It's a question of reframing life with a deep sense of gratitude and appreciation. It's taking notice of the joy and beauty all around us. There are many unhappy people who possess a significant amount of money!

When Viktor Frankl wrote the book, *Man's Search for Meaning*, his experiences in a concentration camp were so devastatingly brutal. However, on the inside, he looked for and found beauty in the suffering. This may be a far-reaching example, however, it demonstrates that success is an inside job.

Wright

What inspires you?

Richmond

I am moved most by people who live a life of purpose. I am inspired by the people I've coached or treated as a therapist who have suffered greatly and have found the strength to keep moving forward. The inner strength and resources I see people access is amazing. I have worked in some extremely difficult therapeutic environments. I would often ask my clients where they got their strength. When people are facing fierce adversity and have the faith and strength to stay focused on their goals and purpose, it gives me great inspiration.

Wright

So how did you become a coach?

Richmond

My dad was a coach in the sixties. He had a flattop haircut, a bullhorn, and a whistle—he was a track and a physical education coach. He was also a rebel! The rebel part of him definitely was something that influenced me to become comfortable developing my sense of self.

I started participating in sports when I was in elementary school. It was the beginning of my discipline-building skills. After a few broken bones in high school, I decided to stop playing competitive sports and gravitated back to playing guitar more seriously. My father was my first coach. My mom was also a coach to me in my personal development. She has always had a good sense of strategizing and has helped me see things from a greater perspective. It's amazing how much my parents have influenced my life. They are extremely loving, kind, and non-judgmental. I could not have asked for better role models. They're my coaches for life!

Wright

In your opinion, how is coaching different from consulting?

Richmond

Coaching is about helping someone come to his or her own conclusions and answers by asking clarifying questions, brainstorming, and accepting accountability. Coaching is not telling people what to do. It's about holding a safe space so clients can access their own wisdom, and then developing and refining skills that can be integrated.

Consulting is a hands-on role that includes offering advice.

There is also a coaching-consulting hybrid model. This model incorporates both roles throughout the process. I use this model quite frequently when I work with artists, entrepreneurs and small business owners who want to take their companies to the next level. Some of the marketing work I might do along with the client. I will also use the language of the coach to help direct the process, and to help draw out the intentions and marketing direction of the small business owner.

Wright

You don't blow whistles and make people run laps, so what kind of coaching do you do?

Richmond

I really like working with highly creative artists, entrepreneurs and small business owners. There are certain dominant learning styles that radical right-brain dominant people possess naturally. They are usually big-picture, visionary people who have a gift for creating their lives no matter what field they may be in.

Right-brain dominant people learn best by seeing the big picture before breaking it down into action steps. The use of examples helps to anchor new information along with the use of visuals and metaphors. Right-brain dominant people generally learn very well in group settings, yet may need help in organization and follow-through.

The hybrid marketing coaching-consulting model I use helps highly creative people capture their vision in addition to breaking down the action steps with accountability. It's not that I can't work with a real left-brain dominant person who is much more linear in thinking. I can help left-brain dominant people access their right-brain creativity. I have developed my marketing and personal coaching to resonate more with right-brain dominant people because it's how I am wired as well.

The language of coaching radical right-brain dominant people is very unique. I structure my sessions and my coaching around this style of learning. By doing so, I help radical right-brain dominant folks do more left-brain dominant tasks. This would include the implementation, application, and follow-through required in order to achieve their desired outcome.

Wright

So how do you help others identify what success means to them?

Richmond

I help people assess what is living for them today. By this I mean that I help people get current with what is most exciting to them, and to help evaluate through assessment tools how well their lives are in balance at the moment. This personal self-discovery inventory helps people identify what's working for them now, what's not, and what they would like more of in their lives. This applies to either a marketing or a life-coaching client.

How building and growing an ideal business impacts someone's personal life should also be considered. Finding balance between professional and personal life is a big part of what I do. The definition of success may have some common denominators for many. At the same time, one man's floor is another man's ceiling. Everybody is unique and has his or her own values and vision of what success looks like.

Wright

So how do you coach from a creative point of view?

Richmond

I begin with creating a safe environment that allows my clients to get real and honest with themselves. I help people envision in detail their ideal business and personal lives. What does this look like? For a creative person, it may be helpful to invite him or her to draw a picture of success or use pictures gathered from magazines to connect with purpose and meaning in the vision the person has. This visual connection can help creative people capture their big picture in a non-linear way before getting linear with the written word. The language is grounded in meaning and purpose.

Facilitating a process to help bring someone's personal vision into a written road map with action steps, timelines, expectations, and accountability is what I do to help highly creative artists, entrepreneurs and small business owners achieve their desired outcomes. With regular on-going coaching sessions, I help people overcome challenges, take action, and stay focused, balanced, and on-task.

Wright

So why would I hire a coach?

Richmond

That's a really good question. Most people hire a marketing or personal coach because they are ready to take their businesses or personal lives to the next level. They have reached a plateau. They have realized they no longer know how or what to do to make their business or life more enjoyable, meaningful, or profitable.

Many businesses and entrepreneurs now have coaches or consultants. The coaching industry has boomed over the past two decades and it has become more common to hire a coach because the focus is on solutions not problems. Personal coaching is not therapy. It may feel therapeutic, however, the focus is on strategies, tactics, and facilitating a collaborative, co-equal relationship with a coach for brainstorming, support, and accountability.

Wright

So tell us, what is "Duct Tape Marketing"?

Richmond

John Jantsch is a really bright small business coach and consultant who spent over twenty years working with small business owners developing a marketing system. His book, *Duct Tape Marketing*, outlines his principles, which are simple, straight ahead, and practical to apply. John's Duct Tape Marketing principles are broken down in great detail in workbook form in his *Ultimate Marketing System*, which has been approved by Forbes Business Review, and Harvard Business School. John is one of the world's leading small business marketing experts with an award-winning blog and a loyal following of high profile business leaders including, Michael Gerber, author of *The E-Myth Revisited*, Seth Godin, author of *Purple Cow*, John Batelle, co-founding editor of, *Wired*, and Guy Kawasaki, author of *The Art of the Start*. John's marketing expertise has also been tapped by American Express and Hewlett Packard.

Wright

How is it different from other types of marketing programs?

Richmond

David, it's unique because it's a marketing system—it's not just a bunch of marketing concepts. I've never seen a marketing system so simple to understand and to apply. Once the system has been installed at a company, the heavy lifting has been accomplished. It is then just a matter of adding to the content and keeping a company's Web site up to date. It's pretty exciting because the road map for marketing in today's Internet savvy world is already laid out in the Duct Tape Marketing system. So, it's a matter of coaching and consulting with artists, entrepreneurs and small business owners to help them apply the principles with their unique company strengths in their market.

Wright

So who would your ideal clients be?

Richmond

I help highly creative, radical right brainer artists, entrepreneurs and small business owners with fewer than one hundred employees who are looking to take their companies to the next level. I also work with creative professionals as a personal coach for those looking to bump up their personal lives to the next level. I help professionals restructure, regroup, reassess, and develop a new life-map with a sense of purpose and meaning. By doing so, I help people re-engage in life with more focus and energy.

Wright

How can you coach people around the world?

Richmond

Well, it's pretty easy these days with a telephone or with a computer and the Internet. I have coaching clients in a number of states across the country. Skype is a great, free service to connect via webcam and audio with an Internet connection and no need for a phone. My coaching fees can be made with PayPal.

Wright

So you've been one of those people who has really used new technology to get you where you want to go, haven't you?

Richmond

Yes, it's called Cyber Coaching. Cyber Coaching has been around for a number of years. I think it's a really effective way to coach small business owners and professionals because it offers the opportunity to make significant professional and personal progress without getting in a car and sitting in someone's office. I still offer opportunities for those who are local to have their sessions in an office environment. However, it seems that with the time it takes to travel, it's more time efficient to work via phone or Internet for the convenience of the client.

Wright

In your experience of coaching throughout the world using this kind of technology, have you found that people have similar problems, similar dreams, and similar goals?

Richmond

There is no question that there are a number of common issues with people no matter where they live. I believe most people are looking to create happiness in their lives, and a sense of purpose and meaning. There is a universal need for balance between work and play. There is strong desire to create a healthy family life.

People can also experience similar suffering including depression, anxiety, and substance abuse. I coach from a solutions-focused perspective. I believe coaching is a series of questions searching for solutions. We've all got questions and we all have areas in our professional or personal lives that, if we really want to get down to it, can be helped by coaching.

David, I think we're living in an exciting time where we're able to have a lot more conversations with more people around the world using visual and audio technology that's free to use! I do see more commonalities than I see differences with people, and that's helped me as a person to grow and be more accepting of others.

Wright

Sounds exciting. Do you have any last thoughts?

Richmond

I really enjoyed the opportunity to reflect on these questions, and it's been helpful for me to recalibrate my own concepts of what success means to me. I'm already there. I feel very, very successful because I feel joy, bliss, and a deep sense of appreciation for life. I feel that I'm in a really good spot in my life. So, it's been fun to share some of that with you, David. You have been a champ to guide me through this wonderful conversation. So, thank you!

Wright

I've learned a lot here today. I'm going to have to think about some of these things you've talked about. I think you're the first right-brain dominant coach I've ever talked with.

Richmond

All right, I take that as an honor. I'm glad I was able to stir a few concepts for you.

Wright

Well, I really do appreciate all the time you've taken to answer these questions for me.

Today we've been talking with Miles Richmond, MA. He is Founder of Radical Right Brainer (what a great name for a company). He has over twenty years of experience coaching and consulting small business owners, professionals, and Fortune 1000 Companies in advertising and broadcast production. He is an authorized Duct Tape Marketing Coach, incorporating the Duct Tape Marketing System we discussed earlier, which has been endorsed by Forbes Business Review and the Harvard Business School. Miles is also a Certified Professional Coach.

Miles, thank you so much for being with us today on *Success is a State of Mind.*

Richmond

Thank you very much.

ABOUT THE AUTHOR

Miles Richmond, MA helps highly creative, radical right-brain dominant artists, entrepreneurs and small business owners install a marketing system, and offers personal coaching for those seeking life balance, accountability, and support. His coaching is laser focused, fun, and rewarding. He is Founder of Radical Right Brainer. He has a master's degree in Counseling Psychology, and is a Certified Professional Coach. Miles graduated from the TV and Film Scoring programs at the Grove School of Music in Los Angeles where he studied with top Hollywood composers and arrangers. Miles spent fourteen years as an Executive Vice President with Tuesday Productions with musical advertising credits including Disney, American Airlines, NBC, Target, Domino's Pizza, Kodak, and Chevrolet. Miles also has over twenty-five album credits as a producer, arranger, or musician. Miles is an authorized Duct Tape Marketing Coach. He has been a keynote speaker at radio and television conventions, advertising clubs, and small business marketing seminars across America. He lives on the Sandy River with his wife and lots of four-legged critters just outside of Portland, Oregon, in the United States.

Miles Richmond, MA
Radical Right Brainer, LLC
P.O. Box 822
Sandy, OR 97055
800-277-1687 office
503-816-4960 direct
miles@RadicalRightBrainer.com
www.RadicalRightBrainer.com

SUCCESS IS A STATE OF MIND

19

An interview with...

Sue Stevenson

David Wright (Wright)

Today we're talking with Sue Stevenson, a highly regarded global business leader. She has coached CEOs, HR leaders, and executives working internationally. Her company, Lifted Fog LLC, is a global executive coaching firm with over fifteen years of international, organizational, and individual coaching experience. Her mission is to stimulate *curiosity*, create *clarity*, and inspire clients to take *action* for results. During her rich and varied career, Sue has spoken at many international forums and has been recognized as an honored VIP by *Cambridge Who's Who*. While studying at the Hudson Institute of Santa Barbara, she authored research titled *Thrive or Survive, the Impact of Working in Different National Cultures*. A University of Aberdeen graduate, Sue is a Fellow of the Chartered Institute of Personnel and Development, accredited by the International Coach

Federation, and is currently serving as a Board member of the HR Strategy Forum in California.

Sue, welcome to *Success is a State of Mind!*

Sue Stevenson (Stevenson)

Thank you. Good morning, David.

Wright

How do you define your own success?

Stevenson

Success is deeply personal, David, and is about *achieving results* based on your own life's purpose. The following story illustrates my constantly evolving definition of success.

How I define success today is markedly different to how I may have described it at different stages of my life. It's perpetually changing. What constituted success for me twenty years ago is very different today. And it would be true to say that it's only in the last few years that I've shifted my mindset from an externally driven view of success to one that's much more internally focused. However, there are definitely a few constants through my life that have contributed to my success: hard work, persistence, energy, curiosity, a genuine interest in others, and a passion for learning.

A key question for us to figure out for ourselves is: who is really defining our success—is it our own free choice or are we living a life that we were *supposed* to live? Sometimes messages about what we are *supposed* to do come from our families and are unspoken or indirectly expressed in terms of others, such as, "Oh, did you hear that Mary is marrying that rich, successful landowner?" At other times the messages are blatant and the expectations are made crystal clear.

I was a recipient of both types of these *"supposed* to" messages. I was brought up on a farm on the east coast of Scotland. My father, an elder of the Kirk (Church of Scotland), instilled in me a very strong work ethic, appreciation of nature, and a sense of the proper ways of social interaction for a lady.

My mother married my dad just before she finished studying to be a physiotherapist. When she informed her supervisor of her engagement, she was given an ultimatum, "Finish the course or get married and quit!" She left and became a traditional farmer's wife who raised three children, volunteered for local causes, and hosted elegant dinner parties.

My destiny seemed to be mapped out quite clearly: study hard, mix with the right social set, and marry well. Careers in business were not for young ladies! I distinctly remember how my older brother was invited to sit behind closed doors in the drawing room with my father and grandfather to discuss business. My curiosity was piqued and I longed to be a part of these conversations. I wondered what on earth they were talking about. It was many, many years before I really understood what the world of business was all about.

Schooled and educated in elocution and etiquette by my grandmother, I learned how to conduct myself in social situations, which has served me well throughout the years. Her ambition for me was even grander than that of my parents—to become a nanny to royalty that would lead to the right connections for marriage, ideally into an aristocratic family. In fact, one of the most interesting pieces of advice she ever gave me was that upon meeting a gentleman, in any environment, I was to raise my eyes up to meet his, then cast them down and ask him if he has ever been to Hong Kong, then shut up! I was never to give any indication that I had an opinion or even a brain. No surprise—almost every man I have every tried this with has responded positively and, in many cases, regaled me with their stories of Hong Kong with glee!

So my initial path, although not quite as was intended for me, allowed me to go to college at the young age of sixteen to learn how to become an elementary school teacher. I focused my studies on educational psychology and was fascinated by how children developed and learned. When I first landed a teaching job at a private school, rather than follow the curriculum in the traditional way, I tried new ways of helping the children discover their own strengths and abilities, not just in arithmetic, reading, and science, but in all the "seven intelligences," as described by Howard Gardner in his book, *Frames of Mind*. These included interpersonal, intrapersonal, and musical intelligences. I believe that this approach helped them grow their confidence and their desire to learn and ultimately discover different ways of thinking, even if it got me in a little bit of trouble with my school principal! After two years of teaching, I knew that I had not strayed too far off the *supposed* route, although the expectations for my marriage plans were far from being realized.

My curiosity in all things led me to temporarily leave teaching behind to see more of the world, and I set out to grow personally and become a better teacher. I moved to Australia with the intention of trying something new, and I took a job selling restaurant discount books door to door. I learned quickly about how to communicate effectively in a different culture, adopt a positive and optimistic outlook, and persist in achieving objectives despite all odds. I quickly realized I was very good at sales, and that started me on a career route from sales to marketing, human resources to organizational development, and onward and upward for the next twenty years, never to return to teaching at the elementary school level.

I would set goals voraciously—daily, weekly, monthly, yearly, five yearly, even twenty yearly—all written, measured, and reviewed on a regular basis. I was achieving results. However, during this time my success became more and more *defined by others*. This time, rather than by my family, it was defined by my peers and my bosses at large—blue chip, multinational companies. I truly got caught up in the material rat-race and addicted to power and achievement in the corporate world.

Culturally, I was sucked into believing that success meant going faster up the job ladder with bigger job titles, grander homes, luxury international travel, fast cars, and so on. My ego was getting in the way. All I had done was exchange one set of external expectations for another. Worse still, I now had a conflict between the sets of expectations. Still unmarried with no time in my busy life to be dating, I was now a woman operating at a senior level in the predominately male dominated, highly stressful world of business.

So today, I'm redefining what success means to me once again, and it looks quite different. This time, *I* am defining success. It means having great health, meaningful work, fulfilling relationships with my colleagues, friends, and family, having energy and enthusiasm for life, emotional stability, a sense of well-being, and, as a peer and good friend put it, "peace of mind."

I'm grateful to my younger brother who has shown me, through his great compassion for others and advocacy for those less fortunate, the importance of slowing down. Serenity is my new focus, and I do find it hard when I try to *think* about it, rather than just *be* and live in the present. My goals are now much more balanced. Alongside the financial, business, and client oriented objectives, I've integrated other goals such as walking daily on the beach with my cute wee dog, Maggie Mae, photography, playing golf at Torrey Pines, good nutrition, and self-care. Now I see life as a fascinating journey with different twists and turns along the way. I truly believe that as long as I hold true to my real self, live my values consciously, and stay connected to my passion to make a positive difference in other people's lives, I will continue to achieve results and be successful. So if the *state of mind* is healthy, I believe very strongly that success will follow.

Wright

Would you tell me more about why you believe that success really is a state of mind?

Stevenson

I think it's a very broad subject concerning human behavior, consciousness, and thought, and there's no simple answer. The mind is conditioned by the past and very often, when we set out to make changes in our lives, we are faced with unexpected obstacles and bumps in the road. These bumps, often based on limited beliefs conditioned in the past, can be paralyzing and are often grounded in fear—fear of success, of failure, and of the unknown.

I was once attending a Tony Robbins seminar where fire-walking was the culmination of the first day. This was designed to be a metaphor of facing our fears. We worked on a process to get into a state of mind to overcome these fears, and as we got closer to the fire-walk I saw confidence rise in myself and in others. Then came the moment of truth. The fire was there—it was 2:00 on a frosty November morning—and it was time. The terror started to overtake me; the voices in my head created self-doubt saying, "I can't do it!" I was frozen and paralyzed by fear and could not *think* my way out of the situation. Emotions—the body's reaction to the mind—affected my thoughts and were driving my behavior.

At that moment another person noticed my hesitation and stepped in when I needed help. He challenged my competitive spirit, helped me visualize success, and tap into my strengths. I walked all the way over the white burning coals. To this day, the metaphor, "If I can walk on hot coals I can do anything!" stays with me, and I can tap into it when I want to make a leap into the unknown in other areas of my life. It also taught me that we can't always do it alone however much preparation we do because it is hard for us to see the resistance in ourselves and raise our own awareness. That's why it is so helpful to have a friend or coach by our side as we face our fears or step into the unknown.

And for anyone who faces personal change, the same is true. Think about how often we see people set goals, create plans, and eagerly set out to achieve them, only to stumble after only a few setbacks. New Year resolutions are a perfect example. We can have a lot of thoughts that don't support the performance or change that we want; it is often our inner voice and prior conditioning that is winning the battle.

In business, leaders and managers who resolve to change their behavior and negative habits often find it more difficult than they anticipated. They can have 360 degree feedback, do their analyses, and create a plan for change, but when they are ready to move forward to implement their plan they can get stuck. Often leaders assume that they can just *think* their way through the process of change, but their emotions and self-talk drive their behavior or their state of mind. The negative emotions like impatience or frustration are toxic, use up a lot of energy, and do not serve high performance. Developing new muscles or habits and investing the energy positively can help leaders to negate old habits and create new positive practices or behaviors.

In her book, *Change Your Questions, Change Your Life,* Marilee Adams explains, "When we get stuck, it is natural to look for answers and solutions, but it can lead to stumbling blocks. First we need to change our questions, or else we will keep recycling the same old unhelpful answers." For example, she uses three questions that she might ask clients to consider when facing a communication challenge with their CEO: "What assumptions am I making? How else can I think about this situation? And what is the other person thinking, feeling, needing, and wanting?" She continues with the following advice, "What is important is that we observe our own thinking and notice how our moods, thoughts, and feelings drive our behaviors. This ability to intentionally change the internal questions and *choose* rather than react, puts us in charge of our own thoughts and therefore the actions and results."

Our physiology can also give us clues about our state of mind, and by creating awareness, we can take action. The field of somatic (defined as "of the body" Wikipedia 2007) coaching is gaining ground and, as informed by the work of Richard Strozzi Heckler and what he calls "conditioned tendency," we can begin to understand how our experiences shape our body. By altering our posture, centering ourselves, and paying attention to our breathing, we can change our emotional state. Further, by introducing new rituals and practices, we can bring new awareness and choice into our daily life.

Our energy and how it flows through our bodies is a signal about our state of mind. Conversely, this state of mind affects our health and well-being—with more and more research demonstrating that those with a positive attitude and less stress suffer less from major disease. A highly published singer/songwriter, Marian Law, told me that, "When you truly believe you're a success with every fiber of your being, it emanates from your pores, is contagious, and everyone you come in contact with feels the charge." It is really a state of mind.

Wright

Sue, you are running a highly successful global executive coaching business. Tell me how you got started.

Stevenson

In my life I've consistently observed that external events or deep suffering serve as a trigger for major transformational change. This was especially true for me. Over the last six years I gradually came to the realization that I had lost focus on what really mattered to me and what I originally considered factors in my success—helping others to identify and have confidence in their strengths and abilities, inspiring curiosity and thus a desire to learn, and then seeing them take action for results. When I started out as a school teacher, this was important to me, so in essence I had come full circle. Yet, I had not taken real action regarding my realization of what mattered most.

When I relocated to the United States from Switzerland with a global pharmaceutical company, I moved into a fabulous penthouse with a stunning view of the Manhattan skyline. As I mentioned, I'd fallen into the trap of valuing material possessions, working excessively, being highly stressed, and having my ego run my life. This was mid-2001. Then everything changed. It was the affect of the tragedy of 9/11 right in front of where I lived that jolted me into a much more reflective frame of mind.

As I watched the horror unfold and wandered through the eerily quiet halls of our residential building, praying for people to come home, it made me question what was ultimately important. In the days and weeks that followed, as I talked to my neighbors (many of them were survivors of the attack on the Twin Towers), I realized that now was the time to make a change—a big change. This was a defining moment. I was getting too far removed from really making the difference that I desired. What did the huge salary and the big title mean anymore if I was purely furthering company profit at the expense of truly harnessing the talent and energy of the people and organization that I served?

By examining the threads of my passion and listening carefully to my internal voices, it was clear it was time to take new action. I knew that my talent in facilitating positive change at the organizational, team, and individual level was where I needed to focus my efforts and that I could best achieve this by starting my own business. However, I also knew that to have the quality of life, meaning, and balance that I sought, I needed to find a place that nourished and enriched my soul. So I moved to San Diego and the sunshine state of California. With its mild climate and more laid back approach to life and work, I knew I had found a place that would aid in my healing and renewal and would help me to redefine my version of success.

Filled with new intentions on arrival in San Diego, I realized that having a thriving network of business associates was fundamental to starting a new business. While I was making lots of new connections and building new relationships, I slipped back into my old paradigm, "working in the corporate world gets you noticed" and took another global HR position for a biotech company. Although hired to develop their new Global Leadership and Talent Management program, the reality was that I spent two years developing global compensation and stock option programs to serve a few top leaders, which meant that I was no longer playing to my strengths or contributing in a meaningful way to the lives of the majority of people in the organization. It was time to get back on track and live my life with purpose.

Lifted Fog LLC was created so that as an executive coach I could devote my time and energy to helping people tap into their full potential and be the best that they can be. I believe that we all have immense capacity for change and that this can be realized, especially when working with a great coach or leader. Whether people want to transform their performance at work, thrive in a new culture, or make long-lasting personal change, this business could offer them a professional coach to work with them to get the results they sought. When I embarked on this new journey from the corporate world to the entrepreneurial world, I decided that if I were to become the best coach that I could possibly be, then I needed to continue my learning with the best, so I enrolled with the Hudson Institute of Santa Barbara. I had no idea how powerful this new path would be.

Along with the latest theories and research in the fields of Adult Development, positive psychology and emotional intelligence, as well as the tools and processes of coaching, there was great emphasis on how to manage oneself as a coach. This led to some incredible, powerful learning and a greater awareness of how emotions and thoughts drive behavior. I continued to be fascinated with growing people's strengths, asking powerful questions, and creating the space for them to think differently and be present in their lives.

I also began to reflect on who had influenced me, who I most admired, and how I could learn from their lives. I thought of my grandfather, the late Ian MacDonald. He was a prominent and innovative banker, and even when he was Chairman of the Royal Bank of Scotland, I was always amazed at his humility and his gentle, yet engaging nature. My grandfather had a recipe for success: "If success is used in a material sense, the recipe must have hard work as the main ingredient, and a good measure of lively interest in human relationships." I constantly strive to meet these qualities of humility, hard work, and a genuine interest in people; and through my business I am so thankful that I have been able to learn and grow every day to be a better, healthier person.

I also realize that success is situational and cultural. I saw Richard Branson being interviewed on CNN by Glenn Beck, and he was asked, "With over 200 companies in the Virgin Group and a net worth of $7.8 billion, at what moment did you decide that you were successful?" Richard Branson squirmed, a bit uncomfortable, and replied, "The dollar discussion of success is something you talk about in America, but we might in Britain do it differently. Success comes for me from the satisfaction of someone coming off the plane after a Virgin flight and saying, 'That was the best flight ever!' " And as a coach, when clients tell me that their work with me has led them to think differently and has dramatically changed their course in life or, as one said recently, "That was the best investment in myself that I have ever made!" I regard that as success.

Wright

What is behind the name, "Lifted Fog"?

Stevenson

I'm very fortunate to live by the beach in La Jolla, California, and being on the coast we have fog. I frequently look skyward asking the fog to lift so I can see the beautiful blue skies that I love so much. I also made the discovery that just as the fog lifts and provides clear skies, so too can powerful and authentic coaching assist leaders who are "in the fog" or stuck regarding their career, professional choices, or their thinking about personal change. The use of metaphors is powerful in the life of a coach as in my previous example of fire-walking. As human beings, we often think and speak using metaphors, and like questions, we can create new connections and mindsets that change our thinking, alter our physiology, and interrupt our patterns or our state of mind. My clients often say, "Sue, I am stuck. I am in the fog; help me gain clarity!" hence the name or metaphor "Lifted Fog."

Wright

Your mission is to stimulate *Curiosity*, create *Clarity*, and inspire clients to take *Action* for results. Let's start with *Curiosity*, what does this mean to you?

Stevenson

To quote Samuel Johnson, "Curiosity is one of the permanent and certain characteristics of a vigorous mind." This "vigorous mind" helps us in making new connections, discovering where we might have limited beliefs that hold us back, uncovering where any resistance lies, helping us to build greater levels of self-awareness, and most importantly, discovering new possibilities. Curiosity means being open for exploration, new ideas, new thinking, and continuous learning. With my passion for learning, I find myself reading voraciously, constantly researching new ideas, and inquiring of myself, friends, peers, and clients on every subject. This curiosity certainly keeps my own mind active and vigorous.

In recent years, there has been an exciting upsurge in new research and findings in the field of neuroscience and how it influences the way we think and process information. This new area has been coined "NeuroLeadership" by one of the leaders in this field, David Rock, author of *Quiet Leadership*. He has articulated a brain-based approach to leadership to increase our understanding of how we can help others to think differently. He explains that "the underlying functionality of the brain is one of finding associations, connections, and links between bits of information. Our thoughts, memories, skills, and attributes are vast sets of connections or 'maps' joined together via complex chemical and physical pathways." The maps or wiring in our brains can be altered and new ones can be created. The "ah-ha!" moment that we experience when we have a new idea or insight is the precise moment when new connections have been made. Curiosity is fundamental to the process of rewiring the pathways, making new connections, and generating energy for fresh action.

Alternatively, when facing dilemmas and problems, it can be limiting if we try to solve them with the same mindset with which we started. Not only do we limit our choices, but we can activate the amygdala—the part of the brain designed to protect us from threat—and close down our ability to think through any new options at all. We get stuck or mired in fog. How to help ourselves and others out of this limited route and into making new paths and connections is not simple, but can make all the difference between success and failure. It starts with stimulating the curiosity, clarifying our thinking, and believing that we have the potential and energy to discover new solutions for ourselves.

Without feeding the curious mind, I believe that we stagnate, get stuck, and often lose our confidence to take the actions that move us forward toward realizing our full potential. With *curiosity*, the world can keep expanding and so can the possibilities. But we also may need to get clearer on which are the right choices for us to make.

Wright

From what you have said about *Curiosity* on its own, it does not lead to success, so where does *Clarity* play a role?

Stevenson

One of my very first clients, a highly successful businesswoman who founded and ran a major childcare corporation, said, "Success is entirely achievable if you start by crystallizing to your mind the key goals in life that you are passionate about or that move you or set you alight or float your boat or, to put it another way, if you don't tell the taxi driver where to take you, he can't get you there."

There are a number of ways that we can view the question of clarity. It can refer to "one's ability to clearly visualize concepts, ideas, and thoughts" (definition from Wikipedia, 2007). When communicating with others—seeking to understand and be understood—we seek clarity. When we're overwhelmed with choices or cannot see what is going on with a clear view, we can become stuck or lack clarity. Sometimes we may not know consciously what we want, but with focused energy and attention we can gain insights, find the clarity, and hence, lift the fog.

We all have basic needs such as the need for love and belonging, achievement, freedom, and so on, and our behavior is usually motivated to protect or satisfy one or more of these needs. In his book, *A-ha! Performance: Building and Managing a Self-Motivated Workforce*, Doug Walker explains that by understanding what we need, we move a step closer to determining what we want and visualizing how it will look when the need is met. He continues that unless we know clearly what we've got, we won't fully know whether we are satisfying our needs and/or getting what we want and that all problems and opportunities are gaps between something we want and something we've got. He calls the energy generated by the gap, the "GapZap."

I see many people who hastily identify changes they think they wish to make, and rush into a solution before they adequately understand the implications or are prepared for such a change. It takes discipline, focus, and an understanding of each step of the journey to be clear about the gap, the size of the gap, and how to change. Then, the way we invest our energy to create the change through new practices or habits greatly affects the likelihood of success.

The process of gaining clarity can be facilitated using different tools and techniques such as decision maps, identification of strengths and core passions, meditation, and framing. For example, by changing the language, reframing, or changing the questions we ask ourselves, we can look at the situation differently and gain a clearer view of what we need to do to achieve the results we seek. This may require identifying and letting go of limiting beliefs that have been deeply embedded into the subconscious and thus hardwired in our brain, becoming repetitive habits that hold us back from living to our full potential. With clarity, the energy and motivation to create new patterns and habits can be harnessed, thus leading to improved performance or change.

Often the act of seeking *clarity* will lead to a better understanding of our true purpose. A great question to ask ourselves is, "Am I having a life of significance?" This is taken from Frederick Hudson's outstanding work in adult development. It also helps us understand that we want different things at different stages of our lives, but finding our core passion or purpose is the key. Success is then achieving results based on our clearly defined life's passion and purpose.

Helping clients gain *clarity* is one of a coach's challenges, as *clarity* is a state of being. I believe that it requires us to be totally in the present, focused, centered, and physically relaxed. Being in this state allows the brain to seek new connections and find energy in seeing possibilities rather than being overtaken by the demons that sometimes haunt us and lead us down the paralyzing path of being stuck in fear and anxiety. Focusing on possible solutions rather than problems facilitates the path to making these new connections.

When working with clients in a coaching setting, I always have to remember that my role is to enable others to have their own insights and reach their own solutions rather than imagining what I would do in their situation. We all have very different brains and ways of thinking. The risk is that coaches see problems through their own filters and lenses, which most often leads to very different ideas or solutions that are probably not the best for the client. By focusing on *other* people's thinking, however, and helping them make the new circuits in their brain, the client's personal path to clarity and thus insight is being created.

Another client of mine, who is the founder of an interior design company, believes that "success is being clear with where we are in life, peacefully living in the present, and anticipating the future." She has *clarity!* Her personal definition of success is based on being clear about her mission and purpose in life.

But of course, self-awareness and clarity must lead to action, or it can be classified as merely fantasy or dreaming. Another way of viewing this was expressed by businessman Bruce Cleckley, "If the mind is not in a state of preparation, through necessity or desire, there will be no action and no success. And in this manner, success is truly a state of mind."

Wright

It is clear to me that *Curiosity* and *Clarity* are essential ingredients for success, but without *Action*, success will not be realized. Will you tell me more about how you see *Action* contributing to success?

Stevenson

"Some men dream of worthy accomplishments, while others stay awake and do them." I don't know who the author of that is, but it demonstrates that even if people have both the Curiosity and the Clarity about their dilemmas and opportunities, they still have to have the final ingredient for success, and that is Action.

It is so liberating to be crystal clear about the solutions and what needs to be done, but making this a reality is the next real challenge. Even when we have the energy for action, this energy can dissipate quickly. With a new thought or insight that a particular deeply engrained habit has to change, paying attention to the new habit and practicing requires discipline and focus. David Rock makes the distinction between a thought—the map held in our working memory—and a habit—a map that is hardwired in the deeper parts of our brain. The challenge is how to bridge this gap between the thought and the habit so that the new habit becomes hardwired and thus automatic. Paying a great deal of attention to the new habit is essential, and this understanding of how we think affects what needs to happen next to make our desired change a reality.

To illustrate some proven, effective approaches to changing deeply engrained habits, let me share one client's story. The client is an ambitious, smart woman who is in her company's High Potential program. She consistently exceeds the profit goals for the Business

Unit she manages, is well respected, and is seen as a strong leader with a brilliant future.

The company had chosen to offer executive coaching to all those identified as High Potential as part of their ongoing leadership development and as a retention tool for their key talent.

After some initial coaching sessions and following interviews I conducted with her boss, peers, and direct reports, she realized that she had one particular habit that, if not corrected, was a potential derailer for her ongoing success. During the process of gaining clarity around the issue, this client had gained insight into her habit of starting her responses with "no," "but," or "however." She began to see the affect of this behavior and how it led others to see her as opinionated, having to always be right, and stifling open dialogue. As she grew her self-awareness by observing how often she would say these words, she decided to act and change this behavior. Not only did she wish to stop and change this deeply engrained, unwanted habit, she wanted to create a new one in its place, which was to say "thank you" or "yes . . . and" to build on another person's point in a conversation or meeting.

She was very committed to the change and was certain that it was attainable and that the payoff would be worth the effort. At first she got stuck and frustrated that it was not as easy as she thought to stop the old habit because it was very deeply engrained in her subconscious.

To help her, we built a plan to start not only practicing the new habit, but embedding it, so that it became the natural response. The key components of the plan were a set of strategies to keep her attention focused on the new habit or connection. Initially she decided to invite her boss, peers, and colleagues to provide positive feedback to her whenever they observed her responding with a "thank you" or "yes . . . and." This helped her enormously by reinforcing her new habit and giving her greater confidence as she saw real progress toward her goal. Knowing that others were reminding her and paying attention to her new habit further strengthened the new connections in her brain.

She also wrote down her goal very precisely and created mini reminder cards that she attached to her meeting folder, put up in her office, and stuck on her BlackBerry phone. Although she had not done so previously, she would take specific time out during her drive home each day to reflect on how well she was doing in applying her new habit and then write down her thoughts and feelings each evening.

During our coaching sessions we would consistently review exactly what had happened since we last met, how often she had noticed practicing the new habit, and how it felt. She would identify when perhaps she had slipped into old behaviors and without beating herself up about it, she would acknowledge every effort she had made.

With encouragement, new insights were being created that also led to new learning. Momentum soon gained pace as she also noticed a change in the conversations she was having with others—they were less adversarial, there was less defensiveness, and the outcomes were becoming more creative. It was becoming more common for her to agree and support other people's comments than to use "no," "but," or "however."

During regular review meetings I had with her boss and other key stakeholders, the feedback was increasingly positive as they noticed the affect of her changes. This client has continued to flourish and is in line for further promotion. The combination of all the methods she utilized to pay attention to her new desired habit made a difference to how effectively it became engrained, and her action got her sustainable results.

Alongside Curiosity and Clarity, the final ingredient in the recipe for success—Action—is not as simple as being clear on what to do, being committed, and just doing it. To get the desired outcome requires time, focus, practice, reflection, more practice, positive reinforcement, follow-up, and the right state of mind.

Wright

Your research paper, *Thrive or Survive: The Impact of Working in Different National Cultures,* helps throw some light on how our state of mind can be intensely affected when we find ourselves with very different ways of viewing the world. Would you tell us a little bit more about it?

Stevenson

Yes, I will. When I was living in Switzerland, I was the Global Head of Organization and Leadership Development for a consumer health business. Part of my role was coaching leaders who were on an international assignment. Very often these leaders were in an environment that was very, very different in terms of culture, belief system, language, work habits, et cetera, from what they were either accustomed to or even felt comfortable with. Consequently, many of them would begin to redefine success for themselves, not only in terms of the business results they needed to achieve, but also how they and their families would engage themselves in their new world. This new perspective, and thus *state of mind*, would alter how they would set out to be successful and upon what criteria they would judge their own success during their assignment.

Curious about this area, I conducted research to find out whether leaders working on an overseas assignment were *thriving* or *merely surviving*, and what the affect was on them and their organizations. Through interviews and online surveys, participants were asked about their experiences and how they viewed success before, during, and after working on their assignment.

The results produced a fascinating insight into the state of mind of these leaders, as well as clear evidence of the lack support and encouragement that many were provided. Only 6 percent either had a coach or felt properly supported for success by their company. When asked what they would do differently or what advice they would give to someone else setting out on a similar journey, their answers were commonly about state of mind and navigating change. One said, "Things are going to change; be prepared that it will be different and adapt and work on it." And another one said, "Embrace the differences; your world as you know it is going to change in every respect. Work will be more challenging, everyday life will be more challenging, and your personal relationships will be tested in ways that you never knew possible. Keep an open mind and embrace the change. Open your heart and mind to new possibilities, and it will elevate you to a new level of performance and appreciation for all things and in life." This leader was not only curious, but through greater clarity and renewed action, had redefined what success meant to him.

One of the key measures to determine success in the research was how quickly the leaders felt they were able to adjust and be successful, both in arriving in their new country and on their return home. Only 34 percent of the participants felt that they were fully effective in the first ninety days when they set out, and only 7 percent on their return. This led me to conclude that there was a gaping hole in how international assignments are structured, how leaders are supported, and how international assignment success should be defined.

One client, a Swiss financial officer, was asked to turn around the financial performance of a poorly performing business unit in a foreign country. He appeared to be struggling after the first few months, facing rebellion within the employee ranks. He had made certain assumptions on arrival in a country whose culture was unlike any he had ever encountered. Without any formal training, preparation for this assignment, or having a coach, he was deeply in the fog. We began to work together to examine his thinking and assumptions, and with an open mind he was able to discover that the gap was related to perceptions about time, culture, and history. Although the business objective about changing the financial viability of the operation remained unchanged, this client realized that his approach to achieving his goal was going to be radically different than he had anticipated. By changing his mindset and opening himself up to new thinking, he was able to engage his team and organization, turn the business around, and demonstrate a successful assignment outcome.

Many participants in the study discovered new learning for themselves when asked about critical success factors. They said, "Natural curiosity, an open mind, and a desire to learn. Get rid of any closed mindset." So once again it is about state of mind, it is about choosing how you want to view and participate in your day, and how much you want to stretch yourself. Does an individual get out of bed in the morning thinking, "I need to just get through this day" in the *survive* mode or "I am looking forward to making a difference in my world!"—the *thrive* mode?

When coaching leaders, particularly those facing new uncomfortable situations, I sometimes use a model I've created called *"Comfort to Discomfort and Back."* It uses language and a visual image to help people communicate their experience and the affect they are feeling in the moment.

Wright

So, the *Comfort to Discomfort and Back* model that you created is used as a tool to help someone adapt to new circumstances. Will you explain how this works?

Stevenson

I have created and used this model for many years to demonstrate to leaders how they may see themselves moving between different levels of emotion and thought, from *Comfort to Discomfort and Back*. There are three zones, each depicting feelings from *Comfort* to *Stretch* to *Panic:*

1. The *Comfort* Zone in the middle is a place where many of us sit, and it reflects the hum-drum of normal everyday activity and the status quo.

2. The *Stretch* Zone is where people begin to step out and push themselves to where they can be creative, curious, experimental, and experience change. I call this *eustress*, or positive stress in which we can thrive, learn, grow, and make new connections in the brain.

3. The *Panic* Zone is where people might find themselves either by accident or through external circumstances, and there they may have feelings of anxiety and extreme discomfort, potentially leading to burnout or, in the case of an overseas assignment, failure. This is *distress*.

If the leader is in the *Panic* Zone, I help the person see where he or she is and how to return back to the *Stretch* Zone for maximum learning and growth. If their energy is also diminished, I might also recommend a temporary return to the *Comfort* Zone to recharge themselves to be ready for the next challenge.

I have noticed over the years that both discomfort and stretch are required for people as they experience personal change. My Pilates teacher has certainly caused me discomfort and stretched me, and with her help, belief in me, and positive feedback, I am certain that I will get to my desired results faster than I would (or could do) on my own.

Within the coaching process, the model also serves as a communication tool between my clients and myself to name what they might be feeling as they try out new attitudes and behaviors.

Philippe Rosinski found the notion of the comfort zone an extremely useful metaphor in the context of human development. As he states in his book, *Coaching Across Cultures*, "The cross-cultural environment provides a unique opportunity to step outside your comfort zone. Coaches should motivate coachees to embrace the opportunity to grow while urging them to regularly come back inside to recharge their batteries." This recharging of batteries helps with reflection, learning, and gaining clarity before taking further action.

My coaching practice now focuses on those who are actually stepping out of their comfort zone and are ready for making a significant personal change. This may include expatriates or executives who are in their first ninety days of a new role and those who are ready to step out into a new way of thinking and being. I act as a catalyst in this process of transformation so that they can perform at their fullest potential in a shorter period of time and be the best that they can be.

Wright

Finally, Sue, you have talked about having a passion for learning; what in particular have your *clients* taught you?

Stevenson

A lot! I have learned and continue to learn so much from my clients, and am inspired and challenged by them every day. It is not a wonder that I am so passionate about what I am doing. I believe that all my clients have unlimited potential, I just need to keep listening and watching for it. When focusing on solutions and enabling clients to have their own insights, it is amazing what can happen *and*, as I have witnessed, can lead to many new, unexpected insights and ah-ha! moments. When clients have been *most* curious and open to new ideas, I can just see or hear the connections being made and the energy change. It is so rewarding to be given these opportunities to create partnerships for change with really inspiring, committed leaders which build value for the individual and for the organization.

A client who used to be filled with anxiety when making presentations to his board of directors had a goal to be calm and have a confident presence every time. One of the positive rituals he introduced was daily silence and meditation. He has shown me how his meditation practice has positively affected his success in this area by creating the space he needed for awareness, observation, and greater well-being. It has reignited my desire to build meditation as a consistent and integral part of my own life. I am also reminded, through working with my clients, why it is so important to continue the journey to greater self-awareness because without it we are unable to see with clarity how we show up and affect our families, our friends, our work colleagues, and ourselves. I believe that awareness is the greatest agent for change and helps us to be better connected to the greater field of consciousness.

Another client, the CEO of a software company, with whom we worked on how to create full employee engagement and greater staff retention, has shown me that the will to ask for and receive feedback openly has changed the culture of his company. He also demonstrated that ruthless, regular self-scrutiny, reflection, and a constant questioning of his own motivation and thinking has served him well as a CEO.

The nature of follow-up actions between coaching sessions makes a very big difference in the process of embedding new circuits in the brain and I learn from each and every approach my clients choose to take. I help them to be specific and systematic about what they have decided to do, when they plan to do it *precisely*, and how they are going to repeat the practice so it becomes a conditioned response in the future. I help them build some forward momentum, create sustainable high performance, and provide accountability. Although I have a resource library with books, CDs, articles, et cetera, for my clients, many of them are avid readers and share information with me when they find a great book, Web site, or new material. This rich exchange brings great pleasure and new sources of learning and inspiration to me and in turn, to other clients.

There are times when I find myself asking questions of my clients that I realize I should be asking of myself. For example, questions about how long they have been thinking about making a particular change or how being present and creating stillness in their mind is influencing their clarity or how often they are noticing and seeing themselves as an observer of their thoughts and emotions. By reflecting on the questions I ask, and picking a few to answer myself daily in writing, there can be deep learning, awareness, and growth about myself.

Finally, although not married into the ranks of the aristocracy, my life's journey to this point has contained suffering and great joy, ignorance and insight, but most of all the passion to follow my instincts, live with purpose and thus achieve what I deem, success. I believe that most of us only use about 10 to 15 percent of our full potential, but I know that we can access much, much more to not only improve our performance and potential, but to have the capacity and energy to truly *thrive*. This requires stimulating *Curiosity*, creating *Clarity*, and inspiring people to take *Action* for results. Success *really is* a state of mind.

Wright

Thank you, Sue, for your insights and the valuable answers you have given to these questions. I've learned a lot here today.

Today we have been talking with Sue Stevenson. Sue is a highly regarded global business leader who has coached CEOs, HR leaders, and executives working internationally. Her company, Lifted Fog LLC, is a global executive coaching firm with over fifteen years of international, organizational, and individual coaching experience. Her mission is to stimulate *curiosity*, create *clarity*, and inspire clients to take *action* for results. From what she's said here, I think she knows what she's talking about.

Thank you, Sue, for being with us today in *Success is a State of Mind*.

ABOUT THE AUTHOR

Sue Stevenson is a highly regarded global leader. She has coached CEOs, HR leaders, and executives working overseas. Her company, Lifted Fog LLC, is a global executive coaching firm with over fifteen years of international, organizational, and individual coaching experience. Her mission is to stimulate *curiosity*, create *clarity*, and inspire clients to take *action* for results. During her rich and varied career, Sue has spoken at many international forums and has been recognized as an honored VIP by *Cambridge Who's Who*. While studying at the Hudson Institute of Santa Barbara, she authored research titled *Thrive or Survive, the Impact of Working in Different National Cultures*. A University of Aberdeen graduate, Sue is a Fellow of the Chartered Institute of Personnel and Development, accredited by the International Coach Federation, and is currently serving as a Board member of the HR Strategy Forum in California and the Torrey Pines Women's Golf Club.

Sue Stevenson
Lifted Fog LLC
8144 Paseo Del Ocaso
La Jolla, CA, 92037, USA
Phone: 858.344-4632
E-mail: suestevenson13@gmail.com
www.liftedfog.com
Curiosity–Clarity–Action